# WHY THE
# GERMANS LOST

## By the same author:

*Lightning War: A History of Blitzkrieg*, HarperCollins, London, 1985

*Knights of the Black Cross: Hitler's Panzerwaffe and its Leaders*, Robert Hale, London, 1986

*The Czar's British Squadron* (with Anthony Lord), William Kimber, London, 1981

*The Battle Book: Crucial Conflicts in History, 1469 BC to the Present*, Brockhampton Press, Leicester, 2000

## Published by Pen & Sword

*North Sea Battleground: The War at Sea 1914–18*, 2011

*The Hunters and the Hunted: The Elimination of German Surface Warships around the World 1914–15*, 2012

*The Real Hornblower: The Life and Times of Admiral Sir James Gordon*, 2013

# WHY THE GERMANS LOST

## The Rise and Fall of the Black Eagle

Bryan Perrett

Pen & Sword
**MILITARY**

First Published in Great Britain in 2013 by
PEN & SWORD MILITARY
an imprint of
Pen & Sword Books Ltd
47 Church Street, Barnsley, South Yorkshire S70 2AS

Copyright © Bryan Perrett, 2013

ISBN 978-1-78159-197-0

Typeset in 11/13pt Palatino by
Concept, Huddersfield

Printed and bound in England by
CPI Group (UK) Ltd, Croydon, CRO 4YY


Pen & Sword Books Ltd incorporates the imprints of Pen & Sword Archaeology,
Atlas, Aviation, Battleground, Discovery, Family History, Fiction, History,
Maritime, Military, Naval, Politics, Railways, Select, Social History, Transport,
and True Crime, Frontline Books, Leo Cooper, Praetorian Press, Seaforth
Publishing and Wharncliffe.


For a complete list of Pen & Sword titles please contact
PEN & SWORD BOOKS LIMITED
47 Church Street, Barnsley, South Yorkshire, S70 2AS, England
E-mail: enquiries@pen-and-sword.co.uk
Website: www.pen-and-sword.co.uk

# Contents

# CHAPTER 1

# The Feldherr and His Army

At the end of the seventeenth century the area of northern Europe known as Prussia was poor, backward, barren and of little or no interest to the powers of the day. One of the few ambitious families living within it were the Hohenzollerns, who were feudal lords of the small enclave of Brandenburg. By degrees, they expanded their holdings partly by purchase and partly by services undertaken for the Holy Roman Emperor, whose subjects included all of the German nobility. In due course, by adding force to his methods, the Elector of Brandenburg had won a major concession from the Emperor in that he was granted the right to call himself King of Prussia.

In 1713 the Prussian throne passed to Frederick William I, who was aged twenty-four. In character he was vigorous, energetic, determined, ruthless, violent and capable of inspiring great fear among his subjects. His ambition was to raise his country's status to that of one of Europe's great powers. To do that he recognised that he must acquire two things, namely wealth and military power. He promptly set about placing his national finances upon a sound footing and increased the strength of his small army to 89,000 officers and men. This he did by conscripting officers from his nobility and squirearchy and either impressing his own subjects or offering incentives to foreign recruits.

Training was thorough, drill was constant and discipline harsh. One means of punishment was the wooden 'horse', on which the defaulter was seated on its painfully thin back, consisting of three or four sloped planks each side, with heavy weights strapped to his legs. Even more painful was the 'pole', which had a spike on either side of its base or two rings near its top. The defaulter stood with his bare heels on the spikes and his wrists were pushed through the rings and fastened together. Granted that strict discipline was necessary

1

given the nature of the battles fought, the sheer cruelty of this sort of punishment made the British Army's employment of flogging as the major corrective seem mild by comparison. Nevertheless, it was Frederick William's intention that his soldiers should be more afraid of their officers than they were of the enemy. Drill and parades were his passion, to the extent that it was said, privately, of course, that he would have been just as happy if he had been born a drill sergeant. Certainly, he was as crude and foul-mouthed as the contemporary worst of the type.

However, even foreigners agreed that no infantry regiments in all of Europe's armies could be considered to be as ready for war as Frederick William's, with one notable exception. That was known by the rest of the Prussian Army as the *Riesen Garde*, or Giants' Guard. It was a grenadier regiment in which all the men were well over six feet, and sometimes even seven feet, tall. The king's agents scoured Europe from Ireland to Russia for such men and were paid handsomely for the recruits they brought in. By no means all came voluntarily; more than a few had to be sandbagged and carted away unconscious and under guard, including at least one priest. The regiment's running costs amounted to eight times that of a normal regiment. This might be surprising when one considers that the king was one of the meanest men alive, but it was his pride and joy and he fed its members better than he did the Hohenzollern princes. The problem was that it was utterly useless when it came to active service. Height apart, many of the men suffered severe ailments of the heart, other organs and the digestive system and were in generally poor health. Apart from giving drill demonstrations for distinguished visitors to the Prussian court, they would have been physically unable to stand the rigours of campaigning for more than a few days. When Frederick William died the regiment was reduced in size and those of its members who were released did their best to find their way home.

The king had fourteen children. He disliked thirteen of them but reserved a special hatred for Frederick, the fourth of them to arrive, and who would in due course become known to history as Frederick the Great. Brought up by a governess and tutor, both of whom were French, he developed a preference for French rather than German language and culture. He played the flute, enjoyed literature, studied art and took pleasure in civilised discussions. None of these things, in his father's eyes, were masculine activities and they earned him frequent thrashings. His father also tried to strangle him with a length of cord, frequently had him whipped and occasionally expressed the wish that he was dead. Thrust into the Army at seventeen, Frederick decided to desert with a friend and escape abroad. The two were caught and imprisoned. The king forced Frederick to watch the execution of his friend and would have executed his son as well had it not been for intense pressure from the diplomatic corps.

On his release Frederick became less rebellious and in 1732 accepted the colonelcy of a regiment, which he commanded from an estate at Ruppin given to him by his father. During this period he developed a friendship with and was greatly influenced by the French writer and philosopher Voltaire. Perhaps the most important result of this relationship was his conviction that the ruler was the servant of his state and that war was an acceptable instrument of policy if the state benefited from it.

Frederick William died on 31 May 1740, leaving behind a healthy treasury containing nine million thaler. It is commonly said that he also bequeathed his heir a magnificent army, but the truth was that this was only true of its fiercely drilled infantry, the quality of which he had further improved by issuing it with iron ramrods that produced a higher rate of fire than the wooden ramrods in use with other armies, which were inclined to jam, bend and snap in use. While moving into action or in action itself, the Prussian infantry moved at the same slow march that can be seen on Horse Guards Parade, London, during the annual ceremony of Trooping the Colour. Frederick did not believe this was fast enough when a change of position, such as moving from column of march to line of battle or from the latter to square as a defence against cavalry was needed, and increased it to seventy-two paces per minute, executed with straight knees and pointed feet. This, he held with some justice, equalled the average beat of the heart and kept the men in a calm frame of mind. It should not be confused with the goose step, in which each foot was slammed on the ground in turn. This was not actually introduced until the period of the German Empire and, while often mocked as idiotic, did strengthen the leg and stomach muscles over a period. In particular, Frederick insisted on absolute precision in the spacing between his advancing columns, the reason being that when the order was given for them to wheel to left or right and so form the line of battle, if the distance between columns had been wrongly calculated, either gaps would appear in the line or the companies would become crowded together in an unworkable tangle.

The Prussian cavalry consisted of heavy and light elements. The heavy cavalry included cuirassier regiments whose members wore breast- and back-plates and were intended to deliver smashing charges against their opponents. Dragoon regiments, originally conceived as mounted infantry and still armed with firearms as well as swords, lacked body armour although they, too, were intended to deliver decisive charges when the moment came. The light cavalry consisted of hussar regiments, recognised by their fur busbies and heavily frogged jackets. The origin of the hussar lay in Hungary and, while a number of hussar regiments formed part of the Austrian Army's order of battle, they were a comparatively recent inclusion in the Prussian service. The formal roles of the hussar included the provision of vedettes, mounted screens during an advance or withdrawal, reconnaissance, the pursuit of a beaten enemy, providing escorts and, whenever suitable circumstances presented themselves, carrying out aggressive charges against enemy infantry or cavalry. Lancer units also formed part of Frederick's army from time to time but took longer to establish a permanent place for themselves. Their functions were similar to those of the hussars but, while they were at their most effective and dangerous when carrying out a pursuit of the enemy, they were at something of a disadvantage in a close-quarter mêlée with other types of cavalry.

When Frederick first took his army to war at the end of 1740 the cavalry's performance left a great deal to be desired. In due course it would be rated among the best in Europe and the credit for this belongs to two senior officers. The light cavalry benefited enormously from the leadership of General Hans Joachim von Ziethen, a man of exceptionally small stature and quiet voice but quick temper who would brook no personal criticism. Those who sought some amusement at his expense quickly regretted the impulse as he was reported to have survived no less than seventy-four duels; as to the fate of his opponents, there seems to be no detailed record. Having been born in 1699, Ziethen could reasonably have been regarded as too old for active service, a view with which he strongly disagreed. He retired in 1763 at the end of the Seven Years' War, but on the outbreak of the War of Bavarian Succession in 1778 he announced that he was quite ready to resume his active service career and had to be restrained by a direct order from Frederick himself. He died in 1786.

The heavy cavalry owed its success to General Friedrich Wilhelm von Seydlitz, the son of a cavalry officer. Following his father's death, the family's straitened circumstances resulted in Friedrich being sent at the age of fourteen to serve as a page boy at the minor court of the eccentric Margrave Friedrich Wilhelm of Brandenburg-Schwedt. Here he learned to enjoy the pleasures of tobacco and the opposite sex and became noted for his skill as a horseman. Most of his feats involved riding through or over dangerous obstacles at the full gallop, on one occasion passing through the sails of a windmill turning at full speed.

In 1740 he received a commission as a cornet in the margrave's cuirassier regiment. Two years later, now a lieutenant, he was surrounded by Austrians but put up an incredibly tough fight before being overwhelmed and captured. This was witnessed by the king, who offered to exchange a captured Austrian captain for him. Promoted captain himself in 1743, he transferred to a hussar regiment and brought his squadron to such a pitch of efficiency that by the end of the Second Silesian War he had been promoted major at the age of twenty-four. In 1752 he became commander of the 8th Cuirassiers with the rank of lieutenant colonel. The regiment quickly became recognised as the best in the Prussian Army and its methods were adopted as standard.

It was, however, as a general officer that Seydlitz made the Prussian cavalry as highly regarded as any in Europe. Time and again, at the head of large numbers of cavalry squadrons, he inflicted dis-organisation and rout on the enemy, or held off their pursuit when the Prussians were themselves compelled to retreat. On the conclusion of the Seven Years' War in 1763 he was appointed inspector general of cavalry in Silesia, where much of the Prussian cavalry was stationed in peacetime. His worth can be appreciated by the fact that Frederick sent his most promising officers to him to learn the finer points of their profession. Seydlitz retired shortly after being promoted to the rank of general of cavalry in 1767 but his later years were marred by a quarrel with the king and an unhappy domestic life in which neither his wife nor his two daughters considered fidelity to be compatible with matrimony. He died in 1773 but his name was commemorated in one of the Imperial German Navy's most famous battle-cruisers.

Superficially, Frederick's artillery resembled that of most con-temporary European armies. On paper, it seemed numerous but closer examination revealed that some of the bigger guns were simply dinosaurs from another era, their performance neither justifying the effort of bringing them onto the field nor the expenditure of excessive powder. Most of the guns, however, were known as battalion guns and fired a three-pound projectile. Two were issued to each infantry regiment and manned by infantrymen, often with the assistance of a professional gunner. In action they were manhandled by their crews, conforming to the movements of the battle line, for which they provided immediate support. The dinosaurs were soon retired and although the battalion guns continued to serve for some time, Frederick standardised most of his artillery to 6- 12- and 24-pounder guns, which fired solid shot or anti-personnel canister rounds, and 10-pounder howitzers, which fired explosive shells. These weapons were manned solely by professional artillerymen and served in batteries deployed along the battle line. In 1759 Frederick formed a 6-pounder horse artillery regiment to provide support for cavalry operations, but his favourite weapon was the 12-pounder gun, which was considered to be a battle winner. On the other hand, he was not a little impressed by the performance of the high angle 10-pounder howitzer, one of which formed part of the equipment of every battery. Depending upon wind and weather conditions, it had a maximum range of 4,000 paces and its shells burst with shattering effect, making it particularly useful in the counter-battery role. Another high-angle weapon was the short mortar, which also fired explosive shells and was usually employed against buildings and fortified towns.

Artillery and engineer officers were drawn from a slightly lower strata of society than their counterparts in the infantry and cavalry. This, and the technical nature of their work kept them a little apart from the rest of the Army's officer corps. There was, too, an aura of the sulphurous black arts about the artillery, inherited from the Middle Ages, which a number of arcane, and probably illegal, customs did nothing to dispel. The Prussian artillery, for example, exercised what they considered to be a right to the church bells of captured enemy towns. These were sent to the Army's gun founders in Berlin who cast them into new guns. No doubt money changed hands at some point in the transaction and if the clergy raised objections they were told to discuss the matter with St Barbara, who was the patron saint of artillerymen.

In addition to becoming known to historians as The Great, Frederick had another title, employed as the highest compliment possible in German military circles, who would refer to him as The Feldherr. The term does not have an exact translation, for while the dictionary will simply put its English equivalent as 'General', this is somewhat bald and fails to describe the full scope of what was involved. It would, in fact, be almost impossible to encapsulate it in a single word, for the Feldherr, at his simplest, was a commander of well above average abilities who instinctively recognised how to employ terrain and the qualities of his troops to obtain a decisive victory. When Frederick first went to war these qualities were not apparent, but as time passed they became the hallmark of the Fredrician battle, notwithstanding uneven results.

# CHAPTER 2

# Mistakes and Methods

On 20 October 1740 the Holy Roman Emperor Charles VI breathed his last. Lacking male children, he had ensured his succession with a measure known as The Pragmatic Sanction under the terms of which the Empire was to remain intact and be ruled by his daughters in accordance with the principles of primogeniture. This had originally been accepted by all the major European powers, with the exception of Bavaria, but when Maria Theresa, eldest daughter of the late Emperor, assumed the throne, objections were raised not only by the Elector of Bavaria, but also by the kings of Spain and Saxony.

In Prussia, Frederick believed that a situation had developed that he could employ to his country's benefit. He generously recognised Maria Theresa's right to the succession, and indeed offered to assist her in the event of her being attacked by rival claimants, but only on condition that he occupied the prosperous and populous province of Silesia, to which Brandenburg had an ancient and unproven claim. Naturally, the Empress rejected the proposal.

Frederick, therefore, invaded Silesia on 16 December 1740. During the next two months Prussian troops established control over the province, with the exception of a few towns held by Austrian garrisons. On 9 March 1741 the most important of these, the fortress town of Glogau, fell to a successful assault. In the meantime, the Austrians had not been idle and were assembling an army in neighbouring Bohemia under General Count Adam Neipperg. Frederick was convinced that the Austrians would not move while the mountain passes from Bohemia were still under snow, and in this he was gravely mistaken. Neipperg began his advance in March 1741 and before Frederick could concentrate his own troops from their scattered winter quarters the Austrians had not only relieved their besieged fortress of Neisse but also severed their opponents' communications with Prussia.

8

Despite being caught wrong-footed, Frederick reacted quickly. The two armies met at Mollwitz on 10 April, the Prussians with 22,000 men and the Austrians with 19,000. The latter, however, included 8,500 good quality cavalry while the Prussians could only field 4,000 of mixed quality. In later life Frederick was fond of commenting that he never repeated his mistakes, but at Mollwitz he made one serious error that was only corrected by another.

Both armies deployed in what had become something of a tradition, with the infantry in the centre and the cavalry on either wing. Unfortunately, on the right wing of the Prussian army, the last infantry units to deploy from column of march found their designated places in the line of battle occupied by cavalry regiments which refused to give ground to the right. Consequently, the infantry units were forced to halt at right angles to the rest of their army. What happened next might have ended in a disaster. After winning a short exchange of fire, the cavalry on the Austrian left charged home and drove their opponents into a confused retreat. Frederick, situated close to the scene of action, was promptly advised by his senior general, the elderly Field Marshal Count Kurt von Schwerin, to leave the field, which he did, accompanied by his escort.

It was in Schwerin's mind that the victorious Austrian horsemen would abandon their pursuit and simply roll up the Prussian line from the right while it was also under attack from the front. That was, indeed, its intention, but it ran straight into those Prussian infantry units that had been unable to take their place in the formal line of battle and were now facing to the right. Already disordered, the troopers were beaten off by sustained volleys of musketry. Elsewhere, iron discipline kept the Prussians' line firm and the Austrian attacks simply melted away in the face of a blizzard of musket balls. In the end, though their losses were the heavier, Prussian discipline proved to be the decisive factor and it was the Austrians who backed off. Prussian losses included 3,930 killed and wounded and 690 missing; Austrian losses amounted to approaching 3,000 killed and wounded plus 1,400 captured or missing. The term 'missing' at this time might refer to men captured by the enemy, but more probably it meant those who had no wish to continue in the hard life of a soldier and who took advantage of battlefield confusion to make themselves scarce.

A long operational pause followed, but in 1742 Frederick invaded Bohemia and, on 17 May, inflicted a second defeat on the Austrians at Chotusitz. Maria Theresa, believing that Prussia was the least dangerous of her numerous enemies, decided that Frederick could retain Silesia for the time being while she was fully engaged elsewhere and concluded a peace treaty with him, so ending the First Silesian War. Apart from the considerable material gain to the Prussian exchequer, Frederick's subject population had increased by half, enabling him to increase the size of his army.

Frederick gave much thought to the near disaster of Mollwitz and reached the conclusion that there were better ways of fighting a battle than forming up in a manner which differed little from that employed in the Middle Ages. As finalised, his new system was known as the oblique order of attack. It involved locating the enemy's chosen line of battle and then overwhelming one flank of it by bringing a superior force to bear upon it. This would involve reinforcing the wing of his own army that was to deliver the attack, while the Prussian centre and other flank demonstrated against the rest of the enemy line, only advancing when the main attack was making good progress. The main attack would be made either by marching diagonally across the flank of the enemy line that had been selected as its target, then wheeling into line of battle once it had been outflanked and partially enveloped, with reinforcements following the advance. The approach would be made in columns, which would wheel together into line to deliver the attack. To succeed, the distance between regiments had to be precisely calculated so that there would be no overlapping or gaps in the line. This required endless drill in battalion movements. Cavalry, deployed *en masse*, would swing round the threatened flank, isolating it from the rear and denying it any chance of reinforcement. In addition to battalion guns, heavier pieces of artillery would also take part in the attack.

In 1744 it became apparent to Frederick not only that Maria Theresa and her allies were more than holding their own against their opponents, but also that the Austrian empress intended to recover Silesia at the earliest opportunity. He therefore initiated the Second Silesian War by launching a pre-emptive strike into Bohemia, during which he captured Prague. It was soon clear, however, that he was in real danger of being cut off from Silesia by the resurgent Austrian armies. The Austrians, however, were slow to follow up and it was not until the spring of 1745 that a 72,000-strong army, including 12,000 cavalry, under the command of Prince Charles of Lorraine emerged from the passes. Apart from Ziethen's retiring cavalry screen, there was little or no sign of Frederick's army, which in itself ought to have aroused suspicion.

On 3 June Charles established his headquarters in the walled town of Hohenfriedberg, some distance to the west of the small river Striegau. The rest of his army was strung out in bivouacs to the north with its left flank, consisting of Austria's Saxon allies, resting on the village of Eisdorf. During the evening, Charles sent the Saxon contingent an order to the effect that at dawn they were to drive out the Prussian detachment known to be holding Striegau town, which possessed a good bridge over the river.

He little suspected that Frederick's army, consisting of 49,000 infantry and 28,000 cavalry, was lying just a few miles to the east of the river. Furthermore, the Prussian cavalry were keeping the king fully informed of every move Charles made. It was obvious that Charles would attempt to take Striegau and after dusk Frederick sent a mixed force of infantry, cavalry and artillery to hold a line of low hills between Striegau and Eisdorf. In command of this detachment was a General Du Moulin, who was neither the first nor the last officer of French Huguenot descent to render good service to the Prussian Army. Throughout the remainder of the misty night the bulk of Frederick's army was marching in disciplined silence across the Striegau bridge and turning left so as to form a line of battle facing the Austrians at dawn. The exception was Ziethen, whose 10,000 troopers marched south along the riverbank, ready to splash through a ford opposite Hohenfriedberg at first light.

The short summer night ended at 04:00. Things began to go wrong for the Allies almost immediately. Promptly on time, the Saxons began their advance on Striegau but on reaching the low hills they encountered unexpected resistance for, instead of conducting a passive defence, Du Moulin launched a vigorous counter-attack involving all his infantry and cavalry and all six of his guns being pushed forward and fighting aggressively. To the rest of the allied army the roar of battle simply suggested that the Prussian rearguard was putting up a strenuous resistance. However, as the mist shredded away, it revealed all of Frederick's army drawn up opposite their own in equal strength. As the Prussian line began to advance, firing regular volleys, a charge by a brigade of dragoons under General Gessler smashed through the Austrian line, separating its right from its centre. Next, Ziethen's cavalry, having forded the river under cover of the infantry's attack, swept round the enemy flank. By 09:00 Charles, seeing the whole of his now isolated right wing being bundled back in complete disorder, realised that he was in acute danger of being cut off from the mountain passes, and sanctioned a general withdrawal. Having been spent the previous night marching and forming up before then fighting a battle lasting five hours, most of the Prussians were too tired to pursue, although Ziethen brought in a number of prisoners. Total Austrian losses amounted to 9,580 killed and wounded, 5,650 prisoners, forty-five guns and sixty-one colours. For the moment, the Austrian army remained completely impotent. Frederick's loss included 4,750 killed and wounded. To commemorate his victory, the king, as proud of his musical ability as he was of his tactical skill, composed the *Hohenfriedberg March*, which is still played by German military bands.

The Austrians were defeated on several more occasions during the rest of the year, as a result of which Maria Theresa sought and was granted an immediate peace, accepting the Prussian acquisition of Silesia in return for Frederick's recognition of her husband as Emperor.

For the next few years Central Europe enjoyed the benefits of peace. Nevertheless, many of Europe's powers, including Austria, France, Russia, Sweden and Saxony, regarded Frederick as a dangerous *parvenu*, an upstart who must be taught a lesson and deprived of his gains. The exception was England, the king of which was also the Elector of Hanover, which was in a semi-permanent state of war with France that had now been extended to North America and India, a situation that made her a natural ally of Prussia.

Even the most rudimentary intelligence gathering agency would have been able to keep Frederick informed as to what was afoot. He decided to strike first and invaded Saxony on 29 August 1756, thereby initiating what has become known as the Seven Years War or, more locally, the Third Silesian War. He occupied Dresden and the small Saxon army withdrew into a fortified camp at Pirna on the Elbe. When a 50,000-strong Austrian army marched to its relief, Frederick defeated it at Lobositz on 1 October. The Saxons surrendered and were absorbed into the Prussian army.

The following April Frederick invaded Bohemia and laid siege to Prague. Throughout May and into June Marshal Leopold von Daun marched to the city's relief with 60,000 fresh troops. On 18 June Frederick, having stripped his siege lines of every available man, giving him 22,000 infantry and 14,000 cavalry, mounted an attack on

Daun's position, situated on a line of low hills facing south over the Prague–Kolin road. The intention was to mount an oblique attack against Daun's right flank, but everything went wrong from the outset. In the oak forests covering Daun's right, the lanes and clearings had been thoroughly prepared for defence and Ziethen's horsemen met a storm of cannon and musketry fire against which they could not deploy a single gun. The first infantry column, commanded by General von Hulsen, stormed a village but was unable to proceed far beyond. The second column, under General Manstein, swerved off its given axis of advance to deal with some Croat sharpshooters and suddenly found itself engaged with the Austrian main line. The third column, under General Moritz, also veered to the right and was similarly halted by heavy fire from the Austrian front. Each piecemeal assault failed with serious casualties and the battle was lost. Frederick had no alternative other than to abandon the siege and retire from Bohemia. Kolin demonstrated that in a Fredrician battle any attempt on the part of commanders to depart from the agreed plan or use their initiative could have disastrous consequences.

On the other hand, this did not affect Frederick's relationship with his soldiers, which remained remarkably good, considering the heavy demands he made upon them. Once, following a similar battle, a deserter was brought before him. The king asked him why he had left him, to which the man replied that matters were going badly for everyone. Frederick responded that the army would be going into action once more the following day and that if things went as badly again, he would join the man and desert himself. Instead of receiving the fearsome punishment meted out to deserters, the man was sent back to his regiment and resumed his service. Such stories, with their hint of wry humour, spread quickly throughout the ranks and did far more to raise Frederick's standing than any strict application of military law.

Despite the severity of his defeat at Kolin, Frederick was only months away from his two most famous victories. At the beginning of November his headquarters were located in the small Saxon town of Rossbach. Behind the town was a range of low hills with gentle slopes and among these, sheltered by a hollow, was the small Prussian army, numbering just 18,600 infantry, 5,400 cavalry and seventy-two guns. Early on the morning of 5 November, Frederick was informed that a much larger Franco-Austrian army was approaching from the west. The king climbed to the town hall roof and surveyed the approaching enemy through his telescope. They were moving in three parallel columns, led by masses of cavalry. A keen eye quickly established the enemy's numbers as being in excess of 40,000 men with no fewer than 109 guns trundling along in the intervals between them. Suddenly the columns halted and threw out a protective screen in the direction of Rossbach. Evidently their commanders had decided to take their mid-day meal and Frederick decided to do likewise, sending orders for his own army to be drawn up along the crest of the hills.

The allied army was commanded by a prominent French courtier named Charles de Rohan who made himself so popular with Louis XV and the latter's mistress, Madame de Pompadour, that he was now generally referred to as the Prince de Soubise and had reached the rank of Marshal of France. In fact, he knew very little about soldiering and nothing at all about reconnaissance, which would prove to be most unfortunate in the present circumstances.

When the French columns began to move again, they headed towards the shoulder of Polsen Hill, the most easterly feature of the range, and it became clear that Soubise intended to outflank the Prussians. It would have been a very good idea for him to find out what they were doing, but he lacked so much as an advance guard. As the French intentions became clear Frederick marched his troops rapidly but unseen towards Polsen Hill. In the lead was Seydlitz with 4,000 cavalry, followed by eighteen guns and the mass of the Prussian infantry.

To its horror, when the French van reached the lower slopes of Polsen Hill, the Prussian cavalry breasted the crest to their left. Without a moment's hesitation, Seydlitz gave the order to charge. Under perfect control, his thirty-eight squadrons thundered down the gentle slope, smashing into the French horsemen on the bridle hand and placing them at an immediate disadvantage as they cut their way through. It had now become an instinctive feature of revised Prussian cavalry tactics that on completion of a successful charge a forward rally took place, after which the charge was repeated in the opposite direction. Four times Seydlitz charged through his opponents, reducing them to a routed mob of individuals interested only in flight. It had taken him just thirty minutes to destroy the enemy cavalry.

Meanwhile, from the adjacent Janus Hill, the eighteen Prussian guns had opened fire, their balls ricocheting and bounding through the ranks of the French infantry columns. Seven battalions of Frederick's infantry also arrived, blasting fresh gaps through the ranks below. The French had ceased to advance but none of their senior officers seemed capable of forming a coherent battle line or regaining the initiative. A ragged but ineffective fire was maintained against those Prussians on the crest of Janus Hill but this ended when, despite a serious wound that kept him out of action for several months, Seydlitz mounted another charge, this time into the enemy's main body. Two hours after the battle had begun, the landscape was filled with fleeing fugitives from the allied army.

In terms of killed and wounded Soubise lost only 2,700 men, but 5,000 of his soldiers were taken prisoner; in addition, sixty-seven guns and twenty-two colours had been lost to the Prussians. Frederick's casualties included 517 men and twenty-three officers killed or wounded. In terms of troop numbers actually involved in the fighting, 10,000 men had beaten 40,000 in less than two hours. Understandably, the memory of Rossbach rankled the French for almost fifty years.

Rossbach alone would have been sufficient to establish Frederick's reputation, yet an even greater triumph was to follow a month later. After Rossbach, he marched into Silesia where an Austrian army commanded by Prince Charles of Lorraine and Marshal Daun had captured the city of Breslau. To retake it he had assembled an army consisting of 11,000 cavalry, 32,000 infantry and an artillery contingent reinforced with ten 12-pounder guns stripped from the fortress of Glogau. The Austrians had barred his path by establishing a position running from north to south across the Neumarkt–Breslau road to the west of the city, with its left among pine-clad hills, its centre in the village of Leuthen and its right protected by marshland and bogs around another village, Nypern. The line was strengthened by fortifying the villages and constructing earthwork redoubts, the whole being held by 72,000 men and 167 guns.

On the morning of 5 December the Prussian army was advancing along the road towards the Austrian position, led by Ziethen's cavalry screen. There had been a snowfall and visibility was restricted by a winter mist. Suddenly, the shapes of a line of Austrian vedettes showed up through the murk. Ziethen gave the order to charge immediately and drove them back towards their main body, taking a handful of prisoners in the process. On receiving the vedettes' confirmation that the Prussians were approaching, Charles and Daun reached the too-obvious conclusion that Frederick would mount a frontal attack and that this was imminent.

Nothing could have been further from the truth. Frederick had no intention of repeating the mistakes of Kolin and he now took full advantage of the fact that the loss of his vedettes had rendered the enemy blind to his intentions. With half his army he swung obliquely off the road to the right and marched through the snow-covered pinewoods, invisible to the Austrians. His intention was to envelope and assault the enemy left with superior numbers. Once it had been driven in, the rest of his army would attack the Austrian front, pinning it down and preventing it from forming a new flank. At about 13:00 the head of the Prussian column entered a hollow through which the now-frozen Schweidnitz brook ran. From this point, the end of the Austrian line was visible, protected by an abattis consisting of felled trees, behind which could be seen emplaced cannon and lines of white-coated infantry.

The Prussian infantry formed line to the left and the artillery's ten 12-pounder fortress guns opened fire, sending a rain of smashed timber and splinters among those behind. Added to the fire from the Prussian infantry, this was too much for those who, minutes before, had thought their position safe and secure. The fact was, the 6,000 Austrians holding their left flank now had 20,000 Prussians on their hands even though Ziethen, attempting to exploit prematurely into the enemy rear, received a temporary check from which he recovered after rallying behind several infantry battalions.

The Prussian advance was remorseless, destroying every Austrian attempt to form a new defensive front. From the direction of the main road, the rest of Frederick's army added its weight to the assault. A furious battle raged in and around Leuthen, where the church, the walled churchyard and two windmills were turned into temporary fortresses that had to be stormed at the point of the bayonet. Two bodies of cavalry under Generals Ziethen on the right and Driesen on the left, protected the flanks of the Prussian advance so that when the Austrian cavalry tried to intervene it was charged in flank and ripped apart by sustained musketry, only a few of its number managing to make good their escape. By the time dusk put an end to the fighting, Charles and Daun had completely lost control of the situation and the remnant of their army was streaming in utter rout along the road to Breslau.

Frederick and his escort actually mingled with the bolting fugitives without being recognised. At the village of Lissa he entered the court-yard of the manor house to find a dozen Austrian officers outside the building. The king greeted them courteously, commenting that while he knew that he was not expected he would be grateful for the opportunity to share their accommodation. In the circumstances the Austrians could hardly refuse.

At Leuthen the Prussians lost 6,000 men killed and wounded. Austrian losses included 10,000 men killed and wounded, 21,000 taken prisoner plus 116 guns, fifty-one colours and 4,000 wagons. On 9 December a further 2,000 were scooped up by the Prussians and on the 19th the 17,000-strong garrison of Breslau and another eighty-one guns fell into Frederick's hands.

Leuthen was Frederick's masterpiece and for the moment Austria was finished. Unfortunately, the war was not and it continued until 1762. During that period he fought almost continuously against Austrians, Russians, Swedes and the French. He won battles and lost them and at one stage Berlin, his capital, was in the hands of his enemies. Gradually, the strength of his army was eroded and his future began to look bleak until Russia's Tsarina Elizabeth, his most dangerous enemy, died in 1762. Her successor, Tsar Peter III, was an admirer of Frederick and he suspended Russia's hostilities against Prussia. The rest of Europe, weary of war, concluded a series of peace treaties that left Frederick in possession of Silesia.

Frederick spent the years between the end of the war and his death in 1786 restoring his country to prosperity. Overall, his achievement was to have turned Prussia into one of the great powers of Europe, although at this stage there was no question of its leading a drive towards Germanic unity. There were scores of independent German states, many of them tiny, and that would remain the case for many years to come. It was for his military achievements that Frederick was best remembered throughout Europe, yet the very essence of these tended to be overlooked. His emphasis on precise drill was slavishly copied by most armies, as though it was this that produced such victories as Rossbach and Leuthen rather than tactical genius. It was forgotten that drill was simply a means to an end and not the end in itself. The Prussian Army became wedded to the past while those officers who had actually served under Frederick came to be regarded as the fount of all military knowledge. There would be a price to be paid for this.

# CHAPTER 3

# The World Turned Upside Down

Following the ending of the Seven Years' War in 1763, the states of Central Europe enjoyed a generation of peace and prosperity under the rule of benevolent despots. With the exception of religious and topographical differences between north and south, it was possible to travel from state to state without knowing that one had crossed a boundary. Some, like Prussia, Hanover and Bavaria, were the size of nations, but many others were little larger than the average English county. The most obvious differences were in their soldiers' uniforms but even then one could watch them drilling in states far apart and performing the evolutions perfected by Frederick the Great's army. Indeed, these same evolutions were also being carried out in many armies beyond the geographical limits of Germany, so great was the prestige of the Prussian Army.

There were exceptions, of course. The British infantry preferred to fight in a two-deep firing line that extended the length of its units. In addition, instead of simply blazing away at the enemy's line of battle, it now aimed its shots at individual men or horses, with dramatic results. The first major occasion on which this took place was at Minden in 1759, when three charges by the French cavalry only ended in their destruction, while every infantry unit, be it French or Saxon, was simply chased off the field by the ferocious advance of scarlet-coated battalions. Nor was that quite all, for in its protracted struggle with the French for the possession of North America, it had learned the value of light infantry in skirmishing or fighting in broken country.

Naturally, the French had also learned light infantry skirmishing skills in North America, but they were concentrating on developing a system of land warfare that would guarantee success against the

Prussians and their imitators. As luck would have it, in General
Jean Baptiste de Gribeauval the French possessed one of the most
far-sighted artillerymen of the age. Starting in 1765 he began to
revolutionise the arm, standardising the field artillery into smooth-
bore 4-, 8- and 12-pounder guns and 6-inch howitzers cast in iron
or bronze. The weight of the pieces was reduced and they were
equipped with tangent scales and elevating screws to improve the
ease of laying, while their carriages were strengthened to improve
mobility. Compatible caissons and limbers were also produced. Horse
teams became harnessed in pairs rather than in tandem, and the
practice of employing civilian drivers, who were apt to vanish with
their mounts if a situation became dangerous, was discontinued, their
place being taken by disciplined soldiers. Within a dozen years he
had produced the finest contemporary artillery system of any nation.

The French Army was also introducing a new method of attack,
the column of battalions, although it was not credited with doing so
until somewhat later. The advantages of the column over the line in
these circumstances were that it gave men the reassurance of fighting
in close proximity with large numbers of their comrades and also
provided a sufficient combination of weight and speed to smash
its way through the opposing line. Of course those in the leading
battalion might suffer severely if the enemy did not give way before
their onset, and a further disadvantage was that if it was halted by the
enemy's fire only its leading ranks could reply. Against this, it was an
excellent means of employing even semi-trained troops in a mass
attack.

The French treasury had all but emptied itself after France took part
in the American War of Independence on the side of those colonists
seeking political separation from the United Kingdom. Since then,
the monarchy, the nobility and the functionaries of church and state
appeared to have done everything they could think of to provoke a
revolution, not, of course, because they sought their own overthrow,
but because they wished to preserve the status quo. Unfortunately for
them, the mass of poor, under-privileged, unrepresented, over-taxed
citizens had no wish to continue supporting the *ancien régime* and, in
1789, the revolution erupted, becoming progressively more violent
with every year that passed.

As far as the Army was concerned, some of its officers and men
escaped abroad and fought against France during the wars that
followed, although the quality of these *émigré* units left a lot to be

desired. Those that remained were joined by men who were idealists, those who had no intention whatever of returning to the bad old days, and those whom the revolutionaries forced to become soldiers. They had most to lose and fought with a degree of fierce personal motivation that was lacking in the professional armies they opposed. As far as the Army's officer corps was concerned, the cavalry lost most of its aristocratic officers and the infantry a lower proportion, the shortfall often being made good by the promotion of experienced NCOs. In the artillery and engineers, both branches of the service that demanded technical skills rather than social standing, most of the existing officers remained, among them a junior subaltern by the name of Napoleon Bonaparte.

The question facing revolutionary commanders was how to employ the diverse human material under their command to best advantage. As luck would have it, the methods were already to hand. The enemy line would be plagued by clouds of skirmishers. If the enemy infantry charged them, they would simply disperse and their own cavalry would charge through their opponents. If they were attacked by the enemy cavalry, they would form defensive squares as usual. Once the opposing battle line had been worn down, it would be assailed by deep columns of attack. If these could not be halted, they would break through the opposing lines and drive their survivors from the field. This was not the way the professional armies of Europe, brought up in the Fredrician school of tactics, had been trained to fight, and for a while they found it impossible to deal with.

Nothing could have emphasised the point more than the astonishing engagement that took place on 20 September 1792. Prussia was one of several continental nations which had formed a coalition with the intention of restoring the old order in France by means of force. A Prussian army under the command of Charles, Duke of Brunswick, who had served under Frederick the Great, was operating in the area of Verdun, accompanied by King Frederick III. Significantly, Brunswick's troops included a contingent of *émigrés* whom he neither liked nor trusted and it is quite possible that he felt disinclined to sacrifice too many of his own men pulling French chestnuts out of the fire. To the north-west of Verdun a 36,000-strong French force with some forty guns, commanded by Generals Kellerman and Dumouriez, had established itself across the Prussian lines of communication, its position centred on a low hill crowned by a windmill. It did not seem to present much of an obstacle and Brunswick simply detached

34,000 men and thirty-six guns to deal with it. A foggy dawn greeted
the day and out of it loomed the Prussians, pitching the French out of
an outpost in the village of la Lune. For some reason it took longer
than had been expected for the two forces to draw up their respective
lines of battle and the opposing artillery did not open fire until noon
had passed. Few had expected Kellermann's volunteer units to stand
for long but they did, keeping up their spirits with stirring patriotic
songs such as the inflammatory *Ça Ira* and cries of 'Vive la Nation!
Vive la France!'

At 13:00 Brunswick decided that the time had come to drive his
opponents off the field. His grenadier regiments formed line and began
their steady, measured advance on the enemy. The artillery fire on
both sides rose to a crescendo. That of the French regulars with their
Gribeauval guns quickly proved to be the more telling, bringing the
advance of the grenadiers to a standstill after they had covered just
200 yards. At this point a Prussian shot exploded three ammunition
limbers near the windmill. It unsettled the French and the moment
had come for the grenadiers to resume their advance. They did not,
largely because Brunswick claimed that they would be in immediate
danger of being charged by the French cavalry. In the meantime
Kellerman had rallied his volunteers and Dumouriez sent two fresh
batteries to the threatened sector. Firing continued until about 16:00,
when a heavy downpour put an end to the fighting. By then,
Brunswick had left the field, having given up hope of dislodging
Kellermann. The French had lost 300 men, the Prussians just 185.
These were astoundingly low figures, especially when one considers
that each side had fired over 20,000 cannon shots. However, the range
of the artillery battle was 1,350 yards, the maximum for contemporary
field guns, and the majority of the rounds simply buried themselves
in sodden clay that deprived them of the ricochet effect. One could
hardly dignify Valmy with the title of battle and it has always been
referred to as a cannonade. Nevertheless, both Sir Edward Creasy
and Major General J. F. C. Fuller include it in their studies of the
world's decisive battles. If Brunswick had not allowed himself to
be diverted by the French force at Valmy, he could have marched
on Paris unopposed and occupied the seat of the Revolution. Yet
somehow he had lost the will to win and within a month had
retreated into the Rhineland. Johann von Goethe, the great German
literary genius and polymath, was present with Brunswick's army
and quickly identified the changed nature of warfare, commenting to

his companions as they trudged off the battlefield: 'From today and at this spot there begins a new era and you can say that you were present. Thirty years will be required to make good this day and its consequences.' In other words, the small-scale dynastic wars of the past century had given place to the nation in arms and its commitment to total war.

In the French capital, the Revolutionary government went wild with joy. Kellerman and Dumouriez had repelled the most formidable army in Europe and the Revolution was safe! Two days later the monarchy was abolished and the following year King Louis XVI and Queen Marie Antoinette were executed. There would be other occasions when the new Republic seemed to be on the verge of collapse, but none were as potentially dangerous as that which had existed on the eve of Valmy. The year 1793 also saw France gripped by the infamous Reign of Terror in which none could consider themselves safe and the idealism of the Revolution was held in place by merciless discipline imposed by fear. It also saw the introduction of the *levée en masse* which made the entire male population liable for conscription, administered by the Republic's brilliant Minister for War, General Lazare Carnot, which produced no fewer than fourteen armies in a matter of weeks.

Fighting continued to rage around France's frontiers, without decisive results. The Prussian king, Frederick William II, had none of the energy and single-minded sense of purpose possessed by his late uncle, Frederick the Great. Indeed, his army failed to produce worthwhile results as the war progressed and this, coupled with the continuous strain on Prussia's exchequer, seemed to erode his self-confidence. He began to suspect the motives of his allies, Austria and Russia, and concluded a separate peace with France in 1795. Under the terms of this, the Treaty of Basel, Prussia shamefully abandoned German territories along the Rhine, yet secured a number of eastern provinces when Poland was partitioned. The latter almost doubled Prussia's size, yet they were of little value and did nothing to enhance her power. The result was a loss of national prestige, accompanied by a weakening of the army and a reduction in economic activity.

In 1797 Frederick William III succeeded his father. He attempted to repair some of the damage inflicted on his country during his father's reign but was indecisive by nature and was unpopular with his subjects because of it, so much so that his beautiful queen, Louise of Mecklenburg-Strelitz, was known as 'the only man in Prussia', mainly because of her detestation of the French. Following its spectacular defeat of Austria and Russia at Austerlitz in 1805, the former had made peace and most of Napoleon's Grande Armée had withdrawn into cantonments in central Germany. Napoleon himself was contemptuous of the Prussian king and did everything in his power to humiliate him publicly. This was not something that Queen Louise was prepared to tolerate and it was said that her husband's conjugal rights were withdrawn until he played the man.

Be that as it may, Frederick William ordered the Emperor of the French to remove his troops from Germany and see that they remained on the left bank of the Rhine in future. Given that Napoleon had crushed Austria and chased the Russians back across the Vistula, this was an astounding piece of cheek that must have made numerous Parisian jaws drop in astonishment. When the officers of the Prussian Garde du Corps Cuirassier Regiment trotted along to the French Embassy and sharpened their swords on its steps, the average Berliner may have felt that in the event of hostilities a Prussian victory was the most likely outcome. The fact was, when Prussia began to mobilise on 9 August 1806, she was in no condition to fight any sort of war. Her army general staff consisted of a few semi-trained individuals given to squabbling among themselves. The divisional organisation, containing elements of all arms, had been adopted but did not bear comparison with the much larger and more flexible corps, containing several divisions, employed by the French. Frederick the Great's large bodies of cavalry had been dispersed throughout the army and lacked the hard-driving leaders of old; even odder, the cuirassier regiments retained their title but had ceased to wear the cuirass. In the glory days an artillery reserve had been maintained; now, no such thing existed. Light infantry tactics were not popular and only a handful of regiments had been trained in these essential skills. As for mobility, divisions moved at the speed of their long supply trains, which was very slow indeed and added nothing to their tactical flexibility.

Naturally, Napoleon was hardly likely to ignore the challenge and began making plans for the invasion of Prussia immediately. The Prussian army also took the field under the operational command of the Duke of Brunswick, now aged seventy-one. Frederick William himself knew nothing of military matters and brought along a personal advisor, the aged Field Marshal von Möllendorff, with him into the field. The problem was that the field marshal was at, eighty-two, unlikely to be physically equal to the demands of active campaigning. Also present were most of the army's bureaucracy, including the various inspector generals and departmental heads. They could not be expected to get on with each other, let alone the various divisional commanders, and they did not. Needless to say, when the army marched south towards its operational area there was some disagreement about where this might be. One idea was to deprive Napoleon of his supply depots along the river Main, yet in this respect it lacked so much as one reliable map.

In fact, on 10 October the bulk of the Prussian army found itself near the town of Jena, with the bulk of it west of the Saale river and other elements to the north and east. In the meantime, during the early weeks of October the Grand Armée had passed through the difficult, wooded and hilly terrain of the Thüringer Wald in three main columns, led by six of Napoleon's most experienced Marshals – Lannes and Augerau on the left, Soult, Ney and the Bavarian contingent on the right, and Bernadotte and Davout, plus the Reserve Cavalry, the Imperial Guard and General Headquarters, in the centre. The French marched at speed – there was a saying among the French infantry that the Emperor made greater use of their legs than he did of their arms – and were soon in less difficult country. On 10 October, near Saalfeld, Lannes' V Corps encountered an 8,300-strong advanced Prussian detachment under Prince Louis Ferdinand, one of his army's more vigorous commanders, and the first major clash of the war took place. Despite being heavily outnumbered – Lannes could deploy over 21,000 men – the Prince courageously chose to engage and a fierce two-hour engagement took place. During this he was killed in hand-to-hand fighting while leading a desperate charge of five cavalry squadrons. His troops, routed, fled in disorder, leaving behind 2,800 of their comrades and abandoning twenty-five guns.

Lannes resumed his northward advance, as did the rest of the French corps to his right. Meanwhile, Brunswick had ordered the rest of his army, including a Saxon contingent, to effect a general concentration west of the Saale in the area of Erfurt. At this stage Napoleon had no clear idea as to the whereabouts of the main body of Brunswick's army. However, on 11 October his cavalry screen reported the enemy concentration west of the Saale. Orders were promptly given for the entire French army to change its direction of march to the west. The corps of Lannes and Augerau thus became its advance guard, those of Davout and Bernadotte its right wing, that of Ney and the heavy cavalry its left wing, and that of Soult its rearguard.

Both sides were now aware of the other's proximity. On the morning of 13 October Brunswick held a commanders' conference. He announced that he had no wish to fight a decisive battle in the area of Jena and issued instructions for the main body of the army to retreat northwards through Auerstädt and Naumberg towards Halle. A rearguard under Prince Friedrich von Hohenlohe-Ingelfingen would remain near Jena, its right flank protected by a reinforced divisional-sized force under General Ernst von Rüchel, now approaching from the north-west. During the afternoon, Napoleon and Lannes climbed a prominent feature named the Landgrafenberg on the west bank of the Saale, overlooking Jena. Examining the terrain ahead, the Emperor mistakenly believed that the entire Prussian army was present, although this did not affect his determination to attack the following morning. He recognised that the summit of the Landgrafenberg would provide an ideal site for his artillery, although the only possible approach for his guns and ammunition wagons was by way of a narrow, precipitous track. Much of the night, therefore, was spent making the track passable, the work being carried out by the light of flaring torches under the personal direction of Napoleon himself. In Jena itself several fires broke out as troops marching through stripped the town of its food and drink.

Most of the fighting on 14 October centred on the villages to the north and west of Jena. At 06:30 Lannes, his approach covered by fog, surprised the garrison of Closewitz and an hour later, with artillery support, had reached the curiously named Vierzehnheiligen (Fourteen Saints). At 08:15 Soult passed through Closewitz but was halted by stiff resistance outside Rodigen. An hour later Augerau by-passed Cospeda and deployed to attack Isserstedt.

By now, Hohenlohe no longer retained any doubts that he had a major battle on his hands. At 09:30 he ordered Lieutenant General von Holtzendorff, commanding the Prussian 1st Division's cavalry element, consisting of 1,900 cuirassiers and dragoons, to counter-attack Soult. Simultaneously, the remainder of the 1st Division, under Lieutenant General von Grawert, threw the French out of Vierzehnheiligen. Ney's corps had begun to enter the battle at about the same time. Anxious to be in the thick of the action, the impatient Alsatian led his advance guard against Vierzehnheiligen and by 10:15 it was in his hands. He then, rashly, continued his advance beyond the village, thereby losing the support of Lannes' corps on his right. Suddenly, he found himself isolated with only two cavalry regiments, one six-gun battery and three infantry battalions. His infantry was forced to form square as the Prussian cavalry circled round them while Grawert's infantry returned to administer the *coup de grace*.

In the nick of time Napoleon saw what was happening and at 10:30 sent in the heavy cavalry of his Guard. A furious mêlée ended Ney's isolation, but he remained under serious threat until 10:50 when Lannes came up on his immediate right. Forty minutes later Augerau captured Isserstedt and arrived on his left. Satisfied with this stabilisation, Napoleon ordered a general advance at 12:30. Although the Saxons recaptured Isserstedt at 13:00 and held it for an hour, Prussian resolve had been broken and Hohenlohe's retreat turned into a bloody rout when Napoleon unleashed Prince Joachim Murat's 19,000 cuirassiers and dragoons in a pursuit that only ended at Weimar at 18:00. French casualties at Jena amounted to 4,000 killed and wounded, while Prussian losses included 25,000 killed, wounded and captured.

That, however, was far from being the end of the story. On returning to his field headquarters Napoleon received the astonishing news that, while he had destroyed the enemy's rearguard, Davout's corps, fighting alone, had shattered the rest of the Prussian army at Auerstädt, fifteen miles to the north. At 03:00 that morning he had sent an order to Davout to block the Prussians' line of retreat at Auerstädt and inform Bernadotte that his corps was to conform. Bernadotte, however, believed in nothing more important than remaining his own master and, for good measure, he disliked Davout and refused to accept instructions from him. Instead of marching north to join Davout's corps in blocking the enemy's line of retreat, he turned south with the object of joining in the fighting at Jena but arrived after it had ended.

Davout had started moving at 04:30. Of necessity, his men marched hard and at 06:45 were in contact with the leading elements of Brunswick's army near the village of Hassenhausen, to the north of Auerstädt. The village was put into a defensible state by General Étienne Gudin's division. Between 08:00 and 08:45 Gudin stood off repeated attacks. At this point General Louis Friant's division reached the battlefield and took the village of Spielberg on the Prussian left. Simultaneously, Davout's corps cavalry and guns began reaching the battlefield. Nevertheless, Prussian pressure continued to build up and at 10:00 Hassenhausen, in danger of falling, was only saved when reinforcements arrived. During the fierce hand-to-hand fighting, old Field Marshal von Möllendorff was knocked down and became a prisoner. Shortly after, the Duke of Brunswick was mortally wounded and a pause ensued while King Frederick William was informed that he was in effective command. Completely at sea, he was never able to establish real control. Nevertheless, the fighting reached a desperate climax when the Prince of Orange's division came up on the Prussian right and was confronted by that of General Antoine Morand arriving on Davout's left. Some of Morand's infantry helped repel yet another attack on Hassenhausen, then, while the rest of their division formed square quickly and efficiently, lined the village's walls and hedges facing left. Watchers held their breath as no less than thirty squadrons of Prussian cavalry thundered past to attack Morand's squares. First, however, they had to endure flanking fire from the village and then they were torn to pieces by volleys from the squares, fired at thirty paces. Five times they charged, and five times they were thrown back before turning away to count their losses. Morand's division formed square and advanced without hesitation, driving Orange's infantry into headlong retreat.

The collapse of their right wing broke the Prussians' will to fight. Incredibly, Davout, who had stood off an army with a single corps all morning, launched a general advance and pursuit that did not halt until the hills above Auerstädt were reached at 16:30. Beyond, broken Prussian units were streaming away to the west, south and north. Davout had sustained 7,000 casualties, a high percentage of his strength; Prussian losses amounted to 10,000 killed, wounded and captured. A total of 200 Prussian guns were captured at Jena and Auerstädt. In both engagements the Prussians had fought to the best of their ability and sometimes with great courage as well as their traditional stubbornness. The fact was that they were essentially an amateur army commanded either by amateurs or old men who simply did not understand the mechanics of modern war and were therefore unable to plan for it. They had been opposed by a thoroughly experienced professional army commanded efficiently at every level and their defeat was inevitable.

Despite the completeness of his victory, Napoleon had bones to pick with two of his marshals. He was intolerant of any form of stupidity and was sharply critical of Ney for impetuously placing a major part of his corps in danger of being wiped out. He was even more intolerant of disobedience and Bernadotte, who, by his behaviour had played no part in either action, had placed himself within a hairsbreadth of a court martial. He escaped purely because of family connections. Once, Napoleon had been briefly engaged to a notable beauty from Marseilles, Desirée Clary. When the engagement ended Desirée had married Bernadotte, beginning a career that would end in her becoming Queen of Sweden and Norway. Her sister Julie married Napoleon's elder brother Joseph, becoming Queen of Naples and then Spain. Whatever the Emperor may have said to Bernadotte, the latter subsequently had not the slightest qualm about turning on his former sovereign and benefactor. For the moment, Bernadotte was permitted no rest and ordered to lead the pursuit of the shattered Prussian army.

On 16 October Murat's cavalry reached Erfurt and took 14,000 prisoners. The following day Bernadotte was in action at Halle, defeating a force under the Duke of Württemberg. By 20 October the French had reached the Elbe and two days later had secured two bridgeheads over the river. Simultaneously, Ney laid siege to Magdeburg, which surrendered to him on 10 November, yielding a further 22,000 prisoners. Elsewhere, Davout marched into Berlin on 25 October and Napoleon took up residence in the royal palace. Shortly after, Augerau arrived, shepherding numerous prisoners taken during the battles of Jena and Auerstädt, among them a number of the Garde du Corps who had so boastfully sharpened their swords on the steps of the French embassy and now begged not to be marched through the city. Augerau had been present in Berlin at the time of the incident, which he had personally witnessed. Understandably, he was less than sympathetic to their request and had them marched past the embassy itself where they were jeered by Berliners who had little time for the rich young noblemen who regarded the city as their personal property and behaved accordingly.

In the meantime, Napoleon had ridden over the field of Rossbach where he had a small memorial commemorating the French victory of 1757 taken down and smashed. On 25 October he visited Frederick the Great's tomb in the Garrison Church at Potsdam, confiscating the king's sword, hat, general officer's sash, ribbon of the Order of the Black Eagle and the standard carried by the Prussian Guard during the Seven Years' War.

The corps of Davout, Augerau and the recently arrived Jerome Bonaparte were directed eastwards to the Oder to forestall any possible

Russian intervention. Bernadotte and Murat's cavalry were pursuing Hohenlohe, who with the remnant of his force, was heading for Stettin at the mouth of the river. On 26 October his flank guard was overwhelmed at Zehndenick and two days later Hohenlohe surrendered his remaining 14,000 men at Prenzlau. On 29 October General of Division Antoine Lasalle, commanding Murat's Light Cavalry Division, talked the 5,000-strong garrison of Stettin into surrendering without the need to fire a shot.

The last remaining Prussian force still at liberty was Major General Gebhard von Blücher's 22,000 men, heading for Lübeck, near the Baltic coast, and the Danish border, hotly pursued by Murat, Bernadotte and Soult. Simultaneously, Napoleon's brother Louis, now King of Holland, was marching on Hamburg, as was Marshal Mortier's corps from the Rhineland. Rashly, Blücher forcibly occupied Lübeck, which was actually a free and neutral city, and demanded money and rations. Neither were supplied and on 6 November Soult and Bernadotte stormed the city, putting it to the sack. The Prussian Army's former Chief of Staff, Colonel Gerhard von Scharnhorst, was forced to surrender along with 10,000 of his men, but Blücher managed to fight his way clear of the city with part of his force. But, by 7 November, he was forced to surrender his remaining 8,000 starving men at Ratkau; on the same day a 600-strong Swedish contingent surrendered. Magdeburg was to hold out for a few days longer, but the campaign of 1806 was over.

For Prussia, its cost had been enormous. Twenty thousand of its soldiers had been killed, perhaps twice that number wounded, and 140,000 made prisoners of war. In addition, some 800 guns and 250 standards had been lost. These things, however, merely marked the beginning of Prussia's troubles. King Frederick William and Queen Louise found sanctuary with the Tsar, Russia still being in a state of war with Napoleon. The Queen was adamant that Prussia would not conclude a peace treaty with France and, during the 1807 campaign, notable for the battles of Eylau and Friedland, the honour of the Prussian Army was maintained by a corps-sized force, consisting of fugitive officers and soldiers under the command of General Anton L'Estocq. However, there came a time when even Napoleon accepted that there was no real benefit to be had in continuing the fighting. In July 1807 separate peace treaties between the warring parties were concluded on a raft moored in the Nieman river at Tilsit. At one stage Queen Louise was granted a lengthy audience with Napoleon, perhaps hoping to obtain favourable terms for Prussia. She found the Emperor to be quite impervious to her charms and the only terms he was prepared to grant virtually destroyed Prussia. All Prussian territory between the Elbe and the Rhine was to be forfeit, as was the land acquired during the partitions of Poland. The result was a reduction to half her pre-war size and population. Her army was to be limited in size to 42,000 men. She was to pay an indemnity of 140 million francs and, until that was paid, the country would remain under French occupation. It was also made clear that while Frederick William could retain his throne, he would do well to remember that the reality was that his country was a vassal state of the French Empire. Years were to pass before her status changed.

CHAPTER 4

# Picking Up The Pieces

In the aftermath of the Treaty of Tilsit, the priority for the Prussian authorities was to find ways of circumventing its restrictive provisions, particularly those relating to the drastic reduction in size of the country's army. King Frederick William established a reform commission to examine the appropriate steps that should be taken. This included the best and most intelligent young officers of the day and, as the provisions it made held good for the wars of 1866, 1870, 1914, 1939 and indeed during the present, it is worth examining the careers of some of its members.

Leading the commission was the recently promoted Major General Gerhard von Scharnhorst whose expertise was considered to exceed that of the most promising staff officer. Born to Hanoverian farming stock in 1775, he educated himself to the point that he was able to secure admission to the Count of Schaumburg-Lippe's military academy in the fortress of Wilhelmstein. In 1778 he received a commission in the Hanoverian service in which he served in the artillery. To supplement his pay he founded a military journal and wrote extensively on military matters.

His first campaign found him serving against French Revolutionary forces in the Netherlands under the Duke of York during the years 1793–94. His writings had succeeded his receiving invitations to join the armies of various allied states and after the Treaty of Basel he joined that of Prussia, receiving the rank of lieutenant colonel and the patent of nobility, enabling him to prefix his surname with von. He was employed in lecturing at the War Academy in Berlin, one of his junior students being Carl von Clausewitz. During the war of 1806 he served as Chief of General Staff to the Duke of Brunswick. In the final stages of that disastrous campaign he attached himself to General Blücher and was involved in the latter's capitulation. Exchanged shortly after, he played a major part in leading L'Estocq's Prussian corps, fighting with the Russian army, receiving Prussia's highest military decoration, the *Pour le Mérite*, for exceptional services during the Battle of Eylau.

As chief of the reform commission he put a stop to the recruitment of foreigners, abandoned the idea of a long-service professional army and replaced it with a national army in which all males of military age had a liability to serve. This had not quite been achieved by the time of his death but, by employing short service engagements, he built up the army's trained reserves to a point well beyond the limits of availability demanded by Napoleon. His further reforms included the abolition of corporal punishment, save in cases of flagrant insubordination, the granting of commissions to suitable candidates other than the nobility as well as battlefield commissions and general promotion for merit. To achieve a standardisation in the performance of junior officers, military schools for ensigns were set up in Berlin, Königsberg and Breslau while, for the further education of senior officers, the famous War Academy was established in 1810.

Particularly important was the decision to recruit and permanently station individual corps, including infantry, cavalry and artillery, in a specific province, with regiments establishing a permanent connection with a town or cluster of villages, thereby taking advantage of the principle that a soldier will fight harder if his comrades include his neighbours and relatives. Such a system also simplified the mobilisation process as a unit's reserves were already living nearby. In addition, Scharnhorst founded schools for the training of the artillery's junior officers and NCOs and instituted technical testing boards to examine the efficiency of military inventions.

August Neidhardt von Gneisenau was born at Schildau, Saxony, in 1760, the son of August Neidhardt, a lieutenant in the Saxon artillery. The family had very little money available and what there was seems to have been devoted to the boy's education for, in 1777, he entered the University of Erfurt and two years later joined an Austrian regiment quartered in the town. In 1782 he received a commission in the service of the Prince of Bayreuth-Ansbach, simultaneously adding the name Gneisenau, taken from a lost family estate in Austria, to his own. His career then took an unusual turn, for he served in one of the Prince's regiments that was rented to the British government for employment in North America during the American War of Independence. In 1786 he returned home with active service experience to offer and applied successfully for entry into the Prussian service, being granted a commission as first lieutenant in the infantry by Frederick the Great. For the next ten years he was employed in garrison duties, using his spare time to study political and military history.

Appointed to the reform commission, he was primarily involved in the problems of reorganising the army but was strongly supportive of Scharnhorst and his reforms. By 1809 he was a colonel and his activities had attracted the unwelcome attention of the French intelligence service. This led to his retirement, but he immediately undertook a series of confidential visits to Austria, Russia, Sweden and the United Kingdom, all of whom had been or were potential enemies of France. The precise nature of these discussions remains unknown, but clearly their subject matter related to future combined action against Napoleon. On his return to Berlin he again took up his position as acknowledged leader of Prussia's patriotic party.

Hermann von Boyen was born in Kreuzberg, East Prussia, in 1771. He joined the army in 1784 and in 1806 served on the staff of the Duke of Brunswick, being wounded at the Battle of Auerstädt. Following the Treaty of Tilsit he served in the reform commission, being regarded by Scharnhorst as his most diligent assistant. However, when Napoleon forced Prussia to ally herself with France in 1812, he resigned his colonel's commission and spent his time visiting Vienna and St Petersburg.

Karl von Grolman was born in Berlin in 1777 and was gazetted as ensign in 1795, second lieutenant in 1797, first lieutenant in 1804 and staff captain in 1805. He had attracted Scharnhorst's attention prior to the war of 1806 and during the period between Jena and the Treaty of Tilsit he had served on the staff, winning promotion to major for distinguished service in action. Following this he joined the reform commission.

At this point his career was influenced by an unexpected turn of events. In June 1806 a quasi-Masonic organisation known as the Tugendbund (League of Virtue) was founded. Whatever its benevolent aims might have been, its membership included men noted for their patriotism, including Scharnhorst, Gneisenau and Grolman. Naturally, this attracted the interest of the French intelligence service, in particular the activities of a Major Ferdinand von Schill, the son of Saxon officer who had raised a Freikorps, a small raiding unit consisting of cavalry and mounted infantry, during the Seven Years' War.

Ferdinand had entered the Prussian cavalry during his early teenage years. While serving as a second lieutenant in a dragoon regiment he had been wounded at Auerstädt but had managed to make his way to the fortress of Kolberg, in the siege of which he had played a notable part. Following the family tradition, he had raised a Freikorps of his own and raided extensively with it behind French lines. After the Treaty of Tilsit he was promoted to major and given command of a hussar regiment containing most of his Freikorps soldiers.

In 1809 the probability of war between France and Austria encouraged him to make an attempt to liberate Germany from French rule. Many of his fellow Tugendbund members believed that the Kingdom of Westphalia, recently created by Napoleon for the benefit of his youngest brother, Jerome, was likely to rebel against the Bonapartes, given sufficient encouragement. While he was prepared to create the necessary uprising himself, the less practical aspects of his plan involved active support provided by Austria, Spain and Great Britain.

He led his regiment out of Berlin before officially raising the standard of Westphalian rebellion, then marched through Saxony and into Westphalia, attracting a number of officers and a light infantry company along the way. On 5 May 1809 he won a small victory over half-hearted Westphalian troops at the village of Dodendorf, and was soon commanding in excess of 2,000 men. However, he received none of the foreign support he had hoped for and even his own sovereign, Frederick William III, condemned his action, fearing that his already weakened country might be dragged into another war with Napoleon. He was forced to retire north-eastwards to Stralsund where he was surrounded by some 8,000 Dutch and Danish troops under French command. On 31 May the town was stormed and Schill was killed in the fighting. About 1,000 of his men escaped to Prussia, the Prussian officers being court martialled, cashiered and imprisoned but sub-sequently pardoned. Others escaped to Sweden but the remainder were either killed or captured. Most of the 570 prisoners were condemned to pulling an oar in the galleys, while eleven officers and fourteen Westphalian deserters were executed. Schill's body was decapitated, the head being presented to Louis Bonaparte, who passed it on to a Dutch surgeon with a taste for the bizarre; it was returned to German patriots in 1837 and placed in a monument in Brunswick. Schill may be regarded as hopelessly optimistic or even foolish, but in Germany he came to be regarded as a national hero.

Monuments were erected to him, and throughout the country streets and squares were named after him.

Grolman might well have joined Schill's rising but for its early failure. As his sympathies placed him at some risk he entered the Austrian service and received the rank of major on the general staff. He then travelled to Cadiz to assist the Spanish in their struggle against Napoleon, leading a volunteer unit in defence of the city. He took part in the hard fought battle of Albuera and was also present at the engagements of Saguntum and Valencia. Captured on the last occasion, he made a remarkable escape to Switzerland and, in 1813, returned to the Prussian army's general staff.

Another of Scharnhorst's group responsible for the reform of the army was the soldier, philosopher and military theorist Carl von Clausewitz, who was born in 1780 and entered the service as a twelve-year-old lance corporal. He served in the Rhine campaigns of 1793–94 and in 1806 was captured at Jena–Auerstädt. After two years' imprisonment in France he returned to Berlin to assist the reform commission and lecture at the War Academy. It has sometimes been suggested, and as often denied, that his thinking was influenced by the philosopher Hegel, but that is a point best argued by those with a thorough philosophical training. His best known work, *On War*, propositions on the nature of war (a) 'War is an act of force to compel our enemy to do our will', and (b) 'War is merely the continuation of policy by other means'.

When Napoleon forced a compulsory alliance on Prussia in 1812, Clausewitz simply could not tolerate the idea of having to fight France's battles. He left Prussia and joined the Russo-German legion. His subsequent experiences involved the ferocious battle of Borodino and assistance in the negotiations leading to the Convention of Tauroggen, signed jointly by the Prussian General Ludwig Yorck von Wartenburg and the Russian General Hans Karl von Diebitsch on 30 December. The effect of this was to neutralise the Prussian corps that had been serving with the *Grande Armée* in Russia and permit the free passage of Russian troops across Prussia. The result was to induce a widespread popular rising in Prussia, leading Frederick William to sign an offensive alliance with Russia. On 17 March 1813 Prussia declared war on France.

As the remnant of Napoleon's *Grande Armée*, a pitiful remnant of its former self, staggered back from its invasion of Russia, Clausewitz was involved in the process in which the Prussian army turned on it. This was a situation that appealed to the author C. S. Forester who, in his novel *The Commodore*, sent his hero, Horatio Hornblower, into the Baltic with a squadron of warships. Forester arranged for Hornblower and Clausewitz to meet during the siege of Riga and exchange views to their mutual benefit. In 1815 the Russo-German Legion was absorbed into the Prussian army and Clausewitz resumed his career in the Prussian service.

A most important contribution to achieving Scharnhorst's concept of a national army was made not by a soldier but by a senior civil servant, Heinrich Reichsfreiherr von und zum Stein, who was born on the family estate near Nassau in 1757. Following the Treaty of Tilsit, Stein was called to high office and granted wide powers. In brief, his achievements included the abolition of serfdom, the removal of distinctions relating to nobles' or peasants' land, the principle of unfettered trade in land, the abrogation of class distinctions insofar as they affected every calling and occupation, and a measure of municipal reform granting local self-government to all Prussian towns and villages with more than 800 inhabitants. Such measures provided the reformed army with the motivation to fight for the country itself rather than just its sovereign.

Stein was also a deeply committed patriot, a fact of which Napoleon remained in complete ignorance. Thus, when his intelligence service intercepted one of Stein's letters expressing the hope that a national uprising similar to that of Spain would soon take place in Germany, his fury was boundless. Well aware that he was in considerable danger, Stein hurriedly left Berlin on 5 January 1809 and crossed the frontier into Bohemia where a former colleague, Count Frederick von Reden, provided temporary sanctuary for him in his castle in the Riesengengebirge. Stein spent the next three years in Austria, mainly at Brno, but by 1812 he was in increasing danger of being surrendered to Napoleon by the Austrian authorities. Fortunately, in the nick of time he received an invitation from Tsar Alexander I to visit St Petersburg.

Following the Convention of Tauroggen, the Tsar asked Stein to act as provisional administrator of East and West Prussia. While serving in this capacity, Stein established the Landwehr, a militia force, and a reserve for it known as the Landsturm. Frederick William took exception to what he saw as a civil servant exceeding his authority by a wide margin and the relationship between Stein and the king became distinctly chilly for a while. Nevertheless, when the United

Kingdom and Austria joined the Russo-Prussian alliance, Stein's view that the war must continue until Napoleon had been removed from the throne of France won general approval and he received the important task of superintending the administration of the liberated territories. He had played a major part in setting in motion the train of events that would free central Europe from French dominion but his hopes of creating a reconstituted Germany as a single political entity were foiled by the Austrian Prince Metternich and the rulers of the minor German states. In fact, the idea was not all that far ahead of its time.

# CHAPTER 5

# Hollow Victory

Having to take over a battle that is failing, let alone one that is lost, is the nightmare of every general. As the remnant of the *Grande Armée* staggered out of Russia into Poland at the beginning of December 1812 its capacity for war barely existed and had not the equally exhausted Russians called a temporary halt to their pursuit its destruction would have been assured. On 5 December Napoleon left the army to return to France and raise fresh troops, leaving Marshal Joachim Murat, more commonly referred to since 1808 as the King of Naples, in command of the army. Murat brought it out through Vilna, Kovno, Königsberg and Elbing. On 1 January 1813 the Prussian corps that had been serving in the *Grande Armée* went over to the Russians and there were anti-French risings right across Prussia. On 18 January Murat reached the conclusion that life in winter at Naples was infinitely preferable to that on the Baltic coast and handed over to the Emperor's stepson, Eugene de Beauharnais.

Eugene was the son of General Alexandre de Beauharnais, who was guillotined during the Terror, and Josephine Tascher, later Napoleon's first wife. He was no fool and when the Prussian corps defected he adopted a defensive stance pending the arrival of the Emperor's reinforcements. Garrisons were put into Danzig, Thorn, Stettin, Kustrin and Frankfurt on the Oder. Eugene himself withdrew to Magdeburg on the Elbe where, in late January, the first of the reinforcements arrived, raising his strength to 68,000 men. This was offset by the desertion of the Austrian contingent serving with the *Grand Armée*, which, having reached Warsaw, had turned away to enter Bohemia. During February and March it began to seem as though the whole of Europe had turned against Napoleon. Russia, Prussia, Sweden and the United Kingdom had formed a new coalition and in the Elbe valley had 100,000 experienced troops deployed between Magdeburg and Dresden. In the Iberian peninsula, the Duke of Wellington's Anglo-Portuguese army, including the King's German Legion, consisting mainly, but not exclusively, of exiled Hanoverians, and Spanish patriotic armies had fatally loosened King Joseph Bonaparte's grip on the country and were pushing his French troops across the Pyrenees into France itself.

Nevertheless, in France Napoleon had brought forward the conscription date of his recruits and in April returned to Germany with a 200,000-strong army that joined the remnant of the *Grande Armée*. To an outsider, his army seemed to consist of fresh-faced boys few of whom had reached the age at which they would begin shaving, and hard-eyed men of middle years prematurely worn down by their recent experiences. Yet, curiously, both would respond to Napoleon who was about to fight what some historians have described as the most brilliant campaigns of his career.

As far as Prussia was concerned, her army was commanded by General Leberecht von Blücher who, despite having been born in 1742 and having served as a light cavalryman, was still a dashing hussar at heart. As already mentioned, in the aftermath of the disaster at Jena-Auerstädt he had continued to lead a considerable body of the Prussian army until cornered at Prenzlau and forced to surrender, lacking the food and ammunition with which to continue the fight. In 1813, at the start of the War of Liberation, his Chief of Staff was Gerhard von Scharnhorst who was thus able to experience at first hand the improvement his reforms had brought about in the army's quality. Such was Scharnhorst's reputation for brilliance that the Russian Prince Wittgenstein, in overall command of the allied armies, requested his temporary attachment as his own Chief of Staff, a request to which Blücher generously agreed.

The first major action of the new war was fought at Lützen on 2 May. Napoleon was taken by surprise but rallied quickly, massing his artillery against Wittgenstein's centre and then personally leading a major counter-attack that divided the allies and forced them into a withdrawal. Each side sustained approximately 18,000 casualties. For the Prussians, the battle had not been a success, but neither had it been a disaster as the French conscripts simply lacked the stamina for a pursuit. For Prussia the most serious loss of the day was that of Scharnhorst who had received a wound in the foot. This began to fester and resulted in his death on 28 June in Prague, where he had travelled to negotiate Austria's entry into the war with Field Marshals Schwarzenberg and Radetzky.

Three weeks after Lützen, the war's second battle took place at Bautzen. Napoleon had mounted a frontal attack against the allied armies, which would be trapped and virtually destroyed once Ney, after outflanking them with a night march, fell on their flank and rear at dawn. Unfortunately for the French, Ney did not seem to have understood what was required of him and Wittgenstein was able to break contact and withdraw into Silesia. The battle cost each side some 20,000 casualties.

By now the scales were beginning to tilt against Napoleon. Bernadotte, once a marshal of France and now Crown Prince of Sweden, was approaching Berlin with a 120,000-strong Prusso-Swedish army while in Austria, on the eve of declaring war, which, in fact, she did on 12 August, a 240,000-strong army under Schwarzenberg had assembled in northern Bohemia and was already dangerously close to the French lines of communication. Elsewhere, Blücher had taken over command of Wittgenstein's army which he reorganised and used to check any further French advance. Aware of the situation's dangerous potential, Napoleon requested an armistice. Incredibly, this was granted on 4 June and held until 16 August. Napoleon used the time granted to deploy his troops to their best advantage and achieve a higher standard of training in his conscripts. By 16 August he had 300,000 men immediately available, but was opposed by the allies with 450,000. On the other hand, so great was the latters' awe of Napoleon that their strategy was to avoid engaging him directly and concentrate on attacking his major subordinate commanders whenever possible. This showed signs of successes when, on 23 August at Grossbeeren, Bernadotte trounced his former comrade in arms, Oudinot, while three days later Blücher defeated Macdonald at Katbach.

These successes, while welcome, were deceptive, for on 26 August a major battle developed at Dresden. Schwarzenberg's army, which had been joined by the Emperors of Austria and Russia and the King of Prussia, attacked the city, held by Marshal Laurent de Gouvion St Cyr. All seemed to be going well but the following day Napoleon took the allies by surprise when he suddenly arrived on the battle-field with reinforcements. Despite having only half the strength of his opponents he smashed through their left flank and inflicted heavy casualties. Having lost a crippling 38,000 men killed, wounded or taken prisoner, plus forty guns, Schwarzenberg disengaged before he was completely encircled and retreated.

Perhaps Napoleon's victory would have been greater had he not succumbed to one of his increasingly frequent torpors and left the battlefield to rest. However, the potential was not lost on one of his corps commanders, General Dominique Vandamme, who, completely unsupported, pushed his men into a forced march across the mountains into Bohemia and took up a position across the allied line of communications at Kulm. The result was a complete disaster that nullified the result of the battle of Dresden. On 29 August his corps was surrounded by over 100,000 Austrians, Russians and Prussians and had virtually ceased to exist the following day. A hard, rough-spoken professional soldier, he boasted that he feared neither God nor the Devil yet admitted that he felt a real sense of terror in the presence of Napoleon. Indeed, far from being impressed by Vandamme's bully-boy manner, the Emperor commented that he wished he had two of him in his service so that the one could set about hanging the other! Vandamme was brought before Tsar Alexander I who was well aware of his reputation as a thief and took him to task on the subject, only to receive the defiant response, 'At least I have never been accused of killing my father!'

Matters continued to go from bad to worse for the French. On 6 September Ney attempted to take Berlin but was defeated by Bernadotte when his Saxon divisions deserted him. On 8th Bavaria, normally a reliable ally of France, withdrew from the Napoleonic Confederation of the Rhine and joined the Allies. Here were the first signs that the War of Liberation was bringing Germans to fight together as they had never done before.

Napoleon's response was to concentrate his troops at Leipzig, where he succeeded in concentrating some 185,000 men with 600 guns against Austrians, Prussians, Russians and Swedes with 300,000 men, 1,400 guns closed in around the city. The subsequent fighting lasted from 16 to 18 October and, for obvious reasons, has become known as The Battle of the Nations. Napoleon fought the Prussians to the north-west, the Austrians and Russians to the south, and then Bernadotte to the east, who almost completed their encirclement of the French. The allies then commenced a series of concentrated frontal attacks, forcing the French into the city, in which savage fighting continued. Whatever chance Napoleon may have had of gaining a victory vanished when the Saxon corps deserted him. Further disaster followed when the bridge over the Elster was blown prematurely. Two marshals, Jacques Macdonald and Prince Anton Poniatowski, tried to swim their horses across but only Macdonald succeeded in reaching the far bank.

Leipzig was a shattering defeat for Napoleon. Approximately 60,000 of his men were dead, wounded or prisoners while his material losses included 150 guns and 500 wagons. It was not a cheap victory for the allies, who had lost over 60,000 men. One interesting aspect of the battle was the presence of a British rocket troop serving with the Swedish contingent. The rockets were carefully aimed at their point of departure but tended to please themselves where they went as they streaked noisily across the battlefield on their fiery tails. They caused comparatively few casualties but instilled a great deal of fear.

Napoleon withdrew the remnant of his army towards the Rhine. The Bavarians, learning of his defeat, sent a 40,000-strong army under Prince Karl von Wrede to cut him off but received a mauling at Hanau on 30–31 October, losing 9,000 men and a number of guns, at a cost to the French of 5,000 casualties. Resuming its retreat, the French army crossed to the left bank of the Rhine during the five days of 1–5 November 1813.

On 8 November Napoleon received an unexpectedly generous peace offer. The salient points of this were that Napoleon would be permitted to retain his throne provided the frontiers of France were re-drawn behind the Alps and the Rhine. In the prevailing circumstances the Emperor would have done well to consider these favourably as the Netherlands were in open rebellion and the Confederation of the Rhine was disintegrating. Furthermore, the French garrison of Dresden surrendered on 11 November. Unwisely, Napoleon rejected the offer. The only alternative left to the allies, therefore, was to finish the war by invading France and, on 21 December, they crossed the Rhine at Mannheim and Koblenz.

Such assets as Napoleon still possessed were widely scattered. The garrison of Danzig surrendered on 30 December, and although there were some 50,000 men still remaining in German garrisons, the majority of them in Hamburg, they lacked the ability to influence future events. In Spain there were another 100,000 fighting hard to delay the advance of the Spaniards and the Duke of Wellington's Anglo-Portuguese army into France, and there was no possibility that any of them could be withdrawn. The same was true of Prince Eugene Beauharnais' 50,000-strong army in north-eastern Italy, where it was confronted by an Austrian army of equal strength. Nearer to hand, Napoleon could muster about 118,000 men west of the Rhine along a frontage stretching from Antwerp to Lyon. As the year 1814 dawned, his intention was to operate on interior lines, defeating each of the allied armies in turn. In this he was assisted by the allies' own deployment, the object of which was centred on Paris, which would be approached along separate routes. Bernadotte was advancing west through Holland and Belgium with a 60,000-strong army; Blücher, with 75,000 men, was marching up the Moselle Valley into Lorraine; and Schwarzenberg, the strongest of the three with 210,000 men under command, was crossing neutral Swiss territory and penetrating the Belfort Gap.

Napoleon's conduct of the subsequent operations, lasting from the end of January until April 1814, have been described as being among the most brilliant of his career. His primary objective was to prevent Blücher and Schwarzenberg joining forces. Starting on 29 January he fought a series of actions against Blücher, designed to halt his drive on Paris down the Marne. In most of these he inflicted the heavier loss but the checks he imposed were only temporary. On 18 February he turned on Schwarzenberg, who was advancing on Paris down the Seine, and defeated him at Montereau, forcing him to retire some forty miles. Blücher, meanwhile, had regrouped and had reached a point only twenty-five miles from Paris. Leaving Macdonald to watch Schwarzenberg, Napoleon attacked Blücher on 7 March at Craonne and drove him back north, seriously mauling his Russian rearguard. Shortly after, Blücher received a reinforcement of two corps from Bernadotte, raising his strength to 100,000 men, three times the number available to Napoleon. Simultaneously, Schwarzenberg had defeated Macdonald at Bar-sur-Aube and forced him back towards Paris.

It goes without saying that, however brilliantly he was performing, sheer attrition was taking its toll of Napoleon's army. It was true, of course, that the Prussians were also having to absorb regular losses, but theirs was the national army Scharnhorst had created and their motivation and dogged determination was evident with every battle they fought. This became apparent on 9–10 March when Napoleon rashly attacked a strong position they were holding at Laon. At the critical moment Blücher led a counter-attack during the night, causing a complete French corps to bolt in panic. On 13 March the Emperor had some measure of revenge when he drove an isolated Prussian corps out of Rheims, inflicting serious casualties.

Hardly pausing, he then marched against the Austrian lines of communication, hoping to panic Schwarzenberg into a withdrawal. Schwarzenberg did not panic and effectively repelled the French attack at Arcis-sur-Aube on 20–21 March. Appreciating that he was now dangerously close to the limit of his resources, Napoleon ordered the corps of Marshals Marmont and Mortier to join him. Both corps, however, were understrength and were beaten by Schwarzenberg at la Fère-Champenoise on 25 March, then driven back on Paris, leaving the Emperor's own army marooned far to the east.

Blücher and Schwarzenberg joined forces near Paris on 25 March, effecting a concentration of approximately 110,000 men. With just 22,000 men at their disposal, Marmont and Mortier fought hard to stem the allied advance but on 30 March they were pushed back to the Buttes de Montmartre, from which the allied artillery could fire into the city. Recognising that further resistance was pointless, Marmont surrendered the capital the following day.

By then Napoleon, desperate to save Paris if at all possible, had reached Fontainebleau and halted, uncertain how to proceed next. The members of his marshallate left him in no doubt. The military situation was impossible; therefore, there was absolutely no point in continuing to fight and the Emperor must abdicate. There were no grounds for doubting that the Bourbon monarchy would be restored and they had to consider their own relationships with their future rulers. Furthermore, having been constantly at war for the greater part of their adult lives, they were tired and wished to enjoy some of the benefits that they believed they had earned in the service of France. On 6 April Napoleon abdicated in favour of his son. This was not acceptable to the allies and on 11 April his abdication was made unconditional. He was permitted to retire to the small island of Elba, off the Italian coast, and maintain a small guard.

The return of His Most Christian Majesty King Louis XVIII to the throne of France was not an event likely to inspire his subjects. Now aged over sixty, he weighed in at about 310 pounds and his waddling progress required the assistance of two servants. He was unbelievably rude to the Tsar, whose army had played a major part in the defeat of Napoleon, and was not unduly grateful that, after more than two decades of aggressive war, France was permitted to retain her 1792 frontiers, plus a little more. Louis seemed determined to return his country to its pre-revolutionary state. The *tricoleur*, long since recognised as the national flag, was immediately replaced by the white with golden *fleurs de Lys* of the Bourbon family. The status of the old Imperial Guard was pointedly reduced by changing its name to the Grenadiers of France, while new and militarily useless guard units were formed from overpaid *émigré* popinjays, some of whom barely possessed a fragmentary right to a coat of arms. Hundreds of Napoleon's veteran officers were sent home on half pay, which might or might not be paid. Returning members of the *émigré* nobility were horrified to discover not only that the common folk no longer grovelled to them but also that their medieval property rights had ceased to have much force in law. Nevertheless, they fought hard to recover town houses that had long since been turned into apartments and vast hunting estates that had been turned over to the plough and they had the sympathy of the king and his ministers. The Bonapartist nobility, including the wives of marshals, were deliberately and publicly humiliated. It seemed as though nothing mattered more to the new administration than turning the clock back to 1789, and it was not something that the people, who had enjoyed years of stability under Napoleon, were prepared to tolerate for long. Naturally, these disturbing currents in French national life were reported to governments throughout Europe, particularly in Vienna, where the victorious powers were discussing the shape of the new Europe, and were understandably observed with particular interest in the former Emperor's new home on the island of Elba.

Once he was satisfied that he would be well received in France, Napoleon made preparations for his return to power. On 26 February 1815 he sailed from Elba with three small ships, 1,100 men, forty horses, two guns and a coach. Somehow, the tiny invasion force evaded contact with the British and French warships in the area and landed in the Golfe Juan on 1 March. It immediately set off northwards in the direction of Grenoble, its progress being reported to Paris by means of the telegraph system recently invented by M. Claude Chappe. By 5 March King Louis was aware of the situation. The war ministry and everyone who might be capable of halting Napoleon's progress was informed and the general view expressed was that he would soon be halted and confined to a prison. In fact, at every point along the way the troops sent to intercept him actually joined his expanding army while the civilians sang the old revolutionary songs, broke out the *tricoleur* and damned the king, his ministers, the nobility and the clergy to hell. The politicians in Vienna, whose apple cart had been well and truly overturned, might well declare that Napoleon was now an outlaw, but as far as the French were concerned he was a very popular one.

On 7 March he reached Grenoble; on 10 March he was at Lyon; on 14 March at Chalon-sur-Saône; on 17 at Auxerre. On 19 March he entered Sens and King Louis hastily hurriedly left Paris. On 20 March Napoleon entered Paris while the King prepared to leave Abbeville for the apparent safety of Belgium. Once again, France and the European powers mobilised for a renewal of wars that had already lasted over twenty years.

# CHAPTER 6

# 'Vorwarts!'

While the armies of both sides assembled on either side of the French frontier, there was general agreement that the theatre of war most likely to produce the first decisive results of the new war lay in the Low Countries, and particularly in Belgium. There the allies assembled two armies, one under the Duke of Wellington and the other under Field Marshal Blücher. The first had been hastily raised and its composition pleased its commander so little that he described it as 'an infamous army'. It contained comparatively few of his British Peninsular War veterans, most having been shipped across the Atlantic to take part in the war against the United States, and the bulk of the British infantry present were second-line battalions with only limited experience. The exceptions were the experienced and very formidable King's German Legion, whose hopes of disbandment followed by a return to its German homes had been dashed by Napoleon's escape from Elba. More German units had joined Wellington direct from Hanover, Brunswick and Nassau, but the quality of these varied considerably. For example, during the coming fighting most Hanoverian units stood their ground but at Waterloo one unit, the Cumberland Hussars, named after the second son of George II who had made himself so unpopular in the Scottish Highlands, refused to fight and trotted off in the middle of the battle to warn the good people of Brussels that Wellington had been defeated; curiously, in later years it became to be regarded as a 'fashionable' regiment joined by rich young men. Most of the green-uniformed Nassauers had fought in the Peninsula against the British and were, with one exception, considered to be experienced and reliable with, for their numbers, the finest fighting record of any contingent in Wellington's army. The Duke of Brunswick, whose father had been killed at Jena, was brother-in-law to the British Prince Regent and because of this his small contingent had been placed under Wellington's command. Their black uniform, topped in some units with a silver skull badge on the front of their shakos, gave them a sinister appearance and was said to have been introduced in memory of the late duke. Wellington had formed a poor opinion of Brunswickers in the Peninsula, but during the present campaign they did their duty. The Duke was killed leading a charge at Quatre Bras, and at Waterloo, despite showing signs of acute nervousness, they stood up to the enemy's fire and his cavalry attacks and took part in the final advance. Second only in size to the British contingent was that of the Netherlands, which included both Dutch and Belgian troops. As some of these had been in the service of Napoleon as recently as 1814, there was some doubt as to their loyalty. In the event, some produced an outstanding performance while others had little reason to be pleased with themselves. In total, Wellington's army contained 63,632 infantry, 14,480 cavalry and 174 guns.

Following the campaign of 1814, Blücher had been created Prince of Wahlstatt in Silesia. He was the ideal choice of commander to co-operate with Wellington as, following the first surrender of Napoleon, he had paid a visit to England where he was lionised wherever he went. His chief of staff was Lieutenant General Count August von Gneisenau with Major General Karl von Grolman acting as quarter-master-general. In the circumstances one advantage Blücher had over Wellington was that his Prussian army was entirely homogeneous. Fortunately, any problems that might have been caused by the different languages of the allies were solved by Major General Baron Carl von Müffling, the excellent liaison officer made available to Wellington by Blücher during the most critical days of the campaign.

Blücher's army consisted of four corps. I Corps was commanded by Lieutenant General Count Hans von Ziethen, a professional cavalry-man who had served against France during the War of Liberation. II Corps was under the command of Major General Georg Pirch, who had only received the appointment the previous month following the departure in disgrace of its former commander. III Corps' commander was Lieutenant General Freiherr Johann von Thielmann, who had been born in Dresden and commanded a Saxon cavalry brigade during the invasion of Russia, acquitting himself well at the battle of Borodino. In 1813 he had commanded the garrison of Torgau for the Emperor but when Napoleon had summoned him to take the field he had defected to the allies. While operating against the French communications between Leipzig and Erfurt he had been defeated by Lefebre-Desnouettes, another professional cavalryman, at Merseburg, and repaid the compliment at Altenburg. IV Corps was commanded by General Count Friedrich Bülow von Dennewitz who had commanded a division of the Prussian army in 1813, winning several important actions during the War of Liberation and the following year had received command of his corps with which he distinguished himself at the battle of Laon. Altogether, Blücher's army contained 99,646 infantry, 11,948 cavalry and 296 guns.

There was a certain inevitability about the way in which the campaign in Belgium would develop. Wellington, based at Brussels, and Blücher, who had entered the country through Namur, had agreed to fight the decisive action in concert at Mont St Jean, south of the village of Waterloo, which was itself situated south of Brussels on the Charleroi road, as well as imposing such checks as were necessary on the French progress prior to this. It was entirely logical that Wellington and Blücher should wish to join forces, and equally logical that Napoleon should follow his own tradition of preventing them from doing so. In the past, when confronted by two opponents, he would concentrate on destroying one before it could join the other, and then eliminate his second opponent with his entire army. In the present circumstances his Army of the North, consisting of 80,350 infantry, 13,049 cavalry and 286 guns, had entered Belgium through Charleroi on 15 June 1815 and was advancing northwards on a broad front. On learning of this Wellington and Blucher moved to impose checks at, respectively, Quatre Bras and Ligny, prior to retiring on Mont St Jean. At this stage we are concerned primarily with events as they affected the Prussian army.

At Ligny Blücher deployed the corps of Ziethen, Pirch and Thielmann on a series of low ridges north of the little Ligny Brook with strong detachments in the villages along its banks, notably in Ligny itself. Napoleon's plan was to employ the corps of Gerard and Vandamme in holding attacks while d'Erlon's corps, brought over from Ney's command to the west, enveloped the Prussian right flank. At this point the Guard Corps would deliver the final crushing assault and a considerable body of cavalry would pursue the broken Prussian army as it fled from the field. That, however, was not how the battle developed. Gerard and Vandamme began their assault at 14:30 but met determined resistance. Only after several hours of heavy fighting did the Prussians show any sign of giving ground.

This was the moment d'Erlon should have entered the battle, but there was no sign of him. However, a large body of troops was seen advancing towards the left rear of the French, and if that was part of Wellington's army the implications were very serious indeed. It took time to verify that the newcomers were d'Erlon's. Their commander had misunderstood his orders and they had spent the day marching about between Quatre Bras and Ligny without contributing to either battle. Understandably, Napoleon was furious and sent in the Guard at 19:30. The Prussians gave way immediately. Blücher personally led a cavalry charge in the hope of stabilising the situation but his horse was killed and he was pinned beneath it. Already in considerable pain, he was tossed and tumbled by horses' hooves as the combat raged around him and it was some time before his aide, Captain Count Nostitz, was able to free him and take him to a place of relative safety where he was given a mixture of milk and brandy and recovered slowly.

Meanwhile, the long summer day had drawn to its close. In the gathering darkness the energies of Gneisenau and his staff were fully engaged in rallying their troops. It was immediately apparent that while they had undoubtedly had the worst of the encounter, having sustained the loss of 25,000 men killed, wounded or captured, plus an unknown number of deserters, the reverse was not a disaster and that the army was still a functioning body. In recent years some German historians have suggested that Gneisenau did not altogether trust Wellington, whom he believed, wrongly, would put the safety of his own army before cooperation with his allies. Grolman, the Prussian quartermaster-general, did not share this view and nor did Blücher when he caught up. It was decided to retreat northwards to Wavre as this would leave the Prussian army within supporting distance of Wellington during the next two days.

This was probably the most critical decision of the entire campaign and, as luck would have it, was reinforced by a serious mistake on the part of the French. Napoleon had ordered Marshal Emmanuel Grouchy to pursue Blücher with the corps of Gerard and Vandamme. Unfortunately, the impression given by deserters was that the Prussian army was retreating along the road to Namur. At first, therefore, Grouchy headed in that direction. By the time he discovered his mistake priceless hours had been lost and he did not catch up with Blücher until 18 June, by which time the latter was secure on his new position at Wavre.

Over at Quatre Bras, Wellington had halted Ney's attack after some hard fighting that had cost him some 4,800 casualties. Despite this, the news that the Prussians had been forced to retire from Ligny meant that he must conform to their movement. During the night and on into 17 June he completed a disengagement to carry out a neat withdrawal to Mont St Jean behind a screen of cavalry and horse artillery.

The night of 17–18 June was one of continuous torrential rain from which few on either side could find shelter. When the downpour ceased with the coming of light the ground had become a quagmire in which any sort of manoeuvre would be impossible until it had been allowed to dry out for several hours. On the Waterloo battlefield fighting did not begin until 11:30, when Napoleon's grand battery opened fire.

Most readers will be familiar with the course of events during the battle of Waterloo, but for those who are not the following summary will provide an outline structure of the six major phases of the fighting. At about 11:30 Jerome Bonaparte, briefly the King of Westphalia and now commander of a division in General Honoré Reille's corps, launched an attack on the château of Hougoumont with the intention of forcing Wellington to reinforce his right wing. In this context it produced very poor results, but Jerome, the least able of the Bonapartes, continued to increase the pressure until by 13:00 no less than two-and-a-half French divisions were engaged in the assault, which was stubbornly resisted, despite the buildings having been set ablaze by howitzer fire. Fighting continued throughout the entire duration of the battle, its only result being to involve the whole of Reille's corps to no purpose. Why Reille did not bring Jerome under control is unclear, although dealing with the wilful brother of the Emperor cannot have been easy.

At 13:30 d'Erlon's corps commenced what was intended to be the decisive attack, delivered against the allied centre east of the Brussels–Charleroi road. Heavy casualties were sustained from the allied artillery and the attack was finally stopped in its tracks by the fire and counter-attack of a veteran British division. Two British heavy cavalry brigades then charged through the disordered mass, putting it to rout and inflicting fearful casualties. One regiment continued its charge as far as the grand battery but its horses were blown by the heavy going and it suffered severely at the hands of fresh French lancers.

In the meantime an unexpected piece of luck had come Napoleon's way. A Prussian despatch rider had been captured with a message for Wellington to the effect that Blücher was already marching to his assistance. The Emperor reacted by sending Lieutenant General Count de Lobau's corps to his right flank with orders to create a defensive front between the villages of Frichermont and Plancenoit, facing the Bois de Paris, through which the Prussians would have to pass. When, eventually, the Prussians began entering the battle the growing rumble of gunfire to the east caused many of those facing Wellington's army to glance nervously in that direction. A lie was then deliberately spread throughout the French army that the noise merely signified the arrival of Grouchy, who was engaged in smashing in Wellington's left flank. It was a lie that would have terrible consequences.

At about this time Napoleon, beginning to feel the effects of his torpor coming on, left the battlefield for a while, handing over effective command of the army to Ney. Wellington had begun moving his most forward elements behind the crest of his position to provide them with some protection from the French artillery. Simultaneously, there appeared to be general movement of allied troops to beyond the ridge. In fact, this consisted of wounded men heading for the nearest dressing station, and those detailed to escort prisoners from d'Erlon's corps. Ney, however, believed that it was a general withdrawal and instituted a series of massive cavalry attacks, without adequate artillery or infantry support. These charges were received in square by the allies, and as each was defeated in turn it was chased back down the slope by the allied cavalry and raked by artillery. Napoleon returned to the battlefield to find that most of his magnificent cavalry had been destroyed. Enraged, he put a stop to the massacre immediately, employing the few remaining cavalry units to extricate survivors wherever possible.

Meanwhile, on 17 June, Grouchy had dictated a letter to Napoleon, the contents of which suggested that he had not grasped the reality of the situation:

> By this evening, I shall be concentrated at Wavre and will thus be between Wellington who is, I assume, retreating before Your Majesty, and the Prussian army. I need further instructions as to what Your Majesty wishes me to do ...

Deign, Sire, to send me your orders. I can receive these
before starting my movement tomorrow.

In fact, Wavre was farther away than Grouchy imagined. During
the night he received reports from his cavalry screen to the effect that
contact with the Prussians had been made in the area of Wavre. He
decided to resume his own march in that direction next day and
despatched a courier to Napoleon informing him of the fact and, once
again, requesting further orders.

At 10:30 the following morning he halted at the house of a lawyer
in Smohain, still some twelve miles short of Wavre, where he was
joined by his two corps commanders, Gerard and Vandamme, and
members of his staff, for their midday meal. An hour later they were
finishing this when the thumping of continuous gunfire was heard
coming from the west. The lawyer's opinion was that the sound
originated in the area of Mont St Jean. That being the case, remarked
Gerard, they should immediately begin marching in the direction of
the fighting. Grouchy was aware that the Emperor had given Ney a
verbal flaying for not obeying a specific order at Quatre Bras and he
had no intention of putting himself in a similar position. His response
was therefore somewhat testy:

> If the Emperor had wished me to take part, he would not
> have sent me away at the very moment he was moving on
> the British ... My duty is to carry out the Emperor's orders,
> which require me to pursue the Prussians. To follow your
> advice would be to disregard his orders.

The march to the north continued, but as the French vanguard
approached Wavre a thoroughly unsatisfactory situation became
apparent. Blücher had taken full advantage of his lead over Grouchy
to establish himself to the west of the river Dyle while Grouchy's
troops were still to the east. The Dyle was certainly not one of western
Europe's great rivers but it was enough of an obstacle to an army's
progress to require a series of bridges along the relevant sector, most
of which would be tenaciously held by the Prussians.

Worse still, Blücher was clearly in the process of thinning out his
formations, some of which could be seen disappearing into the Bois
de Paris, through which tracks ran to Papelotte, Frichermont and
Plancenoit on the right flank of Napoleon's army. Obviously, Blücher's
intention was to join in Wellington's battle with the Emperor, and that

was something Grouchy must do everything in his power to stop. The problem was that Blücher had left Thielmann's corps to defend the river crossings and although the latter had just 17,000 infantry and forty-eight guns to oppose his own 33,000 infantry and eighty guns, the Prussians could be relied upon to fight extremely hard to protect their comrades' rear. Time would be of the essence, the critical question for Grouchy being whether he could dislodge Thielmann in time to prevent the rest of Blücher's army influencing the struggle at Mont St Jean.

In fact, much had already been done to deny the majority of crossings to the French. Between Wavre and Basse Wavre Major General von Borcke had deployed the sharpshooters of his own 8th Regiment and those of Major Ditfurth's I/30th Regiment along hedge- and tree-lined banks of the river, as well as knocking loopholes in every building and outbuilding, a distance of half a mile. Simultaneously, in Wavre itself, those buildings fronting the river were also loop-holed.

At about 16:00 Vandamme ordered the French 10th Division to attack the village of Aisemont, approximately half way between Wavre and Basse Wavre. Supported by two batteries of 12-pounders, the assault on the village's bridge was delivered in column of companies. Immediately, the heads of these were shot away by a blizzard of musketry from the far bank and its loop-holed buildings, supplemented by guns enfilading the bridge. Within minutes some 800 of the attackers, including Major General Habert, the divisional commander, had been shot down. Twice more the division attacked, each attack failing with further heavy loss. The survivors took whatever cover they could find, which was precious little as they were under constant fire from Prussian howitzers and a mass of skirmishers.

Elsewhere, a battalion of the 1st Kurmark Landwehr Regiment stripped the wooden decking from the bridge at Bierge under fire and counter-charged any French attempt to interfere with their work. Reinforced by the 31st Regiment and another Kurmark Landwehr battalion, they stood off all further attempts by Major General Lefol's 8th Division to capture the structure which were further hindered by the undrained swampy nature of the ground.

At Wavre itself, however, the French fought their way across the stone bridge but were thrown back after vicious street fighting with two Landwehr regiments. A second assault carried the French farther along the main street only to find themselves shot down by heavy, close-range musketry from side streets and houses, following which they were driven back over the bridge by a bayonet charge. The defenders were reinforced with a further infantry battalion and three guns and, although the see-saw struggle continued into the evening, further progress was denied to the French.

As Vandamme had been decisively halted by tough Prussian resistance, Grouchy decided to try a little farther south, using Gerard's corps and his attached cavalry. Here, luck was on his side as the bridge at Limale had neither been prepared for defence nor demolished to prevent its use. A hussar regiment riding four abreast thundered across the bridge with Major General Teste's infantry division in its wake, routing those Prussians nearest to it and pursuing the remainder to the high ground beyond the village. This was followed by the remainder of Gerard's corps, although Gerard himself was wounded by a sniper. Understandably, Thielmann now saw the major threat developing in the direction of Limale and deployed his reserves to meet it. A Prussian withdrawal to the north seemed to be a strong possibility, although fighting was still in progress at last light.

Meanwhile, the remainder of Blücher's army had been marching along forest tracks and secondary roads towards the fighting at Mont St Jean with Ziethen's I Corps on the right, Bulow's IV Corps on the left and Pirch's II Corps in the centre and some distance behind. The ground, already saturated by the previous night's rain, was turned into a quagmire by the passage of thousands of feet and deeply rutted by the wheels of the artillery's guns, limbers and caissons. Only those at the front of the trudging columns had anything like an easy passage. Those further back quickly became exhausted by heavy going and the constant need to assist in extricating guns and vehicles from the clinging mud. Blücher, however, permitted no rest, riding along the ranks and exhorting the men to even greater effort: 'Vorwarts! I have given my word to my friend Wellington – would you have me break my word?'

Both Blücher and Gneisenau recognised the immense tactical importance of the village of Plancenoit. With that in Prussian hands, they reasoned, they could cut the Brussels–Charleroi highway, thereby isolating the bulk of Napoleon's army. By 16:30 IV Corps was in position to mount an attack and Count Nostitz delivered their order to Bülow, instructing him to capture the village. Unfortunately, the Prussian approach had been detected and Lieutenant General Count Lobau, commanding the nearest elements of the French army, ordered his troops to occupy Plancenoit, which had hitherto been ignored.

The French won the race, taking possession of the village at the run and making it as defensible as possible in the short time available.

For a little while the fortunes of the battle swung towards the French. The farms of la Haye Sainte and Papelotte fell to them, the former because its King's German Legion garrison, after conducting an epic defence, had expended their ammunition, and the latter because its defenders were driven from the walls by short range cannon fire. The effect of these events were first to weaken Wellington's centre to dangerous levels, and the second to provide, albeit temporary, reassurance to the French that the hinge of their line was secure.

Despite these setbacks, Blücher launched von Ryssel's 14 Brigade into Plancenoit, initiating one of the most savage struggles of the entire battle of Waterloo. The Prussians fought their way through the village at the point of the bayonet until they reached its centre, where the walled cemetery had been turned into a strongpoint. From this the French were lacing the streets with musketry, making further progress impossible. Two small cannon were brought up and for fifteen minutes they flayed the walls with canister, not only scything down the French lining the wall but also chopping down trees along its length. This was followed by a bayonet charge in which no quarter was given.

Having been warned of the situation by survivors, Lobau impressed upon Napoleon the need for substantial reinforcements if the village was not to be lost. The Emperor ordered General Duhesme, commanding the Young Guard, to retake the village and its surrounding woods. No fewer than 4,200 Young Guardsmen stormed their way through the streets, ejecting the Prussians and assuming responsibility for its further defence.

At about this time Blücher and Gneisenau received a message from Thielmann over at Wavre to the effect that he was being attacked by superior numbers and was unsure how long he could hold out. In the circumstances the two could only let Thielmann's battle take its course, a victory in their own battle being considered of greater importance than the possible defeat of their remaining troops at Wavre. Gneisenau, appreciating that the situation at Plancenoit was causing the French serious concern, launched a fresh attack with Losthin's 15 Brigade and two of 14 Brigade's regiments. It did not succeed but, having been rallied by Gneisenau personally, the troops returned to the attack, renewed their assault and this time took the village.

By now Prussian cannon balls were reaching the main highway as far south as la Belle Alliance inn. The French situation had suddenly become desperate. Napoleon ordered two battalions of his Old Guard, a total of approximately 1,100 men, to recover the village. They were to advance with drums beating and perform their work using the bayonet alone. The advancing mass of nodding bearskins struck fear into the Prussians holding Plancenoit for two very good reasons. First, it was known that the Old Guard had usually been committed to clinch a victory and in this role had spread terror across Europe. In addition, they believed that the entire Old Guard was present when only a quarter of its strength was present. They pushed Bülow's troops out of the village, inflicting serious casualties, and would have captured his corps artillery had not their small numbers been recognised. While the Prussians rallied, the Young Guard had returned to the village and the two Old Guard battalions were ordered to remain with them.

Elsewhere, the battle was reaching its climax. Ney was deploying five battalions of the Middle Guard for what was intended to be a final shattering of Wellington's position. While the troops were being marched into position the tempo of cannon fire and musketry indicated a marked increase in activity beyond Papelotte. Napoleon's wildly optimistic interpretation was that Grouchy had entered the battle and that the units on the allied left flank were now simultaneously under fire not only from his own troops but also from those who had apparently brushed aside Thielmann's opposition at Wavre. Staff officers were sent galloping along the French lines, shouting that Grouchy had arrived. A great cheer went up as men suddenly believed that victory was in their grasp after hours of hard, bloody fighting. Anxious to be in at the kill, the remnant of Reille's and d'Erlon's corps fell in on either side of the Middle Guard, ready to mount the body-strewn slope to their front and drive Wellington's troops before them in utter rout.

Of course, the new arrivals were not Grouchy's men, but the leading elements of Ziethen's I Corps. Their arrival led to an unfortunate 'friendly fire' incident when his I Brigade, under the command of Major General von Steinmetz, opened fire on the Netherlands 28th Regiment, positioned on the left of the allied army. This, recruited from Nassauers, was wearing blue uniforms similar to those of the French. It had already been involved in heavy fighting and this unexpected attack from the east had actually caused its ranks to break, while its supporting artillery had limbered up and was heading for the rear. Baron von Müffling, the Prussian liaison attached to Wellington's staff, was quickly on the scene and put a stop to the firing. Simultaneously, Lieutenant Colonel von Reiche, Ziethen's Chief of Staff, galloped over to the Netherlands regiment and explained to the shaken and understandably resentful Nassauers how the mistake had arisen, emphasising that they would be relieved very shortly when the rest of I Corps came up. At this point one of Blücher's own staff officers, a Captain von Scharnhorst, arrived with orders for Steinmetz to proceed through Frischermont in the direction of Plancenoit, where the situation had become difficult. Reiche informed him that Müffling had emphasised in the strongest possible manner that Wellington was relying on I Corps joining his left flank. Scharnhorst raged that he was delivering the army commander's own order and that Reiche would be held personally responsible by him if it was not carried out.

At this point General Steinmetz arrived, wanting to know why the advance had halted. He was evidently a difficult man to work for, and Reiche records his reaction:

> He stormed at me in his usual violent manner and insisted upon an advance. He was scarcely willing to listen how matters stood. My embarrassment increased not a little when General Steinmetz let the head of the column resume its march and himself went past the point where the road to Frischermont branches off. Fortunately, General Ziethen came up at this critical moment. I hurried over to him and when I had given my report, he issued orders for the advance to be continued without fail towards the English army.

The troops themselves would have been less than human if they had not enjoyed the spectacle of senior officers bellowing at each other, nor could Steinmetz have expected much sympathy from Reiche when he was hauled back onto the correct route. Nevertheless, notwithstanding the problems that had arisen, within a very short space of time Ziethen's corps was to have a shattering impact on its opponents.

A short distance to the west, the Middle Guard and its supporters had begun to climb the slope towards Wellington's position. It was impossible for its units to maintain any sort of parade ground formation as they were forced to step over or round the huge numbers of dead or dying men and horses that covered the ground and soon some thirty allied guns, double-shotted with canister, began to blast gaps in their own ranks. Yet on they came with the grim determination that had broken their enemies' will in a hundred battles across Europe. There was a retrograde movement among some of Wellington's infantry until the duke ordered Major General Sir Peregrine Maitland's Brigade of Guards to their feet. At just twenty yards distance, the British guardsmen fired volley after volley into the opposing ranks. Officers, soldiers and drummers were sent tumbling but still the Middle Guard, now halted, stood its ground. Then a Netherlands horse artillery battery unlimbered close to its right flank and sent canister scything through it. On its left, the British 52nd Light Infantry wheeled out of line and fired a volley into the column and then closed in with the bayonet. A Hanoverian brigade, coming up from the direction of Hougoumont château, fired into the French rear. It was more than flesh and blood could stand. At first the French began shuffling slowly backwards into the heavy-hanging fog of powder smoke, then they turned and ran wildly down the slope.

A dreadful cry rose from those watching the encounter – 'La Garde recule!' Never before had the Guard been beaten and, now that the unthinkable had happened, the battle must be lost. To emphasise the point, Steinmetz's brigade, followed by the rest of Bülow's corps, emerged from the dead ground near Papelotte and broke through the hinge of the French line. This meant that the Prussians were able to fire into the French rear from two directions – westwards against those confronting Wellington, and to the south against those holding the line towards Plancenoit, against whom Pirch's corps was now approaching in strength.

Already Wellington had raised his hat, indicating that his own troops should sweep down from the ridge, driving their enemy before them. Another cry was raised in the French ranks; 'Sauve qui peut!' 'Save yourselves, those who can!' Napoleon's army disintegrated, fleeing south with the vengeful Prussian cavalry in hot pursuit. At Genappe the fugitives fought and killed each other in their desperation to cross a bridge on which guns, limbers and wagons had become inextricably tangled, although the stream below was just ten feet wide and three feet deep.

At the aptly named la Belle Alliance inn, Blücher and Wellington shook hands. The former had no English, but surveying the concentrated horror of what was to be called the Waterloo battlefield, he summed up both their thoughts with the comment, 'Quelle affaire!' Later that evening, Wellington was moved to tears when the long list of old friends killed in the battle was read to him. His allied army had lost 15,100 men killed and wounded, the Prussians approximately 7,000, and the French Army of the North 25,000 killed and wounded, 8,000 prisoners, and 220 guns captured.

Over at Wavre, Thielmann's corps had stood off Grouchy until dusk put an end to the fighting, each side having lost approximately 2,500 men killed or wounded. By then Thielmann had been informed of the outcome of the battle at Waterloo and, seeing no point in further loss of life, he decided to break contact. Grouchy, watching his troops moving off at about 22:00, decided that he would advance on Brussels. Thirty minutes later he was informed of Napoleon's defeat. Realising that he was in danger of being trapped and overwhelmed, he had no alternative but to march his command back to France by as safe a route as possible, collecting stragglers from broken units along the way.

Following the political fall of Napoleon, he spent several years as an exile in the United States before being permitted to return home, where he was allowed the rank of general, but lost that of marshal. Many Frenchmen of a Bonapartist persuasion still blame him, unfairly, for the Emperor's defeat.

# CHAPTER 7

# Towards the Second Reich

As popular history is sometimes taught, little or no major military activity took place on the continent of Europe between the Battle of Waterloo and the outbreak of the Crimean War. In fact, from time to time, notably during the years 1830 and 1848, armies found themselves actively engaged in support of the civil power suppressing disorders that varied between major riots and nascent revolutions. The causes were usually similar, on the one hand involving reactionary rulers and their administrations, and on the other widespread agitation by 'liberal' politicians and student idealists.

In Germany, the Prussian army was also actively involved in maintaining the *status quo* in several minor principalities, the rulers of which, having little to offer in their marriage unions, tended to marry into each other's families until too-frequent inbreeding resulted in unfortunate consequences. Happily for Prussia, the Hohenzollerns were not involved in this kind of marital merry-go-round, although in political terms their absolutist inclinations could, and occasionally did, lead their subjects to express themselves forcibly in the streets.

For a while such changes as took place within the Prussian army were of interest only to its members. The generation that had fought in the War of Liberation and at Ligny, Wavre and Waterloo grew older but were still hailed as heroes, especially those who had served in the Landwehr. Clausewitz, now a major general, was appointed Director of the War Academy in 1818, a position he held until 1830. The following year disturbances in Poland led Prussia to mobilise an army which was sent to the frontier as a precautionary measure. Gneisenau, who had been promoted to field marshal in 1825, was appointed as its commander, and Clausewitz was chosen as his chief of staff. Within months, both died in Europe's first outbreak of cholera. The latter's greatest work, entitled *On War*, was published by his widow the following year, having been fifteen years in the writing. It came to be regarded as possessing almost the same force as Mosaic Law and was considered to be essential reading for every German officer. Yet, as Sir Basil Liddell Hart was to comment, idiotic misinterpretation of the ideas expressed was to have unfortunate consequences that would have horrified their author:

> As so often happens, Clausewitz's disciples carried his teaching to an extreme which their master had not intended. His theory of war was expounded in a way too abstract and involved for ordinary soldier-minds, essentially concrete, to follow the course of his argument – which often turned back from the direction to which it was apparently leading. Impressed yet befogged, they grasped at his vivid leading phases, seeing only their surface meaning, and missing the deeper current of his thought.

Put a little differently, Clausewitz's *magnum opus* is best regarded as a philosophical treatise on the nature of war. As such, its virtue lies in discussion rather than a study in practicalities. If the average German officer required the benefit of the latter, he would have done well to have studied a translation of *The Art of War*, written by the Chinese general and master strategist Sun Tzu about 500 BC. The author discusses almost all probable tactical and strategic situations that might be encountered in war, using simple uncomplicated language. Sometimes, when stating the obvious, he does so with a hint of quiet humour so that the image comes to mind of a general chatting with his junior officers after dinner. The most remarkable thing about Sun Tzu's work is that so much of what he has written holds good today.

The German landscape and the economy of the Waterloo period remained essentially agricultural for the better part of a generation. As most people lived in the country, towns and even cities were small. Heavy industry and mining barely existed. What did was a country in which the Brothers Grimm collected their folk tales, in which learned debates took place in prestigious universities and the continent's finest music could be heard in the concert halls or opera houses which every city and most towns seemed to possess. Much would change with the coming of the Industrial Revolution.

It did not sweep across the land quite as quickly as it had in the United Kingdom, but the pace of change was rapid enough. New factories of every kind were powered by steam and their products were distributed farther and farther afield by recently introduced railway systems. Both required large quantities of coal which was mined wherever it could be found. All of this drew populations from the land into the towns, where better wages were paid. Prussia was a major beneficiary of the economic changes that were taking place, for at the end of the Napoleonic Wars she had been granted extensive lands along the left bank of the Rhine as a reparation for the Polish territories of which she had been deprived. Initially, the grant was far from popular, but as the industrial revolution took hold it was apparent that the area of the Ruhr contained all the materials required for industrial and economic growth. Against this, industrialisation and urban living produced social problems that had not existed before. In common with the general staffs of every nation involved in the process of industrialisation, that of Prussia understood from the outset that railways enabled larger armies than before to be transported to and maintained at the battle front. In addition, the application of technology to industrialisation produced more effective weapons of war in far greater quantities than hitherto.

Politically, change took place at a slower pace. In Prussia itself the people had forgiven Frederick William III for the catastrophe of Jena, largely because he had taken the field with his troops during the War of Liberation. Prussia had suffered severely as a result of her earlier defeat, but to some extent the effects were lessened by agricultural, economic and administrative reforms introduced by two of the King's ministers, Karl August, Prince von Hardenberg, and Baron Karl Heinrich von Stein. The King had personally promised to introduce a constitution in 1813 but subsequently reneged on this and during the years that followed his attitude hardened towards political reaction.

His son, another Frederick William, succeeded him on his death in 1840. The new king had also served as a soldier during the War of Liberation but he had little liking for the army and was essentially artistic by nature. He was the patron of several artists, architects and the composer Felix Mendelssohn. He possessed a sentimental view of the Middle Ages and their institutions and was thus an instinctive conservative, avoiding outright democracy by restricting its application.

In 1848 the demand for democracy resulted in serious rioting in Berlin. The army was already bringing the situation under control when Frederick William promised the rioters that he would order the troops back to barracks if they demolished their barricades. Needless to say, the army felt that it had been publicly humiliated and was only too pleased when it was recalled to deal with the resulting chaos.

In due course Frederick William did agree to the founding of a parliament with two chambers, the first consisting of the nobility and the second of members elected by a system based on the amount of taxes paid so that the rich always had greater influence than the poor. The king, however, retained the power to appoint ministers as well as retaining control over the army and the bureaucracy. This system was maintained until the downfall of the Prussian monarchy in 1918.

In 1857 a serious stroke left Frederick William partially paralysed and badly damaged mentally. He was without issue and his brother William acted as regent from 1858 until the king's death in 1861, when he ascended the throne himself as William I. He, too, had fought in the War of Liberation, notably under Blücher at Ligny and Waterloo, and was generally considered to be an excellent soldier. During the troubles of 1848 he had recovered Baden from the rioters, grasping the nettle and obtaining a quick result with artillery, thereby earning himself a degree of temporary unpopularity and the nickname of Prince Grapeshot. In fact, William was little interested in the politics of left or right, which was remarkable considering that the next decade was to be one of the most notable in German history.

This was largely the result of the work of three men. Of these, Otto von Bismarck is perhaps the most commonly remembered. Born shortly before the Battle of Waterloo, he was a lawyer and entered the Prussian civil service. He served as ambassador to Russia from 1859 to 1862, and briefly ambassador to France in 1862, when he was appointed Prussia's Minister President (Prime Minister). Though generally portrayed in regular army uniform, his only military service was as a junior officer in the Landwehr and he was scornfully referred to by his political opponents as 'our Landwehr captain'. His diplomatic postings, however, granted him the equivalent general officer's status, with the right to wear the appropriate uniform.

Bismarck possessed two driving ambitions. In 1862 Prussia was fourth largest of Europe's continental powers and was effectively surrounded by its three more powerful neighbours, namely the French, Austrian and Russian Empires. To remove any potential threat to his country, therefore, he embarked upon a long term policy of maintaining friendly relations with Russia, eliminating Austrian influence in German affairs, and destroying the power of France. Finally, he planned to create a united Germany under Prussian leadership with the King of Prussia as its head.

As a professional politician Bismarck played the game with consummate skill, creating situations that required his enemies to react exactly as he desired. This frequently required a ruthless application of the principles of *realpolitik* which he justified by arguing that the major issues of the day could only be resolved by the expenditure of 'blood and iron'. Sometimes his opponents were caught wrong-footed by a disarming use of sincerity, not always a quality welcomed in political circles. Benjamin Disraeli, the British Prime Minister, was certainly taken aback by it when the two met, commenting, 'That man is dangerous – he means exactly what he says!'

Bismarck's ambitions were greatly assisted by the appointment of General Albrecht Roon as War Minster in 1859. Roon was born in 1803 and as a child had witnessed the devastation caused during the War of Liberation. Having received his commission in 1821 he subsequently passed through a higher form of study at what later became the Prussian War Academy, specialising in military geography and topography. He had served under the then Prince William during the suppression of the insurrection at Baden. By 1851 he had reached the rank of full colonel and thereafter his promotions came rapidly – major general in 1856 and lieutenant general in 1859. Recognising that the army was no longer making the best use of its assets, he set about reforming its shape and can justly be regarded as the Scharnhorst of his day. If politicians were reluctant to provide the necessary funds for his reforms he would consult Bismarck who would ensure that they understood that the expenditure was in their own and Prussia's best interests. As completed, the reformed army was still based on the principle of universal obligation to serve without substitution, but service with the colours began at the age of twenty and lasted for three years. During each year the regular army absorbed seven intakes of recruits and discharged seven groups of time-served men. After that, the conscript served for four years on the reserve and was then transferred to the Landwehr in which he served for a further five, in the first year of which he could still be recalled to the reserve. The quality of the Landwehr itself was improved by constant supervision of training by the regular army.

Of particular importance was the local nature of recruiting, training, supervision and mobilisation. The country was divided into corps areas in which the local authorities were largely self-regulating. Within each corps area individual cities contained the headquarters and barracks of the formations and units for which they were responsible. Within these garrisons, units played a constant part in the life of the local community. Regular band concerts and parades enabled the population to watch their own men in a favourable light, while the attendance of officers provided a cachet to the most prestigious social functions. In time of war, the soldiers fought the harder for being among their relatives, friends and neighbours.

Railways played a vital role in the Prussian military system. No one was permitted to construct a railway in Prussia unless he could prove to the General Staff that it would provide real strategic value in the event of hostilities. It was not just that railways could transport and supply larger armies than ever before; the fundamental point of their use in war was to concentrate these armies in overwhelming force at the point of decision. This enabled Prussia and her allies to take full advantage of their central position in the continent. Thus, the operational employment of railways during the periods of mobilisation and critical manoeuvre was something that could only be planned adequately by the best brains, and such was the requirement for admission to the all-important Railway Department of Prussia's Greater General Staff. Likewise, the introduction of the electric telegraph, the basic routes of which could follow those of the railways, enabled signals traffic in both directions to take place as speeds hitherto only dreamed of. When suitably extended at the battle front it was logical that this should be developed not simply between army headquarters and their subordinate formations, but also laterally between those formations to ensure maximum efficiency. Inevitably, the vulnerability of this type of communication led to the development of signal codes and, logically, the science of codebreaking.

The third and oldest member of the trio whose work was to result in the founding of the Second Reich was Helmuth von Moltke. He was born in 1800, the son of a Danish general and spent much of his youth in Denmark where he attended a cadet school in Copenhagen. In 1818 he received a commission in a Danish infantry regiment but four years later he transferred to the Prussian service. In 1826 he completed the three-year course at the future Prussian Military

Academy. Next he was made responsible for the running of a cadet academy at Frankfurt an der Oder for a year, then spent a further year carrying out a military survey in Silesia. In 1833 he received promotion to first lieutenant and was posted to the General Staff in Berlin.

Moltke's undoubted brilliance was already recognised by his superiors. He possessed a dry humour that was not immediately apparent and his pleasures were entirely intellectual and included music, poetry, travel, historical study, archaeology, the theatre, sketching and writing for publication. In addition, he spoke no fewer than seven languages: German, Danish, English, French, Italian, Spanish and Turkish.

In 1835, now a captain, he visited Constantinople on leave and was requested by the Sultan of the Ottoman Empire, Mahmud II, to assist in modernising his army. Berlin approved the attachment, enabling him to travel extensively throughout south-eastern Europe and Anatolia. At that period Egypt was still nominally part of the Sultan's empire, but in 1838 its *de facto* ruler, Mehemet Ali, rebelled against the authorities in Constantinople. Moltke was attached as adviser to the Turkish general commanding the Ottoman Empire's troops in Anatolia and carried out an extensive reconnaissance of the terrain likely to be fought over. In 1839 the Turks finally marched south to engage the Egyptian rebels. The Turkish commander brushed aside Moltke's advice with the result that the latter resigned his appointment and confined his attention to the artillery. On 23 June the two armies met at Nisib (modern Nisibis) on the border of Syria and Kurdistan. The Turks were completely routed and Moltke, accompanied by the only other two Prussian officers present, had to ride almost non-stop for nine hours before reaching comparative safety. He subsequently commented drily that the years he had spent with the Turks had taught him much.

On his return home he was appointed to the staff of IV Corps for a year and was then appointed personal adjutant to Prince Henry of Prussia in Rome. In 1848 he became IV Corps' chief of staff, an appointment he held for the next seven years, rising to the rank of colonel. He was then appointed aide to Prince Frederick (later Emperor Frederick III), whom he accompanied to England, France and Russia. In 1857 he was appointed the army's chief of staff and remained in that position for the next thirty years.

Naturally, he cooperated closely with Roon in developing the army's tactical and strategic methods, its armament, means of communication and transport, mobilisation and the training of staff officers. In the field Moltke acted as sole advisor to the king and he and his staff naturally occupied part of the Royal Headquarters. The staff included the Quartermaster-General and the Intendant-General, both of whom were lieutenant generals, and three major sections dealing respectively with movement, rail transport and supply and intelligence. These worked under Moltke's immediate supervision and were each headed by a colonel. These officers spoke with Moltke's full authority, were known throughout the army as Moltke's 'Demigods' and more feared than actually disliked. Apart from these five officers, the total establishment of the staff included eleven officers, ten draughtsmen, seven clerks and fifty-nine other ranks, which was modest enough for an organisation controlling up to 850,000 men. In passing, it is worth mentioning that Moltke recruited his staff officers from the twelve outstanding pupils of the War Academy's year and if they failed to measure up quickly they were returned to their parent regiments. Likewise, when a staff officer was due for promotion he was returned to his regiment for a period before the event with the object of reminding him of the realities of regimental life.

In addition to the already numerous population of the Royal Headquarters, Roon and his staff had to be accommodated, as had the civilian officials responsible for the continuity of government. Also present were the military attachés of friendly or neutral nations, and the similar representatives of the international press, all of whom were welcomed because of their potential use to the Prussian cause. Less welcome were the rulers of Germany's mini-states, who arrived all a'jingle with the medals and orders they and their friends had conferred on each other, plus their grooms, cooks and valets, all of whom contributed nothing, but regarded war as a spectator sport.

Moltke was a disciple of Clausewitz, but was more practical in his application of the latter's theories. Considerable study was given to the conjoint battles of Waterloo and Wavre, particularly the fact that the armies of Wellington and Blücher had entered the critical battlefield by different routes. It followed, therefore, that to achieve a decisive result, Prussian and allied armies must march separately but fight together. The end product of the ideally conducted campaign would be the complete destruction of the enemy's army, the German name given to the process being *Vernichtungsgedanke* – the annihilation concept. Indeed, in *Jackboot*, his study of the German soldier, John Laffin comments:

> Annihilation was possible, as the examples of Epaminondas and Hannibal, Frederick the Great and Napoleon proved, only when the attacker initiated a mobile battle with the object of falling upon the enemy's flank or of encircling and destroying his army piecemeal.

The Prussian army commander must, therefore, aim to re-create the Battle of Cannae, in which the wings of a Roman army were driven in upon its centre and the whole jumbled mass, unable to use its weapons, was slaughtered where it stood. Moltke recognised that the introduction of modern firearms increased the power of the defence and this in itself reinforced the value of attacks against the enemy's flanks rather than his front. Equally important was the fact that the increase in the size of armies meant that timings and the allocation of routes had to be given the most careful consideration. In Moltke's view, no more than one corps at a time should be allowed to use the same road. If two or more corps used the road, those at the rear would not be able to enter the action until the day after the leading corps. Yet, however much attention is paid to such matters, Moltke is quick to point out, 'No plan of operations extends with certainty beyond the first encounter with the enemy's main strength.'

As well as possessing a brilliant General Staff, Prussia was gifted with two far-sighted armaments manufacturers. The first was Johann von Dreyse of Sommerda, a small town near Erfurt in Thuringia. During the Napoleonic Wars he had worked in the Paris factory of Jean-Samuel Pauly, a Swiss gunsmith and inventor who produced some prototype breech-loading military rifles. Having returned home, in 1824 he founded a company to manufacture percussion caps. These suggested the potential for a bolt-action rifle. The key to the system lay in the ammunition, which consisted of a paper cartridge holding a bullet in the base of which was a percussion cap. The breech was closed by a bolt and when the trigger was squeezed a needle passed through the cartridge's propellant, which was ignited when the needle detonated the percussion cap. The system became known as the 'needle gun' and gave its users the ability to reload from a standing, kneeling or lying position as well as produce rapid fire. A disadvantage was that the breech was not gas-tight, so that expended or even burning powder was blown back into the user's face, and for this reason it was sometimes fired from the hip rather than the shoulder. The needle gun began entering service with the Prussian Army in 1841. During the 1960s the author came across several of these weapons in the hands of Adeni tribesmen who seemed to have no reservations about firing them.

The second was Alfred Krupp, who in 1826 became head of his family's metal-based industrial interests. The Krupps had lived in the Ruhr town of Essen since the sixteenth century. One, Arndt Krupp, had settled in the town shortly before the Black Death and had made a fortune buying up the houses of those who fled rather than expose themselves to the risk of the disease. Alfred's ambition was to cast flawless steel blocks that could be used in the manufacture of gun barrels. When iron or bronze gun barrels were in imminent danger of bursting the opening of a crack usually indicated an internal flaw and gave its users sufficient warning to take the piece out of service. Steel gun barrels could usually withstand the pressures of larger propellant charges, which in turn produced longer ranges, but they could burst without the slightest warning of a flaw and result in death or horrific injuries to anyone nearby. By 1847 Alfred had overcome the technical problems of casting fine quality steel and produced his first cannon made from this material. At the Great Exhibition of 1851 he astonished the engineering world by producing a solid, flawless steel ingot weighing 4,300lb and a 6-pounder cannon made from the same material. This seemed trivial when compared with his exhibit at the Paris Exhibition of 1855, which was an ingot weighing 100,000lb. From that point onwards the reputation of Krupp Steel and the engineering skills of the Essen works were firmly established.

Next, Alfred produced a rifled, breech-loading steel cannon, the prototype of which he presented to King Frederick William IV. The majority of the king's senior artillery officers preferred to continue using the traditional rifled muzzle-loading bronze cannon and the piece was relegated to ornamental duties. However, his brother William recognised that steel breech-loaders were capable of a more rapid rate of fire and were also more accurate than the old bronze muzzle-loaders and when he became regent in 1859 the Prussian Army purchased the first 312 of the 10,666 steel guns that it would buy from Krupp in Alfred's lifetime. Their efficiency in action was soon to be tested.

# CHAPTER 8

# Prussia Triumphant

During the revolutions of 1848 an association of states known as the German Confederation was dissolved by Austria, its most important member. An attempt to revive it as the Frankfurt Assembly was only partly successful and quickly lapsed. Early in 1850, however, Prussia had taken the lead in creating the Erfurt Union, a confederation containing the majority of German states.

Austria strongly resented this attempt to oust her from her traditional position as leader in the German world and used a dispute between the Elector of Hesse and his subjects as a means to humiliate Prussia. The Austrian Chancellor, Felix zu Schwarzenberg, quickly made his intentions clear. The armies of Austria and her allies marched into Hesse, ostensibly to keep order, although the move was clearly nothing less than a blatant challenge to Prussia. The Prussian army was mobilised and advanced against Bavaria, an important ally of Austria, and on 8 November an exchange of fire was narrowly avoided during an incident at Fulda-Bronnzell.

Hostilities were avoided when it became known that Tsar Nicholas I of Russia was siding with Austria. Prussian delegates were summoned to a conference at Olmutz (modern Olomouc) in Austrian Moravia. Prussia simply could not afford to go to war when faced with such odds and her delegates had no other option than to give in to every demand. They agreed to Austrian leadership of a restored German Confederation, to return the Prussian army to its peacetime footing, to take part in the intervention of the German Diet (an assembly of rulers) in solving the internal problems of Hesse and the duchy of Holstein, and to abandon the concept of the Erfurt Union. These details were incorporated in a document entitled the Punctation of Olmutz, signed on 29 November 1850, the use of the word punctation being intended as a statement of Austrian demands rather than an agreement and therefore intended to rub salt in Prussian wounds. In Prussia itself the document was known as the 'Humiliation of Olmutz', and it was neither forgotten nor forgiven.

In 1848 the population of the three duchies of southern Denmark, namely Schleswig, Holstein and Saxe-Lauenburg, contained a large German element that amounted to one-third of the national population and produced half its wealth. Ever since the end of the Napoleonic Wars pan-Germanism had become a political force in Europe and in the three duchies there was considerable resentment among the ethnic Germans that they were ruled by a Danish monarch. An armed rebellion quickly escalated into a potential war of independence to be known as the First Schleswig War or the Three Years' War. Prussia sided with the rebels, ignoring the incongruity of her doing so when elsewhere her troops had assisted other states in actually putting down similar freedom movements. The Danes, however, proved to be extremely tough opponents. In addition, they made the most of their island geography, their navy outclassed that of Prussia and they received assistance from Sweden. Remarkably, they won, and the *status quo* was preserved by the peace treaty of 1851.

The basic problem, however, simply would not go away and erupted into the Second Schleswig War in 1863. In the opinion of Lord Palmerston, the British Prime Minister, the situation was even more complicated than it appeared at first glance and had only ever been properly understood by three men. One of them, Prince Albert, Queen Victoria's Consort, was dead; another was a German professor who had been declared insane; the third was himself, and he had forgotten. Put at its simplest, the Salic Law, denying a female succession, applied in Schleswig and Holstein, and the tie with the Danish crown would cease when the present king, Frederick VII, died, lacking as he did a male heir. Following the Punctation of Olmutz, the Danes had taken advantage of Prussia's temporary political impotence to persuade the other European powers to recognise Prince Christian of Glucksberg as heir not only to the Danish throne but also as heir to the duchies. The agreement was brushed aside by the German Diet and the claims of Prince Christian were dismissed by Bismarck, who supported the case put forward by Prince Frederick of Augustenberg.

Bismarck wished to avoid upsetting Austria a second time, so he politely requested the latter's assistance. Austria assented, wishing to recover some of the prestige she had lost because of defeats in

Italy. Denmark refused to alter her position and the Second Schleswig War began on 1 February 1864. While Prussian troops invaded the disputed territory, Austria despatched a naval squadron to secure the seas around the Jutland peninsula and the Danish islands. On this occasion the Danes were on their own; although the King of Sweden promised help none was forthcoming. Palmerston hinted that the United Kingdom might provide assistance as the previous year Princess Alexandra of Denmark had married the Prince of Wales and was very popular with the British public. This was no more than the suggestion of a threat for the United Kingdom was a maritime power and her army was structured to operate in her overseas territories; furthermore, since the Crimean War, there was no British appetite for further military involvement on the mainland of Europe. Bismarck was well aware of the fact and when asked what he would do if the British Army landed he replied that he would send for the police. The Danes fought doggedly on but the outcome of the war was a foregone conclusion and they were forced to seek terms. Under the provisions of the Treaty of Vienna, signed on 30 October 1864, Schleswig was transferred to Prussian rule while Holstein and Saxe-Lauenberg became Austrian territory. Simultaneously, the candidature of Prince Frederick was accepted as being valid.

It seemed that no sooner had one potentially dangerous crisis been resolved than another with far greater implications for those involved raised its head. Berlin lawyers requested to examine the claims of Prince Frederick produced irrefutable proof that they were illegal. Frederick therefore turned to Austria for assistance and in so doing, having already served once as a *casus belli*, was about to do so again, little suspecting that he was dancing to Bismarck's tune. Having been assured by Roon and Moltke that the Army was now capable of defeating Austria, the First Minister set in train a series of discussions and events that would fulfil his ambition of making Prussia the leading nation of Germany. Italy would gladly ally herself with Prussia in order to free more Italian territory from Austrian rule. Russia was grateful to Prussia for her assistance in putting down a recent Polish uprising and had not forgiven Austria for her attitude of hostile neutrality during the Crimean War. The Second Schleswig War had demonstrated that the United Kingdom was not interested in becoming involved in the affairs of continental Europe. That left France, the old enemy. Bismarck paid a confidential visit to Napoleon III at Biarritz and, during the most friendly discussions, suggested that France would be rewarded with territory if she would stand back from the coming war. As the Emperor had no intention of joining either side he unwisely drew the conclusion that the apparently amiable Bismarck was something of a simpleton, failing to see the implications for France if Prussia became the paramount power in Germany. Discreet soundings among the German states revealed support for Prussia, but slightly more for Austria although the latter would also have to deal with the Italians.

Having received the unfortunate Prince Frederick's complaint, the Austrians had to do something about it. They brought the dispute before the German Diet and also convened the Holstein Diet. Apparently outraged, Prussia declared that the original settlement was now void and marched into Holstein. The German Diet ordered a partial mobilisation against Prussia, after which Bismarck declared the German Confederation, led by Austria, had ceased to exist. That was more than enough to set hostilities in motion, the adversaries being as follows:

**The German Confederation**
The Empire of Austria
The Kingdom of Saxony
The Kingdom of Bavaria
The Kingdom of Württemberg
The Kingdom of Hanover
The Electorate of Hesse
The Grand Duchy of Hesse
The Grand Duchy of Baden
The Principality of Reuss
The Principality of Schaumburg-Lippe
The Duchy of Saxe-Meiningen
The Duchy of Nassau
The Free City of Frankfurt

Total Strength: 600,000 Austrians and German Allies

**Prussia and Allies**
The Kingdom of Prussia
The Kingdom of Italy
The Grand Duchy of Mecklenburg-Schwerin
The Grand Duchy of Mecklenburg-Strelitz

The Grand Duchy of Oldenburg
The Duchy of Anhalt
The Duchy of Brunswick
The Duchy of Saxe-Altenburg
The Duchy of Saxe-Coburg & Gotha
The Principality of Lippe
The Principality of Schwarzburg
The Principality of Waldeck
The Free Hanseatic City of Bremen
The Free Hanseatic City of Hamburg
The Free Hanseatic City of Lübeck

Total Strength: 500,000 Prussians and German Allies; 300,000 Italians

The war is known by several names, but more commonly as the Austro-Prussian War or the Seven Weeks' War. Its first action took place on 16 June in Hanover, which had severed its long connection with the United Kingdom in 1837 on Queen Victoria ascending the throne of the latter, a female sovereign not being permitted by the Hanoverian constitution. During the period leading up to the war Bismarck had offered its current king, George V, the alternative of maintaining an armed neutrality. Unwisely, this was rejected in favour of providing active support for the Austrian cause. Unfortunately, Hanover had no natural defensive boundaries and was flanked by Prussian territory to the east and west. In addition, she was a comparatively small state that could not hope to compete militarily with Prussia and her isolation placed her beyond assistance by Austria and her allies.

On 16 June a 50,000-strong Prussian army under General Vogel von Falkenstein invaded Hanover from the west. To everyone's surprise, on 27 June, the 19,000 Hanoverians of General Alexander von Arentschildt's command trounced one of Falkenstein's corps at Langensalza. Some years had passed since King George had lost the sight of both eyes in separate incidents but now, in his delight, he asked the Almighty to let him have them back just long enough for him to watch the Prussians running for their lives. Unfortunately, by 29 June, his little army was surrounded and forced to surrender and he was forced to flee to Austria. The battle was remarkable for being the first occasion on which the Red Cross tended wounded on the battlefield.

In the meantime, Moltke and Roon had employed the strategic railway system to deploy Prussia's three major armies to the south on a wide frontage. The First Army, under Prince Frederick Charles, generally known as the Red Prince because he chose to wear the red uniform of the 2nd (Life) Hussars, advanced from its assembly area near Gorlitz; the Second Army, under Crown Prince Frederick William from the area of Landshut; and the Army of the Elbe, under General Herwarth von Bittenfeld from the region of Torgau. Although it was a long established tradition that, whenever possible, Prussian armies in the field should be commanded by a serving member of the Royal Family, it was now accepted that, with the growth of armies and increasing complexity of war, they should be guided by an experienced chief of staff. Thus, while King William was nominally commander-in-chief, the strategy of the campaign lay in Moltke's hands and his intelligence sources suggested that the principal Austrian army appeared to be concentrating to the north-west of Olmutz.

The first part of his plan involved the Army of the Elbe occupying Dresden, the Saxon capital, which it did on 19 June, and then effecting a junction with the First Army in the passes of the Bohemian mountains. Continuing their south-easterly advance, the combined armies defeated retreating Austrian and Saxon elements at Munchengratz on 27 June and again at Gitschin two days later. To the east the Second Army was marching on a converging course, fighting two successful actions at Trutnov and Nachod on 27 June and halting just east of Gitschin on 30 June. Thus far, Moltke had been content to let matters take their course, but as the Second Army settled into its bivouacs he left Berlin by train for the front, in company with the King, Roon and Bismarck. He was already in telegraphic contact with the three Prussian armies, but he wanted to be on the spot while they crushed the Austrian army in a gigantic trap.

In terms of numbers, he could deploy eight corps and three cavalry divisions, a total of 278,000 men. The Austrian army was commanded by Field Marshal Ludwig von Benedek and consisted of one Saxon and seven Austrian corps and four cavalry divisions giving a total of 271,000 men. The Austrian infantry was still armed with muzzle-loading muskets, which placed it at a serious disadvantage with Dreyse needle-gun-armed Prussians. On the other hand, the Austrian artillery was more up-to-date than the Prussian, which had only recently started re-equipping with Krupp weapons. However, the Austrian War Ministry was less interested in supporting Benedek than it was its troops fighting in Italy, who were producing good results. The Prussian commanders had been worried that Benedek would deploy his army along a front behind the Elbe with its flanks resting on the fortified towns of Josephstadt to the north and Königgrätz to the south. This would have provided a very formidable position indeed and it was with relief that the Prussians noted that most of the Austrian army was actually positioned on the Prussian side of the river, behind a muddy watercourse named the Bistritz Brook. This was four miles west of the Elbe and ran almost parallel to it. Villages, farms and woods along its length had been fortified and most of the Austrian artillery was positioned on a low ridge behind it, in an excellent position to support the infantry below. On balance, therefore, the position was only a little less formidable to attackers than that along the Elbe might have been.

It made little or no difference to Moltke's plan. The Army of the Elbe was to circle to the south and then strike north into the Austrian rear. The First Army was to attack due east, across the Bistritz, while the Second Army was to advance down the Elbe Valley to enclose the Austrians in a ring of steel. The attack commenced in driving rain at first light on 3 July. Almost immediately, the ancient truth that no plan survives its first contact with the enemy became horribly apparent. Anxious to get his troops into action quickly, Herwarth von Bittenfeld did not extend his front sufficiently so that his left flank overlapped the advancing right flank of Prince Frederick Charles' First Army. Confusion reigned supreme and was aggravated by a prompt Austrian counter-attack. The confused mass was being ripped apart by concentrated artillery fire and was only holding its ground because of the high output of the infantry's Dreyse rifles.

By 11:00 the attack of both Prussian armies was at a standstill and, to make matters worse, Moltke had lost his telegraphic link to the Crown Prince's Second Army, still stationary some fifteen miles to the north. Everything now hinged on whether that army could be brought into action quickly. Moltke despatched one of his aides, a Lieutenant von Norman, with an order in the king's name, to advance immediately and fall on the Austrian right. Norman had the ride of his life. For a while he was pursued by an entire squadron of Austrian lancers but managed to break free despite a lance point tearing away part of his tunic.

Meanwhile, the battle had become one of attrition, centred on the villages and farms along the Bistritz. The village of Banatek, on the

Austrian right, was set ablaze by shellfire. It was not abandoned by its garrison so that when a Prussian division advanced to take possession it became involved in furious hand-to-hand fighting. In the centre of the line the Prussians penetrated the village of Sadowa and its wood where fighting took place at such close quarters that local struggles were only decided by the bayonet.

Those with most to lose, including King William, Moltke, Roon and Bismarck, had no idea whether von Norman had reached the Crown Prince or not and they could only wait. The king was becoming restive and ordered an assault against an entrenched artillery position without, for once, consulting Moltke. It was obvious that the result would have been a virtual massacre of the attackers had not Moltke managed to put a stop to it, at the risk of incurring the royal wrath. Throughout, he maintained the silent, expressionless calm for which he was famous, pausing in his progress only to exchange a minimum of words with local commanders. Among less senior officers there was a saying that he possessed the ability to remain silent in seven languages. In fact, he was desperately worried that Benedek would employ his greater numbers of cavalry to charge into the confused area where the Elbe and the First Armies overlapped, his entire right wing might be driven off the field and he would have to retire with the remainder. At one point he offered his cigar case to Bismarck. The latter was also rattled by the course of events, but he subsequently recalled, 'If Moltke was calm enough to do that , then we had no need to fear after all'. In the circumstances, it seems more probable that Moltke was seeking the soothing properties of tobacco to allay his own anxieties.

Despite this, Bismarck was still worried by the non-appearance of the Crown Prince and his army. His search of the northern horizon with his telescope spotted something he had not noticed before. Some thought it was nothing more than furrows in the fields, but to Bismarck it suggested ranks of men moving towards them across country. In due course the smoke of several Austrian artillery batteries confirmed his thoughts as the guns were firing to the north and not in support of the fighting along the Bistritz. It was soon apparent that the approaching troops were the advance guard of the Crown Prince's army, the main body of which would enter the fray in mid-afternoon. They had made a forced march in the most difficult conditions, for although the rain had ceased and the sun occasionally appeared in gaps of the scudding clouds, the fields had remained sodden. Yet, just as Blücher had urged on his men from Wavre to Waterloo in similar circumstances, the Second Army was being driven on because its presence was desperately needed. The news of its arrival generated a huge cheer among those Prussians fighting along the line of the Bistritz. At that moment the king was questioning Moltke as to his opinion on the outcome of the battle, and in his calm, collected manner the latter replied, 'Today, Your Majesty will win not only the battle, but also the campaign'.

Benedek had established his headquarters near the village of Chlum, behind the centre of the Bistritz line. Thus far, he had held his own, but with the unexpected appearance of another army closing in on his right flank came the dreadful realisation that the battle was lost. He would, indeed, do well to get as much of his army away as possible, for with the advance onto the battlefield of the Crown Prince's army, those troops presently defending their positions along the Bistritz could only make good their escape through a constantly narrowing corridor. Inevitably, therefore, he would lose part of his own army as it covered the withdrawal of the rest.

Soon, the Second Army, which included the Guard, had turned Benedek's flank and had trapped those Austrians still holding their positions on the Bistriz while their comrades made good their with-dawal. Simultaneously, the Guard Artillery, directed personally by Prince Kraft zu Hohenlohe-Ingelfingen, began hammering away at the retreating Austrian centre. Nevertheless, there were Austrian units that fought with suicidal bravery to stem the Prussian advance, including batteries that fought their guns to the muzzle and died around them. Chlum was captured by the Prussian Guard's infantry, then lost to a counter-attack and finally recovered. There was, too, the devastating charge carried out by an Austrian cuirassier brigade commanded, curiously enough, by an Englishman named Beales. His troopers smashed into the flank of a Prussian dragoon regiment, inflicting heavy casualties with their long, straight swords, but were then counter-charged by lancers and attacked in the rear by red-uniformed 2nd Hussars. A fierce mêlée ensued in which the Austrians were finally driven back and Beales was wounded and unhorsed, but such actions, while costly, ensured that Elbe bridge into Königgrätz remained in Austrian hands, providing an escape route for most of Benedek's army.

After paying his respects to his father, the Crown Prince followed the advance of the Guard and recorded in his diary horror at the scenes he witnessed:

> Around us lay or hobbled about so many of the well-known figures of the Potsdam and Berlin garrisons. A shocking appearance was presented by those who were using their rifles as crutches, or were being supported by other unwounded comrades. The most horrid spectacle, however, was that of an Austrian battery, of which all the men and horses had been shot down. It is a shocking thing to ride over a battle-field and it is impossible to describe the hideous mutilations that presented themselves. War is really something frightful and those who create it with a stroke of the pen, sitting at a green-baize table, little dream of the horrors they are conjuring up. I found my kinsman, Prince Antony of Hohenzollern, who had been shot in the leg by three balls and died of his wounds soon after.

Moltke's plan had borne fruit, but not quite in the way he had intended. Prussian casualties amounted to 1,939 killed and 7,237 wounded. Austrian and Saxon losses included 13,000 killed, 18,393 wounded, 18,000 taken prisoner and 174 guns captured. In the aftermath of the battle the Prussians continued their advance on Vienna but halted when both sides accepted an offer by Napoleon III to mediate, the Austrians because, while they had done well against the Italians, there were stirrings of rebellion in Hungary, always one of the more restless areas of the Empire, and the Prussians because they appreciated that the time might come when they might seek an alliance with Austria. For that reason, when the parties met to negotiate in Prague during August, Moltke chose not to seek the surrender of native Austrian territory. Austria, however, surrendered her influence over the states previously forming the German Confederation which was itself replaced by the North German Confederation under Prussian leadership. Prussia annexed Hanover, Schleswig and Holstein (which amalgamated to become the Province of Schleswig-Holstein), the Electorate of Hesse, the city of Frankfurt, the Duchy of Nassau and parts of Hesse-Darmstadt. The Kingdom of Saxony, the Principalities of Reuss and Schaumberg-Lippe, and the Duchy of Saxe-Meiningen were not annexed but joined the North German Confederation in 1867, which was also joined by three minor 'non-combatant' German states:

Reuss-Schleiz, Saxe-Weimar-Eisenach and Schwarzbur-Rudolstadt. Bismarck wisely took no punitive measures against the south German kingdoms of Bavaria and Württemberg which were allowed to form a confederation of their own. The unification of Germany was almost complete and Bismarck was already giving much concentrated thought to the subject.

# CHAPTER 9

# Creating an Empire

With the possible exception of its southern kingdoms, the victory of Königgrätz and the terms of the subsequent peace treaty ensured a feeling of togetherness throughout Germany and made pan-Germanism a lasting force in politics. Bismarck, however, would not be satisfied until Germany, led by Prussia, became the greatest nation in continental Europe. Austria no longer counted and had given her assurance that she had no further interest in German affairs. Russia, vast but backward, seemed to have no interest outside Poland, preserving the peace in the Balkans and presiding over the probable funeral of the Ottoman Empire, which would gain her access to the Mediterranean through the Bosporus and Dardanelles.

France, the hereditary enemy of many German states, was another matter, for she was ruled by Napoleon III, nephew of the great Napoleon, who had a taste for foreign wars, of which, since coming to power, he had indulged in the Crimea, Italy, the Levant, Mexico, Algeria, Indo-China and China proper. He possessed a very experienced army whose commanders had seen widespread service and generally produced satisfactory results. In addition, he had created a substantial industrial base capable of producing modern weapons within France itself. His ambition was to free France of the inhibitions placed on her by the Congress of Vienna following the fall of his uncle. To Bismarck, all these factors combined to make France a very dangerous enemy indeed and therefore one to be suppressed at the first favourable opportunity.

Yet, appearances were deceptive. In 1866 Prussia mustered about 1,200,000 trained men. In contrast, France could produce only 288,000, albeit long-service regulars, from which contingents had to be found for operations in Algeria, Mexico and Rome, whereas Napoleon was aiming at approximately one million. In 1868 the French Legislature passed a measure which involved two conscript intakes being called each year. The first would serve for five years with the regular army followed by four on the reserve. The second would serve for just five months. It was calculated that by 1875 this would enable the army to mobilise 800,000 men. Another 500,000 would, in theory be provided by the Garde Mobile, which was intended to duplicate the functions of the Prussian Landwehr. It actually did nothing of the kind. The idea was that it should consist of all those men of military age who had avoided the call-up. They would serve for five years in which their annual training liability was two weeks. This would take place a day at a time and not last longer than twelve hours in any one day. Not surprisingly, the result was barely trained, ill-disciplined and frequently disloyal.

Another, and not altogether satisfactory, situation existed in the officer corps of the regular army. The intention was that this should be as inclusive of French society as possible. In theory a man might be considered for a commission if he had already served for two years as an NCO or passed the Military Academy's entrance examinations. One third of new commissions had to be awarded to men who had served in the ranks, yet in 1869 11,374 officers were former rankers, while only 7,292 had passed through the Academy. The officer corps as a whole was therefore so socially mixed as to lack the homogeneity of that in other European armies. Many of the newly commissioned officers had served into their forties as NCOs, which was of benefit at the battalion level, but rarely higher. There was little interest in professional study and even less in service on the staff. If it became necessary to assemble a formation headquarters, its commander would find himself being served by former adjutants, quartermasters and their clerks.

In spite of this, the Army did have reason to feel pleased with itself. In 1866 a breech-loading bolt-action rifle designed by Antoine Alphonse Chassepot entered service. It was a far superior weapon to Dreyse's needle gun in a number of significant ways. First, the breech was sealed by a rubber ring that prevented burnt propellant gas and fragments of cartridge paper being blasted back into the firer's face. It had a calibre of 11mm as opposed to the Dreyse's 15.4mm, but the Chassepot carried a larger charge giving its round a muzzle velocity one-third greater than the German weapon, plus a flatter trajectory and greater range.

The French also possessed a secret weapon called the *mitrailleuse*, which has been described as an early machine gun but was actually a manually-operated rapid fire system. It was the brainchild of a Belgian officer, a Captain Fafchamps, and had been refined in production by Joseph Montigny. It used the same ammunition as the Chassepot, which eased the ammunition supply situation. The *mitrailleuse* consisted of twenty-five barrels inside a tube. The barrels were loaded simultaneously with a steel plate containing the rounds, behind which a breech block was closed. The weapon was fired by means of a crank that enabled all the barrels to be fired simultaneously or singly in rotation. The plate would then be removed, divested of the empty cartridge cases and reloaded with fresh ammunition. By using several prepared plates in succession it was possible to maintain a rate of fire of 150 rounds per minute. The *mitrailleuse* was surrounded by such a cloud of official secrecy that many senior officers had never heard of it. Consequently, no doctrine as to how the best results could be obtained from the weapon was ever evolved. It was agreed that it should become the responsibility of the artillery and was provided with a conventional gun carriage and limber. The problem was that from a distance a battery of *mitrailleuses* resembled a battery of field guns and became an immediate target for the enemy's field artillery which, enjoying longer range, quickly knocked it out. Another error was to take mistaken advantage of the *mitrailleuse*'s range of 2,000 yards by deploying it too far back instead of among the infantry where it could do most damage. Equally important, the French artillery as a whole was the army's weakest arm. The field branch consisted of rifled, muzzle-loading 4- and 12-pounder guns. The former had been introduced in 1858 and performed well, but the latter were older and had formerly been smooth-bores. Both types fired common shell, shrapnel and canister ammunition. The French shell had the ability to ricochet and air burst which its German equivalent lacked although it had a greater explosive effect. Even more important, the various German armies had been re-equipped with Krupp guns that had a higher rate of fire and greater accuracy.

In 1870 a political situation finally developed that Bismarck was able to manipulate so that a war between the German states and France became inevitable. It began with the death of Queen Isabella II of Spain, a sovereign so unpopular with her people that she had been forced to live in exile since 1868. The question was: who was to succeed her? In July 1870 Bismarck arranged matters so that the

Spanish throne was offered to Prince Leopold of Hohenzollern-Sigmaringen, a relative of Prussia's ruling house who would almost certainly be acceptable to the majority of the Spanish people because he was a Catholic. It took Napoleon III the better part of a month to realise that France was about to be sandwiched between one branch of the Hohenzollerns on the Rhine and another beyond the Pyrenees. Alarmed, he asked King William of Prussia to withdraw his support for Prince Leopold's candidature. The King agreed and Leopold withdrew.

There the matter might have rested had it not been for an unbelievably tactless act on the part of the Duc de Grammont, Napoleon's Minister of Foreign Affairs. Grammont seemed to see a mortal insult to France for which Prussia must be made to pay. He instructed the French ambassador to Berlin, Count Benedetti, to obtain from King William an assurance that he would not permit Leopold's candidature to be discussed again. On 13 July the ambassador encountered the King in the public gardens at Ems. William courteously strolled across to him and congratulated him on Leopold's withdrawal. Unfortunately, Benedetti's instructions would not allow him to let the matter rest there. He demanded a guarantee that the king would not consent to any renewal of Leopold's candidature. In the king's eyes the matter was closed and he was not prepared to provide an irrelevant guarantee. However, a little later in the day he received Leopold's letter of resignation and sent an aide to inform Benedetti of the fact, adding that he gave it his 'entire and unreserved approval'. The count requested a further interview at which the question of a guarantee should be discussed. Understandably irritated, William replied to the effect that there was nothing further to discuss.

Only one Foreign Ministry civil servant, Heinrich Abeken, was present in Ems with the king. That evening he despatched a telegram recounting the events of the day to Bismarck, who was dining with Moltke and Roon:

> His Majesty, having told Count Benedetti that he was awaiting news from the Prince, has decided not to receive Count Benedetti again, but only to let him be informed through an *aide-de-camp*. His Majesty has now received from the Prince confirmation of the news which Benedetti had already received from Paris and had nothing further to say to the Ambassador. His Majesty leaves it to your Excellency

whether Benedetti's fresh demand and its rejection should
not at once be communicated both to our Ambassadors and
to the press.

Nothing could have pleased the diners more. They had been depressed
because they had hoped for a war that humiliated the Emperor of
the French and reduced the status of France in Europe. It had begun
to seem that the crisis sparked by the question of the Spanish
Succession was on the point of being defused. Bismarck was in his
most devious element and about to exploit the French foolishness in
over-playing their hand. Without altering the facts of Abeken's telegram, he edited it in such a way that Benedetti had been unbearably
insolent to the King, who had dismissed him in the sharpest manner
possible. 'His Majesty the King,' wrote Bismarck, 'Thereupon decided
not to receive the French Ambassador again, and sent to tell him
through the *aide-de-camp* on duty that His Majesty had nothing further
to communicate to the Ambassador.'

By next morning the *Norddeutsche Zeitung* had an edition containing Bismarck's version of what became known as the Ems Telegram.
Other newspapers around Europe took up the story. Copies of the
telegram were also sent to Prussian embassies abroad with instructions
that they should be brought to the immediate attention of the governments to which they were accredited. While preparing his edited
version of the telegram Bismarck had commented that its effect on
the French would resemble that of a red rag on a bull, and so it
was. The French believed that their Ambassador had been insulted,
and the Prussians felt the same about their King. Angry crowds
formed in both capitals. In Paris they shouted 'A Berlin!' and in Berlin
the cry was 'Nach Paris!' International attempts to restore calm came
to nothing, for the French establishment knew that it had been
outwitted, even to the extent of being the party that would have to
declare war.

They did so on 15 July. Far from being concerned at having
precipitated a major war, Bismarck, Moltke and Roon believed that
it was a necessary stage in European evolution and that a short,
victorious war would be the least painful way of achieving this. The
defeat of France was never in doubt, for she would be fighting
without allies, whereas Prussia would not only be fighting as leader
of the North German Federation, including those states annexed
after the war with Austria, but also, thanks to secret clauses inserted

in the Treaty of Prague, with the south German states of Bavaria, Württemberg and Baden. Thus, while for many years the conflict was referred to as the Franco-Prussian War, it is now more correctly described as the Franco-German War.

Both sides began to mobilise immediately. Moltke and his staff had prepared all but the most minor details long before. During the mobilisation phase all railway movements were controlled by the General Staff in which the specialist transport and logistic sections produced schedules that would deliver huge numbers of reservists to regional depots. There, they would find their equipment ready for collection, be informed as to their parent regiment's whereabouts and given a railway ticket for the train that would take them there. Within eighteen days of war being declared, 1,183,000 men had passed through this induction process and were embodied into units and formations. Of these, no fewer than 462,000 were despatched at short notice to the French frontier.

In sharp contrast, the French mobilisation system resembled nothing so much as a demented musical ride, despite many previous warnings that no adequate consideration had been given to the subject; in particular, only the vaguest plans existed as to how the railway system was intended to cope with the transport of immense numbers of men and all their equipment to the front. Even the mobilisation orders issued on 14 July created dreadful confusion, for on the one hand reservists were ordered to report to their regimental depots, while on the other those same regiments were ordered to leave their garrisons and proceed to assembly areas on the frontier. To add chaos to confusion, only one third of French regiments were stationed in the same town as their depots. The rest were often separated from their depots by long distances. A handful of examples of many will suffice: a regiment stationed at Dunkirk had its depot in Lyons, while another, stationed at Lyons had its depot at St Malo. Also stationed in Lyons was a regiment with its depot in Ajaccio in Corsica. The real prize for official lunacy must go to the official who insisted that recalled Zouave reservists must report to their depot in Oran, Algeria, before they could join their regiment in Alsace. Three weeks after mobilisation, only half the reservists had reached their parent regiments. As for the wretched Garde Mobile, which was called out on 17 and 18 July, no machinery existed by which they could be formed into units, dressed, armed, housed and fed. No one wanted them and for the moment no one was prepared to take responsibility for them. A similar situation existed with the numberless items of equipment and the mountains of stores needed by an army in the field. These were despatched from central magazines to regimental depots and thence to the regiments themselves. It was a military bureaucrat's paradise, a heaven of requisitions, dockets, receipts and signatures, all of which placed an unbearably heavy strain on railways struggling with hordes of reservists trying to reach their depots or regiments.

The French Army was deployed along the frontier between Luxembourg in the north and Switzerland in the south. The mobilisation plan, originally drafted by General Charles Frossard in 1868, involved the establishment of three armies based on Metz, Strasbourg and Châlons, under the command, respectively, of Marshals MacMahon, Bazaine and Canrobert, all capable experienced commanders. Unfortunately, on 11 July, Napoleon decided that he did not like the arrangement. In its place a single army, named the Army of the Rhine, was to be formed with himself as its commander while the displaced marshals received the consolation prize of an enlarged corps each. The re-arrangement left some corps properly balanced and others lacking essential formations. The question of how the Army of the Rhine was to be employed was the responsibility of General Edmond Leboeuf, the Minister of War. He was aware that his troops were dangerously outnumbered but proposed a general advance into the Palatinate with the object of disrupting German preparations. His hopes that this would encourage Austria to declare war as an ally of France were nothing more than wishful thinking. Napoleon was shown the plan on 28 July and wisely countermanded it, ordering the Army to hold its positions while he decided on the best options for the 112,800 men, 520 guns and 150 *mitrailleuses* under his command.

Moltke had mobilised 1,183,000 men, of whom 462,000 had already been deployed on the frontier, together with 1,194 guns and all their equipment. In the north the First Army had assembled in the area of Wadern with the intention of advancing through Saarlouis to the Moselle, south of the fortress of Metz. In the centre the Second Army, opposite Saarbrucken, was tasked with reaching the upper reaches of the Moselle between Metz and Nancy. The Third Army, still concentrating around Landau, was to strike through Wissembourg and take Strasbourg. The essence of Moltke's plan was to tempt the French Army of the Rhine forward until it became heavily involved with his own Second Army, at which point the First and Third Armies would envelope its flanks and crush it. It would then be possible to occupy the French provinces of Alsace and Lorraine, which contained a sizeable German element within their population.

Moltke appointed army commanders who had distinguished themselves during the recent war with Austria. Prince Frederick Charles, the Red Prince, would command the Second Army, while Crown Prince Frederick William commanded the Third. The officer chosen to command the First Army was seventy-four-year-old General Karl von Steinmetz, who had fought in the War of Liberation, the First Schleswig War and had distinguished himself as a corps commander during the war with Austria. Of the three, Moltke was only fully confident in Crown Prince Frederick. He considered Frederick Charles to be excessively cautious yet unpredictable. Normally, Steinmetz's age would have told against him, but he had demonstrated that he had real ability in Austria. Unfortunately, he was also insubordinate, foul tempered and something of an inverted snob.

The first skirmish of the war took place on 2 August at Saarbrucken, alerting the French to the fact that their opponents were closer than they thought. It caused Napoleon to resume his pointless meddling. He now formed his troops into two armies: the Army of Alsace, consisting of three corps, under Marshal Patrice MacMahon; and the Army of Lorraine, consisting of five corps, under Marshal Achille Bazaine. Apart from their rank, the two had very little in common. MacMahon's remote ancestors had fled from Ireland at the time when Oliver Cromwell was ravaging the country with fire and sword, and had subsequently supported the Jacobite cause and been ennobled in the eighteenth century. MacMahon himself had served in Algeria, commanded the Foreign Legion, distinguished himself during the Crimean War and fought in the Second War of Italian Independence. Bazaine had enlisted as a private soldier in 1831 and was commissioned into the Foreign Legion, with which he served in Algeria and Spain and Morocco. By 1855 he had served with distinction in the Crimean War and become the youngest general in the French Army. In 1859 he commanded a division during the Franco-Sardinian campaign against Austria in Italy and between 1862 and 1865 he served in Mexico, where he was created Marshal of France. Nevertheless, despite his fine record and the numerous wounds he had sustained in the service of France, he was something of a lonely figure, not just because he was a ranker, but rather because he was a ranker from the Legion, an institution regarded askance by many Frenchmen who felt that its very existence suggested that they were incapable of defending their own country. A keen student of military history, he had learned enough from its lessons to comment to a companion regarding the present war, 'Nous marchons á un desastre!' At this particular moment, he had one thing in common with MacMahon – neither of them had been given a staff, and both would have to manage with such officers as they could extract from their corps.

On 4 August the Crown Prince's army surprised part of one of MacMahon's divisions at Weissenburg, forcing MacMahon to pull back his army to a defensive position on a wooded plateau near Worth. The Crown Prince followed on 6 August and turned both French flanks after heavy fighting. Outnumbered, and in danger of complete envelopment, the French withdrew to Froschwiller, where they managed to maintain their position until nightfall. MacMahon then commenced an uninterrupted retreat to Châlons-sur-Marne, while the Crown Prince marched through the Vosges mountains towards the Meuse. German losses in the battle amounted to 8,200 killed and wounded, plus 1,374 missing. The French lost 10,760 killed and wounded, plus 6,200 taken prisoner.

While the battle was taking place, the German First and Second Armies had marched into Lorraine. Steinmetz ignored Moltke's movement orders and instead marched his men across the Second Army's line of march. A row ensued in which Moltke ordered him to remain where he was and clear Prince Frederick Charles' route forward. Steinmetz appealed to the king over Moltke's head and when the latter replied, ordering him to get his troops off the road, he knew he had been snubbed and gave vent to a bout of self-righteous indignation. The incident prevented Moltke from carrying out his original plan, but further opportunities would arise, and quickly, too.

However, on the morning of 6 August the German First and Second Armies, still overlapped thanks to Steinmetz, passed through Saarbrucken. Presently, First Army's leading division approached a series of high, wooded features, subsequently known collectively as Spicheren Heights, to the south-east of the town of the same name. They had been prepared for defence and were held by Major General Laveaucourt's division of General Charles Frossard's II Corps. Throughout the day, this stood off one German assault after another until those formations approaching from Saarbrucken were stalled in a hopeless tangle. At length General Constantin von Alvensleben, commanding the Second Army's III Corps, brought some order to the situation and organised two attacks. Both of these were beaten off by French counter-attacks so that by 19:00 there were no less than thirty German infantry companies stalled in confusion in the Gilferts forest. A French victory seemed more than possible as the French III Corps of four divisions lay within easy marching distance of the battlefield, yet Bazaine made no attempt whatever to reinforce Frossard. The latter, seeing that the enemy were using their far superior numbers to turn his flanks, ordered his men to break contact during the hours of darkness, their movement covered by the fire of no less than fifty-eight guns, firing from in front of Spicheren. As it was, the battle had seriously shaken several German units. German casualties amounted to 4,491 killed and wounded plus 372 missing. Frossard's lost 1,982 killed and wounded, plus 1,096 missing.

These battles on the frontier all contained common factors. The Chassepot had cut great swathes through the German infantry, most of whose units preferred to advance in close order. The *mitrailleuses* had also made a contribution, though not as great as had been hoped, and a number had been destroyed by the German artillery. In fact, the older guns of the French artillery were hopelessly outclassed by the German Krupp guns. It should also have been apparent that the days of cavalry were numbered. Those cavalry units that had attempted to charge infantry armed with bolt-action breach-loading rifles were simply destroyed before they could come to hand-strokes.

During the next two weeks both French armies continued to withdraw with the Germans pressing them closely. On 12 August Napoleon, tired, ill and depressed, handed over direct command of the army to Bazaine, instructing him to retire through Metz with the ultimate object of effecting a junction with MacMahon, who was regrouping at Châlons. Bazaine fought a successful rearguard action against Steinmetz at Borny, to the east of Metz, on 15 August and the following day the Emperor left for Verdun, escorted by two regiments of the Chasseurs d'Afrique. Neither realised at the time that whatever Bazaine intended he was actually inside a trap that was about to snap shut.

Moltke, who had been deprived of one decisive victory by Steinmetz's insubordinate behaviour during the approach to Saarbrucken, had quickly scented the prospect of another. MacMahon was to be ignored for the moment. Instead, the three German armies were to advance south on a frontage of fifty miles, effectively separating Bazaine from MacMahon. The three armies were then to turn north until they were west of Metz, which would thus be completely isolated. Naturally, Steinmetz placed his own interpretation on his orders and advanced on Metz directly from the east, so that two corps from Second Army had to be temporarily attached in case the French rounded on him.

Meanwhile, the bulk of Bazaine's army was commencing an untidy and disorganised march westwards along the Verdun road, passing through the villages of Gravelotte, Rezonville, Vionville and Mars-la-Tour. While the German cavalry kept Moltke well supplied with information, Bazaine knew very little about what was taking place to the south. He would have been less than pleased to learn that by first light on 16 August Major General von Rheinbaben's 5th Cavalry Division had the Metz–Verdun road under observation near Vionville and that Lieutenant General von Alvensleben's command was crossing the Meuse at Corny, some six miles distant, and advancing north at its best pace.

Even before the first shot was fired, the situation along the road was chaotic. In fact, two parallel routes existed between Metz and Verdun, the northern through Doncourt and the southern through the villages already mentioned. The problem was that these routes did not part until they reached Gravelotte, so that the whole army and its 5,000 supply wagons had first to travel along a single road from Metz, the centre of which was already congested with troops waiting to begin their march. It was all too much of a tangle for the staff to unravel. Some corps, camped in the areas of Rezonville and Gravelotte, were already shrugging into their packs ready to march, but others were less prepared. Bazaine himself had become so unsettled by reports of German cavalry crossing the countryside to the south that he postponed the move until the afternoon.

The battle began at about 09:00 when Rheinbaben's artillery opened fire on the camp of General Forton's French Cavalry Division. During the morning Alvensleben's corps came up on Rheinbaben's right, cutting the Metz–Verdun road between Rezonville and Vionville. Alvensleben had spent seven years on the Great General Staff, but the majority of his service had been spent with the Prussian Guard. At Königgrätz he had commanded the advance guard of the Guard Corps and took over his division when its commander was killed, being rewarded with promotion to his present rank and the *Pour le Merité*, Prussia's highest gallantry award.

Now, looking to the north-east, he could see the French holding an arc of rolling downland with their left anchored on Rezonville. He believed that he had only the enemy's rearguard to deal with but when the truth became apparent he decided that, as his corps was in a position to halt the French withdrawal, he would mount a sustained holding attack until the rest of Second Army arrived. Subsequently, he attracted criticism for the heavy losses incurred by his corps but, looked at from the perspective of the battle as a whole, these were justified by the results achieved.

His troops took the villages of Flavigny and Vionville but their further progress was halted with crippling casualties by a storm of Chassepot and *mitrailleuse* fire. Cavalry attacks by both sides were destroyed by the hail of bullets or driven back by counter-charges. By 13:00 Alvensleben had committed all his reserves, his ranks had been torn apart by their dreadful losses, his ammunition supply was approaching exhaustion and his left wing was being systematically destroyed by the French artillery. He could see heavy dust clouds moving westwards beyond the French line, suggesting that an attempt would be made to turn his left and it seemed as though the enemy troops opposite were about to go over to the offensive. In the meantime, a galloping staff officer had arrived to inform him that Lieutenant General Constantin von Voigts-Rhetz's X Corps, consisting of troops from Hanover, Oldenburg and Brunswick, was approaching and would be entering the line on his left. In the meantime Alvensleben must hang on where he was.

Realising that only cavalry could buy the necessary time, Alvensleben conferred with General Rheinbaben, commanding the 5th Cavalry Division, but the only troops the latter had available were Major General Friedrich von Bredow's 12 Cavalry Brigade. Nevertheless, as the situation had become desperate, he agreed to their use. Rheinbaben's aide reached Bredow at about 14:00 and delivered orders to the effect that he was to break the infantry opposite. Bredow expressed surprise as the infantry were deployed behind a line of batteries, to charge which frontally was quite contrary to accepted practice. However, when the overall situation was explained to him, he agreed to make the attack.

Bredow had spent much of his service in the Guard Hussar Regiment and had earned a reputation for steadiness and methodical planning. This was evident in the fact that he had positioned his two understrength regiments, the 7th Magdeburg Cuirassiers under

Colonel Count von Schmettow and the 16th Lancers under Major von der Dollen, in a hollow to the south of Vionville. Examining the ground ahead, he reached the only possible conclusion: that a direct attack in the face of massed artillery and concentrated Chassepot fire would achieve nothing and be little short of suicidal. Nevertheless, if the brigade inclined slightly to the left it would enter a shallow re-entrant, hardly more than a wide depression, leading almost to the crest of the rolling downland, where it entered a wide fold in the ground leading directly to the enemy's right flank. Both features would provide limited cover from view and some cover from fire while the brigade made its approach.

His plan complete, he formed his regiment into column of squadrons and led them out of the hollow at 14:30. The commander of the neighbouring 6th Cavalry Division, Major General von Buddenbrock, was unable to conceal his bewilderment that Bredow was even considering an attack on the French. As the brigade trotted past his headquarters in Tronville Wood he despatched an aide ordering Bredow not to mount an attack even if the opportunity for one presented itself. Bredow simply replied that he had been given an order by General von Rheinbaben and was carrying it out.

The brigade entered the re-entrant at the top of which squadrons swung into line with the lancers on the right and the cuirassiers on the left. They were now trotting eastwards, parallel with the Metz–Verdun road below. So far the rolling ground and battle smoke hanging in the warm, still air had concealed their progress. Then, quite suddenly, the French flank appeared, with long lines of infantry rising from the ground to blaze away with their Chassepots. Bredow promptly ordered his trumpeter to sound the 'Charge' and the troopers worked their mounts into a thundering gallop. The nearest batteries of guns were overrun and most of their detachments cut down. Then the brigade was riding through an unruly, running mob of gunners and infantrymen, in which the long swords and lance points did their deadly work.

Some 500 yards beyond were more guns, some in the process of limbering up, and more infantry. Without pause, the brigade, now raked by the fire of guns, *mitrailleuses* and Chassepots, went straight for them, losing men and horses every step of the way. Once again, cuirassiers and lancers fought their way through the shaken enemy, even temporarily capturing a gun, until they had reduced Marshal

Francois Canrobert's VI Corps to a crowd of frightened, disorganised men.

It was too good to last. The horses were blown and at last the French response made itself felt. The French 1st and 9th Dragoons and 7th and 10th Cuirassiers charged downhill to smash into the flank of the German brigade. A furious mêlée ensued when a Scottish officer, Second Lieutenant Edmund Campbell, serving with the German 7th Cuirassiers, cut down the standard bearer of the French 7th Cuirassiers, seizing the trophy with his left hand. The French, desperate to recover the standard, crowded in and he became the centre of what German historians would call 'The Battle of the Standard'. Campbell was forced to drop the standard when a pistol shot from a French officer shattered his hand and he would have been killed had not some of his regiment charged and broken through the circle of his assailants. At this point Bredow noticed yet more French cavalry closing in. It was clear that what survived of his brigade would be destroyed if it remained and he ordered Schmettow to retire. A trumpeter blew the 'Rally' and the remnant of both regiments headed for home, having to endure the fire of the rallied French infantry before they reached comparative safety. Bredow had led 500 men into action, of whom only 104 cuirassiers and ninety lancers returned. Major von der Dollen, the lancers' commander, was not among them; his horse had been shot under him and he had been taken prisoner, but was exchanged two weeks later.

This astonishing charge, subsequently referred to as 'Von Bredow's Death Ride', had achieved its objectives, having simultaneously removed the threat to Alvensleben's corps and disrupted that of Canrobert, which was already short of guns and trained gunners. Because the terrain had been used to good effect, it was the only cavalry charge of the entire war to produce a decisive result. Future generations of cavalrymen would cite it as a complete justification for the retention of their arm, completely ignoring the numerous charges that had been shot to pieces by the constantly growing firepower of the defence, so that all the major European armies entered the First World War with a large and hugely expensive cavalry arm for which little use could be found.

While von Bredow's brigade was re-forming, Voigt-Rehtz's X Corps came up on Alvensleben's left. Simultaneously, fresh French troops entered the line on Canrobert's right, so that on both sides the battlefront was extended to the west. The battle itself ended with a huge but indecisive cavalry mêlée, the last in the history of Western Europe, near the village of Mars-la-Tour. At about 16:00 Prince Frederick Charles reached the battlefield but there was no further initiative that he could take until elements of Steinmetz's First Army arrived. At about 19:00 these were employed in an attack on the French left near Rezonville, but nothing came of this and fighting ended with the coming of darkness.

The battle, named after Mars-la-Tour or Vionville, cost the Germans 15,780 killed and wounded while the French loss amounted to 13,761 killed, wounded and missing. Technically, the result was a draw, although in reality it destroyed the last of Bazaine's self-confidence. He decided to abandon the attempt to reach Verdun and maintain secure contact with Metz. At midnight he issued orders to his corps commanders that they should fall back to a strong defensive position closer to the fortress, pivoting on the village of Gravelotte, which would provide an anchor for the French left wing. His generals and soldiers alike would have been quite willing to renew the contest next day and they were not merely flabbergasted by his decision, but bemused and resentful as well. Nevertheless, throughout 17 August they carried out the move as ordered, being compelled to abandon some of their wounded in the process and burn such stores as could not be transported.

The new position chosen by Bazaine did, in fact, possess a number of advantages as it enabled him to employ his defensive firepower to the full. It occupied a ridge running from north to south. The southern half of this was fronted by a steep wooded ravine through which the Mance stream flowed towards the Moselle. This would serve to disorder the close-order formations which the Germans habitually used for their attacks. Furthermore, above the tree line the crest provided long fields of fire dominated by the fortified farms of Pont du Jour, St Hubert, Moscou and Leipzig, all of which were connected by trenches and battery positions. Beyond the point where the Mance rose in the Bois de Genivaux, the northern half of the line passed through Amanvilliers to St Privat la Montaigne. On this sector the slopes were gentler and more open but offered even longer fields of fire with no protection whatever for an attacker.

The Germans conformed to the French movement and by the morning of 18 August were ready to attack. Moltke's plan was for Steinmetz's First Army to mount heavy holding attacks against the

French left while Prince Frederick Charles marched north and turned Bazaine's right. In effect, each army fought a completely separate battle.

During the day, Steinmetz flung one formation after another into the attack. As each emerged from the tree line it foundered amid a storm of Chassepot and *mitrailleuse* fire, the latter delivered from concealed positions among the infantry, the French having learned the folly of exposing them in the open. The disorganised survivors tumbled back into the Mance ravine which, as the hours passed, became a congested shambles of infantry, cavalry, smashed limbers and abandoned guns under constant fire from the French artillery. By 17:00 Steinmetz had almost used up all his reserves. However, he was aware that Lieutenant General Eduard Fransecky's as-yet uncommitted II Corps was approaching the field. For the second time, he ignored Moltke, approached the king directly and requested that the corps should be placed under his immediate command so that he could consolidate what he believed to be his 'victory'. Believing that the circumstances were favourable, the king gave his assent. Moltke remained silent and regretted ever afterward that he had done so.

Shortly after, the nerve of those penned under fire in the Mance ravine gave way. In a blind, wild-eyed infectious panic, they came streaming out of the narrow valley, a torrent of running men, hobbling wounded, careering gun teams and cavalry troopers, none caring who they ran down. The progress of the terrified fugitives was illuminated by the roaring flames of burning buildings as they careered through Gravelotte, impervious to the king and his escort using the flat of their swords in a vain attempt to restore order. Not until they reached Rezonville did exhaustion bring the running mob to a gasping standstill.

The sight did absolutely nothing for the morale of Fransecky's men, who were now coming under fire themselves. Shaken, they descended into the valley shortly after 19:00, making their way through the torn and bloody remains of what had developed into a massacre. Emerging from the tree line, they were met by the usual hail of Chassepot and *mitrailleuse* fire. Within minutes no fewer than 1,300 of the new arrivals had been shot down. In addition, some German survivors from earlier attacks had taken possession of St Hubert Farm as the basis for a lodgement on the plateau and now, mistaking Fransecky's troops for the French, opened fire on them. This was returned and Germans continued to kill each other needlessly until 20:00, when those in the farm finally bolted back into the ravine. Fransecky himself, recognising that there was no point in continuing the attack, ordered his men to abandon their firing line on the crest.

By now, the King, Moltke and their staffs had retired to Rezonville, where they formed a depressed group standing around a campfire. On one point they were all agreed. Steinmetz had been well and truly trounced at Gravelotte. Serious doubts were expressed about the troops' ability to go through another such day's ordeal. However, Moltke commented that even at the worst moments of the rout the French had not counter-attacked when the opportunity existed to complete the destruction of Steinmetz's army. Of course, none of the group could have known that Bazaine had set up his headquarters in the unfinished fortress of Plappeville, some miles behind the front and was personally unaware of the German collapse. Furthermore, he had expressly ordered his corps commanders to remain on the defensive. Moltke suspected that something was seriously wrong with the French command mechanism and persuaded the king that the assault should be renewed the following day, although the course it would take had not yet been decided.

During the afternoon the sound of heavy and continuous firing to the north had indicated that Prince Frederick Charles' Second Army had been heavily engaged, but it was ominous that no word from it had been received for several hours, despite the fact that the sounds of fighting had died away with nightfall. At about midnight an aide arrived from Prince Frederick Charles with the unexpected but very welcome news that his army had won a victory, albeit at dreadful cost, and that on his sector the French were withdrawing into Metz. The reaction at the royal headquarters was one of intense relief rather than elation, for the losses in both German armies had been too heavy for that. The king, in particular, was deeply saddened by the report that his Guard had come close to being annihilated in an ill-conceived attack.

Moltke's plan for the Second Army's operations during the day was based on the erroneous belief that the French right was based on the village of Amanvillers, when it actually rested on St Privat, some distance to the north. The plan required the German IX Corps, commanded by General Albert von Manstein, the adoptive grand-father of the future field marshal, to neutralise Amanvillers while the Guard Corps and Saxon XII Corps, commanded, respectively, by

Prince August of Württemberg and Crown Prince Albert of Saxony, swept round from the north, took St Privat and rolled up Bazaine's line. In the event, it was Manstein who was pinned down and in need of reinforcement. By 10:00 Frederick Charles was fully aware that Amanvillers was not the French right flank, but some hours would pass before it could be confirmed that St Privat was the enemy's true right flank. That meant that the Guards and Saxons would have to march much further before they could deliver their attack. His plan was that the Guard would mount a frontal attack on St Privat, but only in conjunction with an attack from the north by the Saxons, who were to be sent on a wide enveloping march to secure their start line at Roncourt.

The problem was that it would take a great deal of time to carry out Frederick Charles's amended plan. First, it involved clearing the French from a strong outpost they were holding in the village of Ste Marie les Chênes. The attack itself, supported with ample artillery, had to be delayed until a Saxon brigade arrived and did not go in until 15:00. By 15:30 the village was in German hands and Frederick Charles was able to redeploy the Saxon artillery to the north of the captured houses and the Guard artillery to the south. Simultaneously, von Alvensleben's III Corps was brought forward between the Guard Corps and IX Corps on its right. Some 180 guns were now able to concentrate their fire against the enemy artillery and positions in St Privat, but left the French infantry relatively unharmed.

At about 17:00 the French return fire seemed to slacken. Although he was elsewhere, Prince August's unsupported argument was that the reason for this was an ammunition shortage and the Guard should therefore launch its attack, with or without the Saxons. Frederick Charles, though elsewhere along the front and unfamiliar with the position at the northern end of the line, sanctioned the attack because of the urgency of the situation, but among the staff of the Guard Corps there was heated disagreement. In the German service, the corps' Chief of Staff, Lieutenant General von Dannenberg, the senior professional as opposed to royal soldier, should have taken charge of the situation, but he seemed unclear about what was happening although he emphasized that the attack must be supported by the Guard artillery. The commander of the latter, Prince Kraft zu Hohenlohe-Ingelfingen, vehemently denied ever having received orders to that effect. Major General von Pape, commanding the 1st Guard Division, angrily pointed out that he could see the advancing Saxon columns and they would obviously not be able to launch their own attack for at least another hour. Furthermore, he could see that the earlier bombardment had left the French infantry positions almost untouched. August brushed his observations aside and ordered the corps to advance at once.

It was the German belief that the essential elements necessary for the success of an attack were combined speed and mass. Led by the Guard Rifle Regiment, which formed a skirmish line, the infantry of the Guard Corps formed assault columns with mounted field officers at their head. With colours flying and drums beating the mass moved off as though taking part in a Potsdam review. The advance would cover a distance of 3,000 yards, most of it up a continuous, open slope devoid of any sort of cover. It would be made in quick time, which would be tiring for men in full marching order with heavy pack, blanket roll slung around the body, haversack, water bottle and full ammunition pouches. Tired or not, they would have to deliver the final assault in double time with levelled bayonets over a distance of 100 yards.

The defenders of St Privat watched the distant mass moving slowly towards the foot of the long slope. They belonged to Marshal Francois Canrobert's VI Corps and had recovered from the effects of von Bredow's charge two days previously. Like the majority of French senior officers, Canrobert had served with distinction in Algeria. He had commanded the French army during the Crimean War, being honoured by his British allies with the Grand Cross of the Order of the Bath, and then served in Italy during the Second Italian War of Independence, being present at the battles of Magenta and Solferino. In 1863 he had married Miss Leila-Flora MacDonald, the daughter of a captain in the British Army and granddaughter of the Flora MacDonald who had assisted the escape of Prince Charles Edward Stuart after his defeat at Culloden. Despite their recent experience Canrobert's men both trusted and liked him.

Once he was satisfied that the German attack was within Chassepot range, Canrobert gave the order to open fire. The French line erupted into smoke and flames. Within minutes the German skirmish line had ceased to exist, its officers either dead or wounded and the survivors commanded by an officer cadet. Then it was the turn of the assault columns. Heavy casualties could hardly be avoided because of their close formation. Time and again the leading ranks were shot down but still the advance continued until the leaders were 800 yards from the objective, which was still beyond the effective range of their Dreyse needle-guns. There they went to ground and not even Prussian discipline could get them moving again. It has been calculated that in any one minute no less than 40,000 Chassepot rounds were in the air. Most were too high to find a target, but in twenty minutes the Guard Corps sustained 8,000 casualties, over one quarter of whom were killed. Few of Prussia's noble families remained unaffected by the loss. Now junior officers were commanding battalions and sergeants their companies. Not until the Saxons arrived could the assault be renewed. In the meantime, some relief was provided by Hohenlohe-Ingelfingen who, on his own initiative, brought his guns into action and began punishing the French.

Canrobert, concerned by his gunners' prodigal expenditure of ammunition, sent to request fresh supplies from Bazaine, still secure in his uncompleted fort. Bazaine had no concept of what was happening at the front and sent up just sufficient to keep the guns firing for fifteen minutes. By 18:00 the Saxons began to make their presence felt. An hour later it was apparent to Canrobert that his supply of Chassepot ammunition would not last much longer. He despatched a message to General Charles Bourbaki, commanding the Imperial Guard, to the effect that, as he was now under simultaneous pressure from two sides, he would have to abandon the village. His request that his withdrawal should be covered by a cavalry charge was granted, but the charge itself barely covered fifty yards before it was broken. As the Chassepot fire fell away to a mere splutter, sharp eyes in the Prussian Guard observed Canrobert thinning out the defenders of the village and interpreted its significance correctly. The Prussians, seeking vengeance for the loss of so many comrades, charged up the last of the slope and broke into the village from the west while the Saxons closed in from the north. Some of the garrison bolted but others formed a determined rearguard that contested every street so that it was not until 20:30 that St Privat was securely in German hands. No pursuit was attempted by the exhausted victors.

In the meantime, Bourbaki had received a second request for help, this time from General de Ladmirault, commanding the French IV Corps on Canrobert's left. Ladmirault believed that he was more than holding his own against Manstein and that he could win his battle if he was reinforced. It might seem odd that corps commanders should be approaching Bourbaki for assistance rather than Bazaine, but the truth was that the latter, in his odd way, had given Bourbaki absolute discretion as to how the Imperial Guard should be used. Bourbaki, the son of a Greek colonel, had served in Africa, the Crimea and Italy and demonstrated considerable ability as a soldier, marred by a wilful and emotional personality. At one period he had been offered the crown of Greece, which he declined, although he still retained taste for grand company. While still a lieutenant he served as *aide de camp* to King Louis Philippe, the last king of France, and his subsequent position as a member of Napoleon III's trusted inner circle had resulted in his being appointed commander of the Imperial Guard. Now, spurred on by the knowledge that the first Napoleon had only committed his Guard to administer the *coup de grace* to a beaten enemy, he set off to join Ladmirault at Amanvillers with one division. Unfortunately, when he arrived within sight of the battlefield, he encountered troops from VI Corps streaming away from the heavy fighting in St Privat. Simultaneously, stragglers were beginning to shred away from Ladmirault's line in growing numbers. At that precise moment, Bourbaki might have attempted to restore the situation on the right wing of the French army, and possibly even achieve a degree of success that might have guaranteed his fame, for neither the Prussian Guard nor the Saxons were in any condition to sustain further serious action. Instead, with his private vision of *La Gloire* vanishing before his eyes, he began to behave like an outraged prima donna. 'You promised me a victory,' he screamed at the aides who had brought him Ladmirault's request. 'Now you've got me involved in a rout! You had no right to do that! There was no need to make me leave my magnificent positions for this!' As if this tantrum was not enough, he turned his Guardsmen round and marched off. Just as they had done at Waterloo the French, believing the retreat of the Imperial Guard signified a battle lost beyond recovery, abandoned their positions and dissolved into a retreat that would take them within the ring of forts defending Metz.

The Battles of Gravelotte and St Privat together resulted in German casualties of 20,163 killed, wounded and missing, while the French lost 12,800 killed, wounded and missing. If Bazaine had counter-attacked during the critical period of the Mars-la-Tour battle he would have won a victory. The war, and history, might well have followed a different course.

# CHAPTER 10

# Creating an Empire: 2

Napoleon reached Châlons safely and, without knowing of the disasters which were overtaking Bazaine, called a council of war at which it was proposed that the Army of Châlons, which had received plentiful reinforcements and adequate equipment, should withdraw to Paris. That suggestion was rejected on the grounds of being politically unacceptable. When the news reached Châlons that Bazaine had retired within the ring of forts surrounding Metz, it was also politically unacceptable for MacMahon's army to do anything save march to his relief. A plan was devised that would alter the whole complexion of the war, ably summarised by Michael Howard in his book *The Franco-Prussian War*:

> In 1792 (General) Dumouriez had carried out a flanking operation in the Argonne against the invading Prussians with spectacular success. Why should not MacMahon, over the same ground and against the same enemy, repeat the triumph of Valmy? To make it easier a stratagem was devised to divide the German armies. A false despatch ordering MacMahon to retire on Paris was to fall into the hands of the Crown Prince, whose army would then continue to march on the capital in supposed pursuit of the foe. Meanwhile the Army of Châlons, a hundred and thirty thousand strong, could fall on the remaining German forces with a nearly twofold superiority. The siege of Metz would be raised, Bazaine would attack, and the German armies would be caught between two fires.

The plan could never have worked for two reasons: first, it was based on pure optimism, and, second, it took no account of what the Germans might be planning.

At this moment, having confined Bazaine's army within the defences of Metz, the Germans were balancing their forces. The Second Army, responsible for conducting the siege of Metz, handed over the Guard, IV and XII Corps, plus its two cavalry divisions to the newly-formed Army of the Meuse, command of which was given to Crown Prince Albert of Saxony in recognition of the competent way he had handled XII Corps at St Privat. The function of this new army was to support Crown Prince William Frederick's Third Army, which was shadowing MacMahon's movements without being strong enough to engage him. Second Army's four remaining corps were attached to First Army, which was to conduct the siege under the overall command of Prince Frederick Charles. Steinmetz objected to the arrangements and pointedly ignored the prince, for which he was finally sent packing to become the Governor of Posen.

MacMahon, bombarded by desperate urgings from the Paris politicians to march to Bazaine's relief, did so on 21 August, accompanied by Napoleon. He left Châlons with 120,000 men and 393 guns, his strength and the direction of his march being extensively reported in the press and consequently communicated to the Germans. For some reason, he adopted a northerly route, dangerously exposed to the possibility of counter-attack. This was hardly an opportunity Moltke could miss. The Crown Prince's Third Army was ordered to force march through the Argonne Forest and intercept him while Prince Albert's Army of the Meuse headed west with an identical purpose.

On 29 August part of MacMahon's army crossed the Meuse at Douzy. Prince Albert's army, advancing on both sides of the river, caught up with it and a fierce clash took place at Nuart the same day. A further action was fought at Beaumont on 30 August. After ten days of continuous marching and fighting the French were seriously tired and MacMahon decided to rest his troops in the area of a bend in the Meuse dominated to the north and south by rolling hills. The floor of the interposing valley consisted of flat agricultural land. On the western leg of the bend was the town of Sedan which, while surrounded by fortifications, could no longer be described as a first-line fortress. On the triangular area of wooded ground rising to the north of the town was the Bois de la Garenne. At the apex of the triangle was the village of Illy, dominated by its Calvary. Down the western side of the triangle was a steep valley in which a stream named the Givonne ran southwards into the Meuse, passing through the villages of Givonne, Daigny, la Moncelle and, closest to but not beside the Meuse, Bazeilles, The opposite side of the triangle was formed by a road running between hills south-east from Illy to Floing, another small village. Approximately seven miles to the north-west was the Belgian frontier.

Meanwhile, Crown Prince Frederick William's Third Army was approaching from the south-east by way of Donchery and Wadlincourt on the left bank of the Meuse. Its engineers quickly completed pontoon bridges across the river and the army crossed onto the level plain north of Sedan. Simultaneously, the Army of the Meuse was approaching from the south-west and closing in steadily on MacMahon's western flank. Although the French were not completely encircled, their chances of breaking out successfully were very small indeed. At first MacMahon did not seem to appreciate the terrible danger he was in and was more concerned about resting his troops after their efforts, although the truth was that there was very little in the way of rations and ammunition in the dump that had been established at Sedan station.

Even before the first shot was fired, Moltke knew that he was on the point of winning the climactic battle of the war, deploying some 200,000 men and 774 guns against MacMahon's 120,000 men and 564 guns with the latter already in the most unfavourable position imaginable. 'Now we have them in a mousetrap,' he commented to the king, issuing an order to the effect that should the French attempt to retire into Belgium and not be disarmed immediately by the authorities, they were to be pursued immediately. As dusk turned to darkness during the evening of 31 August, General Auguste-Alexandre Ducrot, commanding the French I Corps, watched the number of German campfires grow steadily and expand into a circle. Marking their position on his maps, he echoed Moltke's thoughts with soldierly realism: 'Nous sommes dans un pot de chambre, et nous y serons emmerdes!'

Fighting began during the early evening of 31 August. Approaching the bridge south of Bazeilles, the leading elements of Third Army's I Bavarian Corps, under the command of Lieutenant General Ludwig Freiherr von der Tann, spotted French engineers laying demolition charges along its length. Von der Tann ordered one of his battalions to attack at once. The attackers charged across the bridge, driving off the French engineers, threw their gunpowder barrels into the river, and swept on to the outskirts of the village, in which they maintained a toe-hold against counter-attacks by the enemy's marines until they were withdrawn to the river bank at dusk. Both sides exchanged shellfire with the result that fires broke out in the village and continued to burn all night. Meanwhile, undisturbed, the Bavarian engineers supplemented the intact bridge with two pontoon bridges.

At 04:00 next morning von der Tann pushed his men across the bridges through a cold grey mist and commenced the assault on Bazeilles. The village consisted of strongly-built stone houses, was extensively barricaded and held by marines, widely believed to be the finest troops in the Army of Châlons. For both sides, the ensuing battle became one of epic determination, fought out amid the flames of deliberately started fires. The inhabitants joined in the fighting, receiving short shrift from the Bavarians. At about 06:00 the Army of the Meuse entered the fray and, despite fierce French resistance, by 10:00 its Saxon Corps had captured Daigny, forced its way across the Givonne stream and linked up with the Bavarians on their left.

In the meantime, as soon as he received word of von der Tann's attack on Bazeilles, MacMahon had ridden out towards the village to obtain a fuller picture of what was happening. No sooner had he set off than a fragment from a bursting shell penetrated his leg. He was carried back into Sedan, nominating Ducrot as his successor. Ducrot possessed the necessary seniority and was considered to be a capable commander. He believed that a brief opportunity existed for the Army of Châlons to fight its way out of the trap that was forming around it and had just given the necessary orders when he was joined by General Emmanuel de Wimpffen brandishing a dormant commission appointing him commander of the Army of Châlons in the event of MacMahon being killed or disabled. De Wimpffen immediately countermanded such orders as Ducrot had given, thereby setting the scene for the greatest disaster in French military history. In mitigation, he was aware that, at 04:00, the German Third Army had begun crossing the Meuse near the medieval town of Donchery and was closing in on the trapped Army of Châlons from the east. At 09:00 the German IX Corps entered Floing while V Corps turned left onto the high ground flanking the Floing–Illy road. A French cavalry attack across the valley was destroyed by rapid rifle and artillery fire. A considerable body of survivors rode away to the north-east, passing through the village of Fleigneux. Other cavalry units, joined by a huge number of stragglers on foot, followed them in the belief that this was part of a general movement. Some were killed by the fire of the German artillery; some crossed the frontier into Belgium, where they were interned; others wandered about the forest until they were picked up by the Germans; and a tiny handful reached safety in Mézières and found liberty. Soon after this debacle the German Guard Corps arrived to close the gap, filling the space between the left flank of the Third Army and the right flank of the Meuse Army.

The French were now completely encircled and the destruction of their army had simply become a matter of time. Moltke led the king and his entourage onto a viewpoint on the wooded hills above Frénois from which they could see, as would never be possible again, the unfolding of history before their eyes. Present were the King, Moltke, Roon, Bismarck and their respective staffs, a veritable cohort of minor German royalty and, among the foreign observers, General Sheridan of the United States Army, General Kutuzov of the Imperial Russian Army, Colonel Walker, the British military attaché, and Mr W. H. Russell, the distinguished British war correspondent who had laid bare the scandalous treatment of British troops by their own War Office during the Crimean War.

When the morning mist cleared it was possible to see that the French were almost surrounded by a continuous line of batteries. Bazailles had fallen to the Bavarians at about 14:00 and now they were deploying their guns on the slopes to the north. To their right were the Saxon guns above Daigny, then those of the Guard above Givonne, then the Silesian batteries at Flaigneux and then those of the Hessians to the north of Floing. Below the hill on which the distinguished spectators were standing II Bavarian Corps' long gun-line stretched from Wadlincourt to Frénois, while to the right of the hill IV Corps' batteries extended to Remilly, the last two deployments being on the south bank of the Meuse and denying the enemy any chance of a breakout in that direction.

The course of the battle was now set. For the Germans it involved their artillery successfully silencing the out-ranged French guns and then firing a rain of shells into the masses of French infantry patiently waiting for an attack that never came. The German infantry were not going to repeat the disaster that had taken place on the slopes below St Privat and sat tight, periodically repelling local attempts by the French infantry or cavalry to break out. The cavalry found themselves with very little to do. For their part the French commanders made plans to break out, delayed their execution and cancelled them. One frantic attempt to escape after another dissolved in bloody ruin. The sustained killing found sympathy, even admiration, with Moltke, who recorded his impressions of a charge by massed French cavalry:

> General Marguerite, with five regiments of light horse and two of lancers, charged out of the Bois de Garenne. Almost at the outset he fell severely wounded and General Galliffet took his place. The advance was over very treacherous ground, and before the charge was delivered the cohesion of the ranks was broken by heavy flanking fire from the Prussian batteries. Still, with thinned ranks but unflinching resolution, the individual squadrons charged the troops of the 43rd Infantry Brigade, partly lying in cover, partly standing out on the bare slope in swarms and groups; and also on the reinforcements hurrying from Fleigneux. The first line of the former was pierced at several points, and a band of these brave troopers dashed through the intervals between eight guns [that were] blazing into them with case shot, but the [infantry] companies beyond stopped their further progress. French cuirassiers, issuing from [the hamlet of] Gaulier, fell on the [German] rear but encountering the Prussian hussars in the Meuse valley, galloped off northward. Other French cavalry detachments cut their way through the infantry as far as the pass of St Albert, where they were met by the [infantry] battalions emerging therefrom. Others again entered Floing, only to succumb to the 5th Jägers, who had to form front back-to-back. These attacks were repeated again and again in the shape of detached fights, and the murderous turmoil lasted for half an hour with steadily diminishing fortune for the French. The volleys of the German infantry delivered steadily at a short range strewed the whole field with dead and wounded horsemen. Many fell into the quarries or down the steep declivities, and a few may have escaped by swimming the Meuse. Scarcely more than half of these brave troops returned to the protection of the forest. But this magnificent sacrifice and glorious effort of the French cavalry could not change the fate of the day. The Prussians had lost little in previous cut-and-thrust encounters, but in this onslaught they sustained heavy loss; for instance, all three battalions of the 6th Regiment had to be commanded by lieutenants.

This was by no means the last attack made by Galliffet's troopers. In obedience to Ducrot's orders, they charged time and again until all that remained of them were Galliffet himself and a few companions. They charged for the last time to within feet of a German infantry regiment, possibly the 82nd or 83rd, only to find that the Germans had ordered arms while their officers saluted the few survivors. Galliffet returned the salute and the Frenchmen were permitted to ride slowly away. They had saved something of France's honour, which was more than could be said for the infantry regiments who refused to budge when Ducrot ordered them to follow up the cavalry's attack. The story is a pleasant one and is probably true.

In mid-afternoon the morale and discipline of the French army broke. Under pressure from east and west as well as being under incessant artillery fire from which it was impossible to find shelter, those units holding the perimeter of the Bois de Garenne disintegrated and initiated an unstoppable stampede down the long slope to Sedan, only to find the gates of the fortress closed and barred against them. Those that could found a limited degree of protection in the defensive ditch surrounding the walls. Not every unit abandoned its position; some simply stopped fighting, piled their arms and waved white cloths as a signal of surrender; others tried to find alternative ways out of the inferno of bursting shells only to find that there was no escape from bullets or captivity. The final act in the tragedy enacted on the plateau saw it being searched systematically by the German artillery and by 17:00 the Bois de Garenne was firmly in German hands.

At about 16:30 white flags were hoisted on the bastions of the fortress. Napoleon penned a short note to King William:

> Being unable to find death in the midst of my troops, it only remains for me to give up my sword into Your Majesty's hands.

The note was delivered by General Reille, a member of the Emperor's staff, who returned with a courteous but formal reply dictated by Bismarck, regretting the present circumstances of their meeting, accepting the surrender of the Emperor's sword, and requesting him to appoint an officer to discuss the terms of surrender with General Moltke. Having been nominated, Wimpffen objected strenuously, to which Ducrot responded tartly that he had been quick enough to take command and must realise that, as commander, the negotiation of surrender terms was an understandably distasteful part of his responsibilities.

Wimpffen bluffed to the best of his ability but all Moltke would accept was unconditional surrender, the only exception being that officers who gave their parole not to take up arms again in the present war were free to leave. This offer was accepted by 550 officers. In other respects, the Army of Châlons had become prisoners of war, surrendered all its arms and equipment together with the fortress of Sedan. French casualties during the battle amounted to 17,000 killed and wounded. Now a further 104,000 had become prisoners, to be marched off in groups of 2,000 to their final destination in various parts of Germany. A further 3,000 who had crossed the Belgian frontier were disarmed and interned. The spoils of war included three colours, 419 field guns and *mitrailleuses*, 139 fortress guns, 66,000 rifles, in excess of 1,000 wagons and 6,000 horses. German losses during the fighting included 460 officers and 8,500 men killed or wounded.

As if the tale of woe created by the destruction of the Army of Châlons did not create enough gloom for the Paris newspapers, the besieged garrison of Metz had tried to fight its way out in a badly planned sortie on 31 August and had failed badly, although it had inflicted 3,500 casualties on the Germans in exchange for 3,000 of its own. The effort virtually absorbed the garrison's offensive capacity as the fortress commander had already warned Bazaine that he only had enough ammunition for his guns to last for one battle and much of that had now been shot off.

In Paris the news created uproar. Of the country's two most important armies, one had been destroyed and the other was bottled up in a fortress without any real prospect of relief. A bloodless coup took place on 4 September, ending France's Second Empire and creating her Third Republic. Suddenly, Napoleon, deprived of his throne, was of no further importance to the Germans and he was permitted to leave for England. His former soldiers, now prisoners still awaiting adequate rations, watched his coach and personal train of wagons trundle past and made no secret of their dislike.

The problem for the Germans was that with Napoleon gone there was apparently no one with whom they could negotiate. In Paris a politician named Leon Gambetta had formed a provisional government and General Louis Trochu had scraped together men, including veterans, reservists and marines, to defend the city. Indeed, despite the loss of her most important field armies, France was raising fresh formations that actually outnumbered the Germans although they lacked the necessary discipline, training and experience to make any difference at all to the outcome of the war. In addition, the *franc tireur*, a civilian who armed himself and sniped at German troops, had begun to appear in growing numbers. This went beyond the accepted rules of warfare and those who were captured were generally shot on the spot.

Having despatched their prisoners to Germany, the Third Army and the Army of the Meuse advanced on Paris, which was invested on 19 September. Moltke had no intention of storming his way into one of the most heavily defended cities in Europe and his policy was simply to allow starvation to bring the garrison to the point of surrender. His task was not an easy one as his lines of communication were harassed by *franc tireurs*. To make matters worse, on 11 October Gambetta escaped from Paris by hot air balloon and established his provisional government in Tours, from whence he organised national resistance and the operations of the newly-formed armies. For a while, therefore, Moltke found himself engaged in two major sieges, a field campaign against the new French armies, and the need to deal with guerrilla attacks in his rear areas.

Luckily for him, Metz capitulated on 27 October and a further 173,000 men marched into captivity. After the war Bazaine, their commander, would be court-martialled for his inept performance, convicted of treason and sentenced to death. This was subsequently commuted to twenty years imprisonment in exile. In due course he escaped to Spain where he spent the remainder of his life in poverty. The release of the German First and Second Armies from their conduct of the siege eased Moltke's difficulties to an appreciable extent and enabled him to conduct operations over a wider area.

Meanwhile, the German headquarters had been established in the palace of Versailles. There, Bismarck had been pursuing his long term aim of establishing German unity under Prussian leadership. Lobbying of Germany's sovereigns and lesser rulers produced agreement on a federated state. On 18 January King William I of Prussia was proclaimed Emperor of Germany in the palace's Hall of Mirrors. William would have preferred the title 'German Emperor' but his fellow monarchs pointed out that this implied a claim to ethnic German territory in Austria, Switzerland and Luxembourg. The idea was dropped, as was another suggested title of Emperor of the

Germans, as William considered himself to be King 'by the grace of God' and not by popular choice. His position in the new Empire was that of head of state and president of the federated monarchs and rulers. He was, in other words, *primus inter pares*, that is, first among equals.

On 26 January the last sortie of the Paris garrison failed. The inhabitants of the city, long reduced to eating dogs, cats, zoo animals and even rats, were starving to death and General Trochu capitulated. Despite this, a further twelve battles had to be fought elsewhere in France after Sedan, some of these resulting in a short-lived French success, and no less than twenty fortified places had to be captured. Not a day passed on which there was not fighting somewhere until a formal treaty ending the war was signed at Frankfurt on 10 May. By then, no fewer than 21,508 officers and 702,048 men were either prisoners of war or had been interned in Switzerland. Material losses included 107 colours, 1,915 field guns and *mitrailleuses* and 5,526 fortress guns. The terms of the peace treaty required France to pay an indemnity of five billion francs and cede Alsace and north-western Lorraine to Germany; a German army of occupation would remain in France until the indemnity was paid.

Germany lost 6,247 officers, 123,453 men, one colour and six guns during the fighting. In addition to her territorial gains, she had achieved unity, gained Imperial status and was now numbered among the great powers of Europe. Curiously, although in the future her army would achieve numerous successes in many local campaigns, the Franco-German War of 1870–71 was the last major war from which it would emerge the victor.

# CHAPTER 11

# The Long Peace

It would be very difficult, if not impossible, to estimate the number of Danes, Austrians, Frenchmen and Germans who lost their lives because of Otto von Bismarck's determination to achieve German unity under Prussian domination at any price. Against this, the series of wars that produced this result also produced a period of peace and stability in central and western Europe lasting for some forty-three years. As Winston Churchill was to write, 'The world was lapped in deep peace', despite which, of course, there were people who would not be averse to starting a war on their own terms, notably the French, whose ambitions centred on extracting a degree of *La Revanche* for the humiliation they had suffered in 1870–71 and the recovery of the 'lost provinces' of Alsace and Lorraine. Yet, not even the most fervent apostle of these causes would have dreamed of France tackling Germany on her own.

Shortly after the Franco-German War a Victory column was erected close to the Reichstag in Berlin, its shaft ornamented with the barrels of guns captured during the recent wars in Denmark, Austria and France. It was subsequently moved to become the centrepiece of a junction known as the Grosser Stern (Large Star) where five roads met in a manner similar to the Étoile in Paris. Somehow it survived the Second World War bombing of the city and the further destruction wreaked by the Red Army as it fought its way through the ruins in the spring of 1945. Shortly after, the French demanded its demolition for obvious reasons but were overruled by their allies and today it still stands as a memorial to the efficiency of the Prussian war machine.

During the long years of peace the machine appeared to be growing steadily in size and efficiency until it was the most formidable in Europe. Moltke was fully aware that the army's smooth mobilisation had contributed in no small measure to its victory and now he set

113

about improving it. On receipt of a telegram containing the single word 'Kriegs-Mobil' the commanding officers of units would instantly set the wheels in motion. The unit would be marched to the stores where each man's war kit, including a new pair of boots, was kept in a separate compartment with his name on it. The troops would then march to the station and entrain for their mobilisation assembly area. Meanwhile, the reserves had been summoned and were heading for their regimental depots.

The Greater General Staff's Railway Department, still regarded as possessing the finest brains in the Army, had also made further detailed preparations for their disembarkation and deployment. Sleepy country stations near the frontier that normally dealt with daily traffic consisting of a modest number of passenger trains and a few goods wagons were equipped with multiple sidings and facilities for handling steam locomotives, all of which would be under the direction of the Army's movement control staff in wartime. It was calculated that the employment of this system could result in a 300,000-strong army taking the field within twenty-four hours of the Kriegs-Mobil telegrams being despatched. That, however, was far from being the whole story. By the end of the period reserves were so numerous that it was possible for some corps to duplicate themselves. In this manner, therefore, IV Corps might be joined in the field by IV Reserve Corps. In addition, such was the enthusiasm for war in 1914 that volunteers from every walk of life rushed to join the Colours so that the creation of new units became a necessity. The military procurement agencies and industry in general worked so efficiently together that the Army was seldom short of the means to wage war. By 1914 all the world's major armies had been equipped for some years with bolt-action magazine rifles, medium machine guns and breech-loading field artillery with efficient recoil systems – in Germany's case these were, respectively, the 7.92mm Mauser rifle, the 7.92mm belt-fed Maxim machine gun, carried on a two-man 'sledge', the 77mm gun and the 105mm howitzer, the whole producing an output that dwarfed anything seen during the Franco-German War. Despite the huge expansion in its numbers the German Army went to war in the field-grey new uniform that had first been issued in 1910.

During this period between the ending of the Franco-German War and the outbreak of what became known as the Great War it was virtually impossible for a soldier in the ranks to obtain a commission, no matter how great his abilities. To apply when one's father neither belonged to the nobility nor held a position in society and considerable wealth to go with it was a complete waste of time. Yet even those with a 'von' prefix to their names might find difficulty in being commissioned into fashionable regiments such as the Guards or cavalry. Officers without such a distinction would be happiest in regiments containing a lower proportion of 'vons'. Even so, the road to commissioning was a hard one. While in his early teens the candidate would enter a spartan cadet academy where he spent five years. No special educational achievement was required, but in its place it was now considered desirable for a candidate to possess something called 'character', which, of course, was capable of a wide variety of definitions. Having passed the academy's undemanding final examination, the candidate's parent or guardian would offer him to the regiment of his choice. If he was accepted he would spend a year in the ranks as an ensign, a rank roughly equivalent to a British sergeant. Should his progress prove satisfactory, he would spend the next two years on probation under the eye of a reporting officer. He now lived in the officers' mess where his manners would be observed and reported on. In this context he was expected to drink heavily and begin a career of womanising. This was considered to be a vital element of conversation in German messes and could lead to officially encouraged pistol duels that conferred prestige on the participants. Finally, the candidate would sit the important examination that would or would not enable him to be considered for a commission. If he passed, the officers of his regiment would hold a ballot as to whether he should be granted a permanent commission. The social life of a newly commissioned young officer during the period of the Empire involved his attending every social function of note in the area of his garrison and in many cases he would be considered to be something of a 'catch' by ambitious parents.

With some exceptions, the country as a whole held the officer corps in great respect. Officers of all ranks, never to be seen without their swords, strode about their garrisons in considerable style. No officer would be seen carrying a parcel, any purchase he had made being delivered to his quarters by the business concerned. Likewise, no officer would queue for entry to a theatre or opera house and would simply march past the waiting civilians to the box office.

Inevitably, there came a time when some people found all this strutting a mite tiresome. One such was an unimpressive petty criminal and shoemaker named Wilhelm Voigt. For some time Voigt, a resident of Rixdorf near Berlin, had been purchasing bits and pieces of a captain's uniform until he had the full set. Thus attired, on 16 October 1906 he set off for the local barracks. On the way he encountered a sergeant and four soldiers. He told them to follow him, which they did without question. He dismissed the sergeant with orders to report to his commanding officer, but collected six more soldiers from a rifle range. His next move was to take his troops to the town of Kopernick, east of Berlin, by train. There, he marched them to the town hall and ordered them to secure all exits from the building. Understandably curious, the police wanted to know what was happening and were brusquely told to confine their interest to matters of law and order. In the town's telephone switchboard Voigt instructed the operators that no calls to Berlin would be permitted for the next hour.

He was now getting into his stride. He arrested the Burgermeister and town treasurer on suspicion of fraud, confiscated 4,002 marks and left a receipt which he signed with the name of his last prison governor. Next, two carriages were commandeered and the arrested men packed off to police headquarters in Berlin under escort so that they could be properly interrogated. The remaining soldiers were told to remain at their posts for the next half hour. The 'captain' then headed for the station and disappeared.

Ten days later Voigt was arrested. Charged with forgery, impersonating an officer and wrongful imprisonment, he was sentenced to four years in prison. However, his activities had caused amusement at every level of German society and he was pardoned two years later. He emerged from prison to find himself an international celebrity. He appeared regularly not only in the theatres of Germany, but also in those of Vienna and Budapest, toured the United States, wrote a book and was represented by a waxwork in Madame Tussaud's London museum. In more recent years a lifesize statue of the 'Captain' was installed on the steps of Kopernick's town hall, and the centenary of his achievement was celebrated by the issue of a commemorative postage stamp.

The obvious message in the Voigt affair was that, whatever their status, officers would be wise to maintain a sense of proportion. Some officers chose to ignore it, notably two subalterns of the 99th Infantry Regiment, garrisoned in the Alsatian town of Zaberne (French Saverne), who behaved with unbelievable arrogance and even violence towards a civilian population that was, initially at least, pro-German. On 28 October 1913, nineteen-year-old baby-faced Second Lieutenant Gunter von Forstner, addressing a squad of recently-arrived soldiers, referred to the local population in insulting terms and promised the men that if they were attacked and made use of their weapons to defend themselves, he would personally reward them with ten marks.

Two local newspapers published an account of what had been said, generating extreme anger among the civil population. The Governor of Alsace-Lorraine, anxious to defuse the situation, urged the regiment's commanding officer, Colonel Adolf von Reuter, and his area commander, to have Forstner transferred. Both considered that this would reflect badly on the honour and prestige of the Army and they simply ordered the subaltern to be confined to his quarters for six days.

On his release, Forstner was ordered to walk around the town with an escort of four armed soldiers. This was a deliberate provocation and the townspeople reacted by insulting Forstner wherever he went. As the police were unable or unwilling to do anything about it, Colonel von Reuter asked the head of the civil administration, a Herr Mahler, to intervene. Mahler was an Alsatian himself and refused to act because the protesters were acting entirely within the law.

On 28 November the crowd of protestors outside the barracks had grown to alarming numbers. Von Reuter ordered his orderly officer, Second Lieutenant Schadt, to disperse it. Schadt turned out the armed guard and ordered the crowd to disperse three times. When it refused, Schadt and his men drove it across the square and arrested a great many people without the slightest legal authority for doing so. Among the prisoners were the president, two judges and a prosecuting lawyer from the Zaberne court who had simply been caught up in the crowd while they were leaving the court building. No fewer than twenty-six people were imprisoned in a coal cellar for the night, the offices of the local newspaper that had criticised Forstner were illegally rummaged and machine guns emplaced outside the barracks.

The result was uproar. The Emperor, now William II, was informed and on 30 November a conference was quickly assembled at Donauschingen, attended by General Erich von Falkenhayn, the Prussian War Minister, Lieutenant General Berthold Deimling, the local area commander and Chancellor Theobald von Bethmann Hollweg, the last representing the principle of governance under civilian law. The conference lasted for six days but, apart from Deimling despatching a brigade to restore order in Zaberne on 1 December, the only thing it achieved was to lower the prestige of the Emperor who apparently saw nothing wrong with the officers' actions and declared that they had not exceeded their authority.

On 2 December a parade was held through the streets of Zaberne. Forstner, appropriately attired in full dress, appeared from the barracks gate, accompanied by five armed soldiers. He was recognised by a shoemaker, an apparently simple soul who was paralysed on one side. He began pointing and laughing at Forstner, as did many other civilians nearby. As a result of the sustained mockery Forstner completely lost control of himself and, drawing his sword, slashed the shoemaker across the head, inflicting severe injuries.

This was too much. Forstner was court-martialled and sentenced to forty-three days under arrest. He appealed and, incredibly, the sentence was overturned on the grounds that he was acting in self-defence and that the shoemaker had been insulting the forces of the crown. By now, Deimling was rapidly losing patience with the 99th Infantry Regiment, which was proving to be the source of all his troubles. He replaced it with a Saxon regiment, less given to arrogance and throwing its weight about. However, the various incidents caused widespread unrest across Germany. Colonel von Reuter and Second Lieutenant Schadt were subjected to a five-day court-martial at Strasbourg, charged with unlawfully appropriating the authority of the civil police. The court apologised for the behaviour of the two officers, but then acquitted them on the basis that an 1820 Prussian cabinet order required that the highest ranking military officer in a city must seize legal authority if the civilian authority had failed to keep order. The Emperor responded by sending von Reuter a medal by express post, thereby confirming the numerous doubts that had been expressed about his judgement over the years. The affair rumbled on, reaching the Reichstag, but no firm decision about the boundaries between civil and military authority had been reached by the time war broke out.

If a minority of members of the officer corps could behave badly to the civil population, they could be even more unpleasant to each other. Officers who wrote and published critical material on the Army found themselves being ostracised and generally regarded as being *personae non gratae*. One such was Captain Fritz Hoenig who had received crippling injuries and been partially blinded during the war with France. In due course he became an internationally respected military historian but made the serious mistake of criticising the Great General Staff in sharpish terms. This was considered to be disloyal, unpatriotic and probably treasonable. One of the Staff's members was General Friedrich von Bernhardi, who had served as a lieutenant in the 14th Hussars during the Franco-German war and by chance had been the first to ride through the Arc de Triomphe during the Germans' victorious entry into the French capital. In 1895 he was appointed head of the Greater General Staff's military history department in Berlin. Enraged by what Hoenig had written, he challenged him to a duel, apparently unaware that he was making a complete fool of himself. Naturally, Hoenig could hardly be expected to accept, but his declinature resulted in his being called to appear before a so-called Court of Honour which deprived him of the right to wear his uniform, the ultimate disgrace for any German officer. The reader will decide for him or herself where the dishonour lay.

This episode, however, was far from being Bernhardi's sole claim to fame. In 1911 he published a book entitled *Germany and the Next War*. Its subject matter included the author's views on a number of subjects, *inter alia*, 'the biological necessity of war; the right of conquest; the destructiveness and immorality of peace aspirations; Germany's historical mission – world power or downfall', and much else besides. So strident was the tone of some of the language used that the German establishment was at pains to point out that it certainly did not mirror their own attitudes and was simply a reflection of some thoughts held by the country's war party.

As the years slipped away, so too did the men who had established Germany's position as a major European power on the battlefields of Schleswig, Austria and France. Roon died on 23 February 1879. Emperor William I passed away on 9 March 1888. He had been liked and respected by his people and a large crowd wishing to pay its respects gathered for his lying-in-state at Berlin Cathedral. So great were the numbers that several barriers collapsed because of the crush. On duty at the cathedral was a company of the German Army's most senior regiment, Kaiser Alexander Garde-Grenadier Regiment No. 1, under the command of Lieutenant Hans von Seeckt. Such was the noise and confusion following the collapse that Seeckt, feeling that the dignity and solemnity of the occasion were being seriously threatened, ordered his men to fix bayonets and clear the area, earning the highest praise for what might be considered an excessive reaction.

In due course Seeckt, a very capable officer who had been placed in a most difficult situation, would reach the top of his profession.

The late Emperor was succeeded by his son Frederick who, as Crown Prince, had made so great a contribution to the victory in the wars against Austria and France despite the fact that he hated warfare and was essentially humane in outlook. He shared a liberal ideology with his wife Victoria, the eldest daughter of Queen Victoria of the United Kingdom, and was an admirer of the British political system. Believing that Bismarck enjoyed too much power, he urged that this should be curbed, without success. As Emperor Frederick III he reigned for only ninety-nine days, most of which were taken up with his unsuccessful fight against throat cancer. He died on 15 June 1888 and was succeed by his son William.

Emperor William II shared his late father's view that limits should be set on Bismarck's power. Having achieved the unification of Germany, Bismarck had become Imperial Chancellor, responsible solely to the Emperor. It was he who drew up policy outlines and held the power to appoint or dismiss the various ministries' secretaries of state. He introduced administrative reforms including a central banking system, a common currency, a unified civil and commercial legal process, as well as a wide-ranging social security system. It could be argued that his obsession with German unification had cost untold thousands of lives, and it could also be argued that once this had been achieved his political expertise and negotiating skills as Europe's elder statesman continued to be a force for maintaining one of the longest continuous periods of peace in the continent's history. It was a tremendous achievement, yet William II intended to rule as well as reign and was determined to be rid of him. A major difference of opinion on policy was provoked. Bismarck, sensing that his power was slipping away, appealed to the Dowager Empress to use her influence on his behalf. The irony was that the Chancellor had expertly destroyed the influence of those who opposed him whenever the occasion demanded it, so it can have been no real surprise to him when the Empress replied that any influence she might have possessed had long since been discredited by Bismarck himself. On 18 March 1890, he resigned. He died on 30 September 1898, having spent his final years working on his memoirs. Moltke had already passed away on 24 April 1891.

William has been described as being bombastic, impetuous, tactless and too inclined to offer instant opinions on matters of state without consulting his ministers. His forays into foreign affairs sometimes reduced his diplomats to a state of near despair. In part, his strange, erratic personality may have stemmed from his difficult breech birth which left him with a condition known as Erb's Palsy, and a withered left arm that he concealed by resting his left hand on his sword hilt or bridle or carrying a glove. He was jealous of and strongly disliked his British uncle, King Edward VII. It was not enough for him to be the ruler of a major continental power. His ambition was to make Germany a global power in the British manner, with colonies in the far reaches of the earth and a powerful modern fleet with which to impose her will. In fact, such colonies as she acquired in Africa and the Pacific did give Germany what William described as 'a place in the sun' but they barely paid for their upkeep and failed to attract colonists in any number from the home country. As far as the Imperial Navy was concerned, in 1897 Admiral Alfred Tirpitz became its virtual head and he encouraged the Emperor to spend huge sums building a battle fleet capable of challenging the Royal Navy across the North Sea. This was a foolish decision as it induced a naval construction race that Germany could not hope to win. This also absorbed enormous quantities of material and huge numbers of men that could have been put to better use by the Imperial Army. Worst of all, it alienated the United Kingdom quite unnecessarily, causing her to establish a defensive Entente with France, which also had a similar understanding with Russia. At a stroke, therefore, the Emperor and Tirpitz had created the nightmare conditions dreaded by German strategists, namely the probability of having to fight a war on two fronts.

Hoping, perhaps, to establish better relations with the United Kingdom, in 1908 William agreed to be interviewed by the British *Daily Telegraph*. Unfortunately, his emotional bombast not only made matters worse but also caused outrage in the foreign relations departments of the French, Russian and Japanese governments. He implied that although Germany cared nothing for the British he had resisted suggestions from the French and Russian governments that he should intervene in the Second Boer War. Furthermore, Germany's naval build-up was aimed at Japan, not Britain. There was, of course, not the slightest justification for this and the limited fuel bunker capacity of Germany's battleships made it abundantly clear that they were not intended for use beyond the North Sea. Hoping to reassure the *Telegraph*'s reporter, the Emperor concluded the interview by declaiming, 'You British are mad, mad, mad as March hares!'

William fitted easily into the militaristic society into which he had been born. He is said to have possessed some 600 uniforms, a number of which would have been those of foreign regiments, it being a custom of contemporary royalty to award important visiting royals with the honorary colonelcy of one of their own regiments to cement good relationships. As Emperor, William was rarely seen out of uniform, the expansion of his Navy providing him with a new one to wear, that of Grand Admiral, a rank to which not even members of the British Royal Navy might aspire. In truth, despite his dashing appearance, his knowledge of military and naval matters tended to be superficial.

One might have thought otherwise if one had been invited to the annual Imperial Manoeuvres, watched by the Emperor from a suitable hilltop on which his personal standard flew. In attendance were the Imperial Army's most senior officers, visiting royals, numerous military attachés and foreign correspondents from the world's most prestigious newspapers. The whole thing seemed to function according to a script which, the participants would learn shortly, bore no relation to what happened on a real battlefield. The intention was to exercise senior officers in situations that might be experienced by commanders whose ranks were two steps above their own, but very few professional war correspondents were impressed by what they saw. *The Times*'s correspondent, who attended the 1911 manoeuvres, was particularly scathing in his comments. He noted that the initiative of large or small unit commanders was insufficiently tested, while higher formation commanders committed so many mistakes that he and his fellow observers doubted their suitability for employment at that level. He had hardly a good word to say about the infantry, who moved slowly in close order, presenting excellent targets for their opponents, had no idea how to use ground, simply did not understand the connection between fire and movement, and were sublimely ignorant regarding the effects of modern fire. The cavalry were good at horse management and performed well in a parade ground sort of way, 'but the scouting is bad and mistakes are made of which our (part time) Yeomanry would be ashamed'. The artillery was out of date and its methods were slow, ineffective and could hardly compare itself favourably with the French, who had recently introduced their magnificent 75mm M1897 *Soixante-Quinze* quick-firing

The Battle of Rossbach. General von Seydlitz leads his cuirassiers in their decisive charge.

The Battle of Leuthen. Prussian grenadiers storm the village's churchyard.

General Oskar von Hutier introduced the infiltration tactics that narrowly failed to win Germany the war.

General Heinz Guderian provided a stimulus for the development of the Panzerwaffe although his memoirs tend to downgrade the part played by several of his superiors if their opinions did not coincide with his own.

Field Marshall Gebhard Leberecht von Blücher, Prince of Wahlstadt.

The 88mm anti-aircraft gun was also used regularly in the anti-tank role, with deadly results.

The Junkers Ju 52 tri-motor monoplane was the Luftwaffe's workhorse. In addition to employment as a supply carrier it also played a major part in air-landing and para-drop operations.

Instead of employing the panzer divisions in the infantry support role, assault gun battalions were formed specifically for this purpose. The infantryman in the camouflaged foxhole is armed with a *Panzerfaust* anti-tank weapon.

The Karl super-heavy howitzer was capable of firing a 600mm 4,836lb concrete-piercing shell to a range of 7,300 yards. The tracked chassis permitted limited movement only, but, as the combined weapon system weighed 122 tons, it was normally carried aboard specially designed road or rail transporters.

BAYONET CHARGE BY PRUSSIANS AT THE BATTLE OF SADOWA.

German troops driving Austrian infantry out of woodland during the Austro-Prussian War of 1866. The Austrians, armed with conventional muskets, were at a serious disadvantage as the Prussians were equipped with the Dreyse breech-loading 'needle gun'. The battle was known as Sadowa to the Austrians and Koniggratz to the Prussians. (*Battles of the Nineteenth Century*)

German sailors and marines storming one of the Taku Forts during the Boxer Rising. The picture owes a great deal to the artist's imagination.

The charge of Major General Friedrich von Bredow's 12 Cavalry Brigade during the Battle of Vionville – Mars-la-Tour was the last successful cavalry charge in Western European history (*Otto Quenstedt, Historischer Bilderdienst*)

Given that setting an example was a necessary part of an officer's duty, doing so was almost suicidal in view of the volume of French fire originating from the crest of the Mance Ravine during the Battle of Gravelotte – St Privat. (*Battles of the Nineteenth Century*)

Terence Cuneo's painting of German storm-troopers attacking 5 Battery, Royal Artillery, at Bois des Buttes on 27 May, 1918. (*Royal Artillery Institution*)

The Prussian Guard sustained 9,000 casualties in just twenty minutes during their attack on St Privat. Only the failure of the French ammunition supply enabled them to capture the village. (*Otto Quenstedt Historischer Bilderdienst*)

The majority of German officers began their careers at Spartan cadet academies. The most famous of these was at Gross Lichterfelde, near Berlin, where this 1913 photograph shows a sports day in progress.

Ausmarsch. The 7th Infantry Regiment marches out of its Bayreuth barracks to entrain to the front.

The original caption refers to reservists reporting for duty, but the frosty ground and bare trees suggest that the photograph was taken some months after the original mobilisation. Again, the fact that NCOs are nurse-maiding the men's attempts to master their equipment suggests that they are later volunteers. Each man carried some 60-70lbs on the march.

Emperor William II, in light uniform, with his staff at the Imperial Manoeuvres of 1913. The officer third from left is General Erich von Falkenhayn while the tall officer next to the Emperor is General Helmuth von Moltke the Younger, then serving as Chief of General Staff. By 1913 these manoeuvres were more akin to theatrical performances than war itself.

Having cleared a trench, German storm-troopers move on to their next objective. Speed was the essence of their infiltration tactics during 1918 and, for this reason, their equipment was kept to a minimum.

The panzer divisions, one of which is seen here advancing along a road in Russia, was just one element of the Blitzkrieg technique.

Field Marshal Erich von Manstein, widely regarded throughout the Army as possessing its best strategic brain. Hitler was never comfortable in his company and dismissed him in March 1944.

Field Marshal Ewald von Kleist commanded in succession the first panzer group to be formed, then the First Panzer Army and then Army Group A. Professional and efficient, he sought neither place nor publicity. Hitler dismissed him at the same time as Manstein.

German light tanks and infantry in training together in Spain during the Spanish Civil War. Germany and Italy supported General Franco's Nationalists while Soviet Russia aided the Republicans.

The vitally important Fort Eben Emael in Belgium, captured during a daring attack in which German glider troops landed on its roof. (*Bundesarchiv*)

Experimental 'diving' tank intended for use in Operation Sea Lion, the planned invasion of England. The large air hose was attached to a float on the surface.

Group of command vehicles in the North African desert. The group includes a command tank, identified by the 'bedstead' aerial over the engine deck, a communications half-track and a staff car.

The end of it all. The wreckage of a German column destroyed during its retreat to Mortain, France, 1944.

field gun, which was technically years ahead of anything the German Army's field artillery had to offer. Nor did the Army's employment of dirigible airships and aircraft provide any obvious grounds for approval.

In summation, *The Times*'s correspondent concluded that, with the exception of its numbers, unbridled self-confidence and excellent administration, the German Army offered no improvement over the best foreign armies and in some respects even failed to reach this standard. It gave the impression of having gone stale through over-training and he suggested that it would be of benefit if everyone went home for a year. Finally, he risked serious unpopularity in Germany by suggesting that the country's military spirit was beginning to evaporate under the passion for making money. This was unfair and proved to be unjustified. The country was proud that it had achieved Imperial status, and proud of its achievements in science, medicine, engineering and manufacturing. In the field of commerce it had penetrated markets that were once the preserve of Great Britain, and it had built fine, fast luxurious liners that had wrested the coveted Blue Riband for the fastest Atlantic crossings from the British merchant marine. None of this meant that, if and when the time came, its soldiers would not fight as hard and well as they had always done. Such changes as had taken place during the long peace were more subtle in their nature. The Lutheran soldiers who had triumphed at Königgrätz and Sedan have been compared to the Cromwellian Ironsides of the British Civil Wars in that when the fighting was done their regimental chaplains had led them in the old German hymn *Nun Danket Alle Gott* in thanks for their victory and personal survival. By 1914 this seemed to have been replaced by the more triumphalist and slightly unsettling strains of *Deutschland Über Alles.*

CHAPTER 12

# A Choice of Foes

Field Marshal Count Alfred von Schlieffen was born into a Prussian military family in 1833 and entered the Army in 1854. Noted for his intelligence early in his career, he quickly earned a position in the General Staff, seeing active service during the Austro-Prussian War of 1866 and the Franco-German War of 1870–71. In 1884 he was appointed head of the General Staff's military history section, and in 1891, after thirty-eight years of service, he replaced Field Marshal Count von Waldersee as Chief of General Staff.

Schlieffen was best known among his contemporaries as a strategic theoretician whose thoughts were greatly influenced by the campaigns of the Roman Army, particularly the concept demonstrated by the annihilation battle of Cannae on which he wrote a book of the same title that was widely read in military and academic circles in the United States and indeed commented upon by General Schwarzkopf in the First Gulf War. Some of his colleagues felt that his character contained more of the scholar than of the soldier, and indeed his general appearance was more of the Classics master at a public school than of a senior officer of the Imperial German Army. His basic philosophy, however, was entirely grounded in sound military common sense: 'To win, we must be the stronger of the two at the point of impact. Our only hope in this lies in making our own choice of operations, not in waiting passively for whatever the enemy chooses for us.'

As the new century opened, it was marked by a feeling of growing insecurity among Germans, despite their financial stability and the possession of the most formidable army in Europe. It stemmed from the Entente concluded between France, her ancient enemy, and Imperial Russia, creating a situation in which Germany seemed to be surrounded by enemies and might be forced to fight on two fronts.

124

France, though still dreaming of *La Revanche*, was unlikely to attack Germany on her own, for although her population had grown to forty million, that of Germany was in excess of fifty million and rising. Russia, on the other hand, possessed apparently uncountable reserves of manpower. Of the two armies, that of France was the more efficient, but that of Russia possessed mass. In 1905 German worries eased a little when Russia not only sustained a humiliating defeat at the hands of Japan but was forced to deal with the revolution that followed. In that year, too, Schlieffen produced the great plan that bore his name and which he hoped would deal with the situation decisively and once and for all.

To understand his thinking, it must be remembered that the conscript armies of continental nation states were far larger than those that had fought the Austro-Prussian War and the Franco-German War. Then, it had been possible for an army commander to have the entire battlefield in view and despatch orders to subordinate commanders whose troops were visible to him. Now, with national armies deployed along the full length of the opposing frontiers, he could see little or nothing of what was taking place. His decisions were taken while he and the most important members of his staff were grouped around a map table, being informed the while by telegraph or coded radio transmissions as to the progress of operations. Generally, his headquarters were situated many miles behind the front at a location from which he could exercise central control through similar means.

The essence of Schlieffen's plan involved a rapid and decisive defeat of France, after which the whole of Germany's attention would be directed against Russia, which it was believed would be the slower of the Entente partners to mobilise. After completing a rapid mobilisation the powerful right wing of the German armies would execute a huge sweep to the south-west, passing through the Netherlands, Luxembourg and Belgium, whose neutrality was to be disregarded if necessary, and on into northern France. Simultaneously, the German centre and left wings would remain on the defensive in the areas of Lorraine, the Vosges and the Moselle. During the next phase of the offensive the German right would by-pass Paris to the west and then swing east while the left wing went over to the offensive, the overall effect being to crush the French armies between the two and compel their surrender. In Schlieffen's opinion, the defeat of France could be achieved in forty-two days, which he believed was precisely the time

Russia would take to mobilise her army. Germany's initial deployment had involved ninety-one per cent of her troops being employed in the west and only nine per cent against Russia, but with France out of the way there was ample room for a drastic re-adjustment of these proportions.

Schlieffen retired on 1 January 1906. He was succeeded as Chief of General Staff by General Helmut von Moltke, the nephew of the hero who had won the Austro-Prussian and Franco-German Wars. He was not to leave anything like as distinguished a record as his late uncle and in due course would be referred to as von Moltke the Lesser. Nevertheless, he made a number of modifications to the original Schlieffen Plan which, on balance, were beneficial. He wisely decided not to violate the neutrality of the Netherlands and, having taken the view that the German right wing was *too* strong, removed a significant number of troops from it to strengthen the armies in Alsace-Lorraine and on the frontier with Russia. Schlieffen had died on 4 January 1913, just nineteen months prior to the outbreak of the First World War, and his last words were said to have been 'Remember – keep the right wing very strong'. In the light of subsequent events there exists a strong possibility that the story is apocryphal.

In recent years the French had done much to correct the shortcomings that had resulted in their disastrous series of defeats in 1870–71. Their Plan XIV, introduced in 1898, involved the use of the national railway system to accelerate the process of mobilisation. In 1903 Plan XV, though essentially defensive in character, examined the employment of reserve formations in a subordinate role. Plan XVI, conceived six years later by General Victor Michel, the French Army's commander-in-chief, anticipated a German invasion of France through Belgium that he intended meeting head on with a counter-stroke into neutral territory. This was rejected and Michel was replaced by General Joseph Joffre who introduced his Plan XVII in 1913, involving a two-pronged offensive into Alsace-Lorraine. Unfortunately, Joffre's planning took no account of three important factors. The first was that the French obsession with offensive tactics, pressed home at the point of the bayonet, ignored the terrible effects of modern defensive firepower. Secondly, while the French 75mm field gun was a better weapon than anything the Germans possessed in the same category, the French artillery was woefully deficient in medium and heavy weapons. Thirdly, although mobilisation of the Russian Army would take three months to complete, Joffre pressured the Grand Duke Nicholas, the Russian commander, into mounting premature offensives that would end in disaster.

Few could remember a summer as fine and pleasant as that of 1914, but it would mark the beginning of the end for Europe's three continental empires. On 28 June a Serbian terrorist murdered Archduke Franz Ferdinand, the heir to the Austro-Hungarian throne, and his wife while they were on an official visit to Sarajevo. General Conrad von Hötzendorf, the Austrian Chief of General Staff, had long nurtured an ambition to teach Serbia a lesson and, although in this case the assassin had acted entirely on his own initiative, he persuaded his government to issue an ultimatum to Serbia. This was delivered on 23 July and contained a number of demands that no self-respecting government could accept. Although some of their demands were met, this did not satisfy the Austrian government, which was clearly intent on war. Serbia therefore mobilised on 25 July.

At this point the German Emperor intervened in his blustering, thoughtless way. Asked for his views on the situation that was developing, he responded by saying that 'The day of Austrian mobilisation, for whatever cause, will be the day of German mobilisation too!' Then, having effectively given Conrad von Hötzendorf and the Austrian war party a blank cheque, he left for a holiday cruise aboard the Imperial yacht *Hohenzollern*. By the time he returned a full-scale European war was in train. On 28 July Austria declared war on Serbia. The same day Russia, the champion of Slav peoples including Serbia, mobilised against Austria. In response, Germany declared war against her on 1 August and then, in accordance with the provisions of her alliance with Austria, declared war against France on 3 August, having initiated the invasion of Belgium and Luxembourg as required by the Schlieffen Plan. At this point Great Britain, a guarantor of Belgian neutrality, declared war against Germany the following day. This unwelcome development generated shock and surprise in Berlin where the German Chancellor, Bethmann-Hollweg, expressed his astonishment that the United Kingdom should consider herself bound by 'a piece of paper', thereby suggesting that in the Second Reich the honouring of treaty commitments was a matter of choice. Finally, on 6 August, Austria declared war against Russia. Italy, allied with Germany and Austria-Hungary, sidestepped involvement on either side for the moment on the grounds that, the war having been started by Austria, her own obligations had therefore been rendered void.

On what became known as the Western Front, Germany had seven armies, numbered One to Seven from the right, deployed along the frontiers of Belgium, Luxembourg and France. The greatest effort would be demanded of Colonel General Alexander von Kluck's First Army which, being on the outer edge of the great turning movement, had by far the greatest distance to march and the largest number of objectives to secure. Kluck had been selected for the job because he had acquired a reputation as a hard driver who would extract every ounce of effort from his men. He had served in the Austro-Prussian War and in the Franco-German War, being wounded twice during the Battle of Colombey-Neuilly and decorated for bravery with the Iron Cross Second Class. Kluck's immediate neighbour on his left was Colonel General Karl von Bülow, the commander of the Second Army, who had also served in both wars. Most of his career had been spent in staff appointments, although at one stage he had commanded the 4th Foot Guard Regiment and the prestigious Guard Corps now formed part of his army.

Both armies cut a swathe across Belgium. The Germans were surprised by the tough response of the tiny and old-fashioned Belgian Army. For their part, the Belgians were horrified by the extent of the brutalities that German troops inflicted upon civilians. The point has been made that the invaders may have intended to stamp out any *franc tireur* activity before it began, but the whole thing quickly got out of hand. Groups were executed instead of individuals, villages and then towns were burned to the ground instead of the isolated cottages belonging to snipers. The ancient cathedral city of Louvain was turned into a ruin in which its priceless library of medieval manuscripts was turned to ashes. The course of the armies could be marked by the columns of smoke from their trail of destruction. For five days the horror continued and then, quite suddenly, it ended. By then, the international reputation of the German Army and the Emperor himself had sunk so low that both were regarded as being little better than barbarians. A situation had been created that, even if they lacked the slightest grain of truth, atrocity stories circled the globe and were believed without question. Germany had chosen to use unbridled terror as a weapon and no further proof was needed than the swarms of pitiful civilian refugees clogging the Belgian roads in their desperation to escape the onset of her armies.

Attached to von Bülow's Second Army was a specially trained 30,000-strong task force under General Otto von Emmich, the responsibility of which was the neutralisation of the forts surrounding, first, Liège, and then Namur. These had been constructed by Henri Alexis Brialmont, the finest fortress engineer of his day, in the period between 1888 and 1892. On the night of 4–5 August, Emmich's attached field artillery, firing from the map, opened up on the Liège forts, which replied in kind. The following morning a surrender demand was sent in and rejected by the garrison commander. German infantry then launched an attack between two of the forts but were beaten off with heavy loss. That afternoon Emmich's siege artillery, consisting of 420mm howitzers, was emplaced and opened fire, shattering the steel and concrete cupolas of Fort Fleron. Time was now of the essence. Throughout the night Emmich's infantry launched continuous attacks until by the dawn of 6 August the German 14 Brigade had broken through the circle of forts and was closing in on the city. By dusk it had reached the heights of la Chartreuse, overlooking the objective. It had, however, incurred serious losses, including its commander, and Emmich sent up Major General Erich Ludendorff, Second Army's Deputy Chief of Staff, to replace him. On the morning of 7 August, accompanied only by 14 Brigade's adjutant, he walked into the enemy citadel and demanded the city's surrender. After terms had been agreed with the Burgomaster and the Bishop, the Germans marched in. After witnessing the terrible power of the German 420mm howitzers, few believed that, after the example of Liège, Namur could hold out for long. Nor could it; between 20 and 25 August it was battered into submission. The Belgians, under the personal command of their sovereign, King Albert, retreated into the fortress of Antwerp.

Meanwhile, between the 14 and 25 August the French had mounted offensives in Lorraine and the Ardennes. They began well. With Gallic élan and cries of '*A la baionnette!*' they stormed forward, the infantry still wearing their traditional blue coat, red kepi and trousers while their officers had donned white gloves so that they might die with a little style, and frequently did. They took some ground but withered away in the face of barbed wire, massed artillery, machine guns, rifle fire and counter-attacks, and were forced to fall back and reorganise, having sustained a horrific 300,000 casualties.

As far as Moltke was concerned the war situation was even better than he had hoped. He ordered the First, Second and Third Armies, the last, operating on von Bülow's left under the command of General

Max von Hausen, to begin wheeling to the south-west and south. Simultaneously he despatched two corps by rail from his right wing to the Eastern Front, where the Russians were achieving better results than had been expected, and diverting reinforcements destined for his right to the Lorraine sector, thereby watering down the entire concept of the Schlieffen Plan. In response to the change of direction by the three right-wing German armies, Joffre ordered General Charles Lanrezac's Fifth French Army into the angle created by the meeting of the rivers Sambre and Meuse. Unfortunately for Lanrezac, the Germans had discovered several unguarded bridges across the Sambre. During 22 and 23 August their Second and Third Armies swarmed across to defeat him south-west of Namur and force him into a retreat.

At this point a new and formidable element began to make itself felt. The mobilisation of Field Marshal Sir John French's British Expeditionary Force and its shipment across the English Channel had proved to be a triumph of organisation. The BEF consisted of I Corps, commanded by Lieutenant General Sir Douglas Haig, II Corps commanded by General Sir Horace Smith-Dorrien, and a Cavalry Division under Major General Edmund Allenby, giving a total of approximately 75,000 men and 300 guns. Unlike the continental armies, it consisted of professional soldiers who were either serving a seven-year enlistment or were recalled reservists. Most had seen active service either in the Sudan, or South Africa or on the North-West Frontier of India. The infantry were trained to fire fifteen *aimed* rounds a minute and use ground and natural concealment to their best advantage whether attacking or defending.

Joffre had ordered it north from its assembly area at le Cateau to co-operate with Lanrezac and 23 August found it occupying the line of the line of the Mons-Condé Canal at Mons. II Corps held the long, straight stretch of canal to the west of the town, its left being extended by the Cavalry Division and an infantry brigade, while I Corps held the British right flank where the waterway looped round the town. The cavalry had warned of von Kluck's approach from the north, while he in turn knew that he was about to be faced with some serious opposition.

It was obvious from the outset that the BEF was seriously out-numbered. Von Kluck's III and IV Corps were closing in on Smith-Dorrien's II Corps, while the German IX Corps was closing in on Haig's I Corps. It was Smith-Dorrien's men, dug in along the canal, who would do most of the fighting. Astounded, the latter watched the dense grey masses, led by officers with drawn swords, moving across the fields towards them. For their part, the Germans saw little or nothing of their enemy until the line of the canal blazed with continuous musketry. The masses seemed to stagger, stumble forward in groups and finally collapse, seeking what cover they could on the ground. Officers and senior NCOs who attempted to get the attack moving again were shot down by the British battalion marksmen. The artillery of both sides joined in, the Germans with twice the number of guns and the British with the bigger target to aim at. Smith-Dorrien's men were quite happy to remain where they were and were astonished to be told to pull back at dusk.

Meanwhile, the German IX Corps was closing in on I Corps from the right. Lanrezac's Fifth Army should have been in position there to protect the BEF's eastern flank, but there was no sign of it. At length Sir John French discovered that, following its recent defeat, Lanrezac had retreated without bothering to tell his allies and was now a full day's march to the south. Obviously, unless the BEF conformed to this movement it would be cut off and forced to surrender.

With the coming of dusk there was no sign of movement from the Germans and their buglers could even be heard sounding the 'Cease Firing' call. The BEF disengaged neatly, passing through the slag heaps that dotted the landscape, and set off to the south with I Corps to the east of the Forest of Mormal and II Corps to the west. The Battle of Mons was a small affair compared with later battles. The BEF sustained some 1,600 casualties and the German First Army approximately 3,000. Von Kluck was sincere in his admiration of the BEF, which had failed to halt his progress but had cost him priceless time. Such was the impression made by the BEF's musketry that when British prisoners were asked how many machine guns each infantry battalion possessed, they were not at first believed when they replied that the answer was two.

The retreat from Mons, carried out in extreme summer heat, continued for the remainder of the month. It was an ordeal that those taking part would never forget. Men slept in snatches as they marched and sometimes hallucinated, exchanging reality for the imaginings and wishes of exhaustion. Blistered feet gave the impression of boots filled with shards of broken glass, boots wore through and horseshoes were reduced to the thickness of tin. It was, of course, the same for the Germans, driven by von Kluck to maintain contact with the BEF. Brief clashes between the respective rear- and advance guards were actually welcomed because they provided an opportunity to stop the eternal marching for a little while.

During the evening of 25 August Haig's Corps was attacked near Landrecies by elements of the German III and IV Corps that had worked their way through the Forest of Mormal. These were repelled after a sharp action, enabling Haig to break contact and continue his southward march the following day. Over at le Cateau, Smith-Dorrien had decided that his exhausted II Corps was in urgent need of rest, his view being that the men could obtain a degree of this while lying down and firing their rifles. He chose a position along the le Cateau–Cambrai road, with a refused left flank based on the villages of Esnes, Haucourt and Caudry. The position offered little in the way of cover, although the enemy's approach from the north and west would be over largely open ground. Unfortunately, little time remained to entrench the position and in many cases the only digging that could be done was with mess tins.

The early summer dawn on the 26th enabled von Kluck to examine the British position. He decided to pin down Smith-Dorrien's front with IV Corps, turn his left flank with IV Reserve Corps and his right flank with III Corps, thereby placing his opponent inside a trap from which there was no escape. The odds against Smith-Dorrien were heavy, for his 40,000 men were opposed by no fewer than 140,000 Germans. Fighting commenced at 06:00 and continued throughout the day. Once again, the British infantry's fifteen aimed rounds a minute, delivered with a high standard of professional marksman-ship, sent the massed grey formations tumbling, and once again a number of British batteries were reduced to a tangle of smashed guns and limbers by the overwhelming strength of the German artillery.

Nevertheless, by 20:00 German casualties had reached such a level that further attacks were halted. Smith-Dorrien's men, having success-fully fought their way out of a double envelopment, disappeared into the dusk and marched off to the south. They had sustained 7,812 casualties and lost thirty-eight guns but they were still a fighting entity and had given von Kluck a bloodier nose than he had received at Mons. In fact, the German commander paid them a most handsome tribute in his report, stating that he had been engaged with no fewer than nine divisions when only three were present. Somehow, the encounter had also shaken his judgement, for he believed that he had inflicted a final defeat on the BEF, which was retreating towards the

Channel Ports when it was actually conforming to the same direction as the Allied withdrawal, with its I Corps still virtually intact.

Joffre, fully aware of the continued German pressure on the BEF, and particularly on its II Corps, ordered Lanrezac's Fifth French Army to strike hard into von Kluck's eastern flank, but declined Sir John French's offer to make the British I Corps available for the counter-stroke. This was a very generous gesture as Lanrezac was already coming under pressure from von Bülow's Second Army, coming down from the north. Despite this, Lanrezac's attack in the direction of St Quentin on the 29th gained several miles before being forced to retire behind the Oise by the superior numbers employed in First and Second German Armies' counter-stroke.

That, however, was far from being the end of the matter. Lanrezac's I Corps, under the command of General Franchet d'Espérey, had thus far been held in reserve, facing west. Lanrezac ordered it to mount a counter-attack of its own against von Bulow's Second Army. Franchet d'Espèrey was a strict disciplinarian and a stickler for detail. His orders required him to turn his corps through ninety degrees to the right, which was no easy matter under pressure. Despite this, he refused to be hurried and only when he was satisfied did he give the order to advance. Given the changed nature of war, the spectacle was astonishing and would be the last of its kind. With their colours uncased, regiments were played into action by their bands while their corps commander, sword drawn, rode along their ranks, encouraging them to forget the enemy's fire and charge home. Head on, they smashed into the Guard Corps, tearing holes in its ranks. The Guards, along with the German X Corps, were bundled back into the area of Guise, where the course of the Oise was from east to west. Crowded together with their backs to the river, they were forced to endure fearful punishment from the 75mm guns of the French artillery until nightfall. Hitherto, the failure to halt the invaders, the long retreats and the fearful casualties sustained during the failed Plan VII offensive on the Eastern frontiers had generated a cloud of black depression that hung over the French armies, but the result of the Battle of Guise raised their morale and self-confidence to new if temporary heights.

Although Lanrezac withdrew during the night, the battle had left Bülow seriously rattled. He requested von Kluck's assistance, as he was entitled to do in the overall planning of the operation. Reluctantly, but with the approval of Moltke, the latter changed First Army's axis of advance to a south-easterly direction in the hope that this would roll up Lanrezac's left flank. This represented a critical change in the most important phase of the Schlieffen Plan. Initially, First Army was to have begun marching eastward from a point south-east of Paris. Now, it was apparent that its new direction of march would take it north of the French capital.

There were, too, other matters occupying von Kluck's thoughts. He had no idea at all as to the whereabouts of the BEF but was firmly convinced that it was now out of the reckoning. In fact, the fighting near St Quentin had pulled him off the BEF's line of retreat and his turn to the south-east was opening the gap still further. The BEF might be desperately tired, but it was still functioning and was actually being reinforced to a strength of three corps, as well as enjoying shorter lines of communication. In contrast, the German First Army was just as weary and its supply lines were getting longer by the day. Kluck was particularly worried about the condition of his cavalry which was seriously short of fodder and had run out of horseshoe nails. There was, too, an unsubstantiated series of rumours that the French were forming a new army to the west of Paris, but these he stubbornly continued to dismiss. The new army, the Sixth, did exist and under the command of General Michel Maunoury, would shortly play a decisive role in events.

These would also be influenced by two incidents. The first involved an allied spotter plane detecting and reporting the German First Army's change of direction. The second witnessed minor clashes between von Kluck's advance guard and the BEF's rearguard at Crépy-en-Valois, Villers-Cotterêts and Néry. During the first two the Germans were easily shaken off, but the last was larger in scale and far-reaching in its consequences. Néry was a small village lying near the confluence of the rivers d'Autonne and Oise, some fifty miles north-east of Paris. During the evening of 31 August Brigadier General C. J. Briggs' 1 Cavalry Brigade, which was screening the withdrawal of the British III Corps on the western flank of the BEF's line of retreat, rode in from the north without contacting the enemy during the day. The brigade's three cavalry regiments (The Queen's Bays, 5th Dragoon Guards and 11th Hussars) and L Battery Royal Horse Artillery, the last with six 13-pounder guns, settled down for the night, intending to move off at 04:30 next morning.

Dawn found the landscape covered with thick, grey mist and departure was postponed for an hour. In the meantime the battery went about its routine business. The mist thinned somewhat, revealing a deep ravine to the east of the village, beyond which lay a plateau of higher ground, dominating the entire area. Suddenly, an 11th Hussar patrol galloped in with a report that enemy cavalry had been encountered in large numbers on the plateau. Almost immediately, the village and the surrounding bivouacs were swept by sustained artillery, machine-gun and rifle fire, causing numerous casualties and considerable confusion.

The enemy were the German 4th Cavalry Division. As was usual, the establishment of this included three horse artillery batteries, each with four guns. L Battery was therefore hopelessly outnumbered. Its strength was quickly reduced to three guns and then to one. This was kept firing for over an hour by volunteer detachments and ammunition numbers, almost all of whom were killed or wounded. At about 07:30 the final round was fired and at last the 13-pounder fell silent.

Just for a moment it began to seem that the supremely courageous efforts of the gun's volunteer detachments had been for nothing, but then the entire situation changed. The Germans had made a grave mistake in employing all their guns against L Battery. Their cavalrymen were reluctant to mount an attack without artillery support, and were now pinned down by the rapid and accurate fire of Briggs' troopers, many of whose mounts had either bolted or been killed or wounded. In addition, two squadrons of the 5th Dragoon Guards had worked their way round the enemy's right flank and were engaged in a dismounted attack. While this was in progress the last of the mist lifted, revealing the reinforcements Briggs had requested closing in on the battlefield. They consisted of 4 Cavalry Brigade, I Battery RHA, which opened fire at once, and several infantry battalions from the 4th Division.

Just what passed through the mind of the German divisional commander at that moment can only be guessed at. What is certain is that he had no intention of fighting it out for he ordered an immediate withdrawal that rapidly became disorderly and quickly developed into panic-stricken, headlong flight. Eight of the division's guns were simply abandoned where they stood, and although the remaining four were limbered up and driven off, they were later discovered in a wood, lonely and apparently unwanted. The 11th Hussars rounded up sufficient horses to mount a pursuit, from which they returned with seventy-eight prisoners. The 4th Cavalry Division, scattered across many miles of wooded country, had ceased to exist as a fighting formation. Not until 4 September did it re-assemble and even then it was not considered to be fit for duty. Kluck mentions in his memoirs that it had made a forced march of twenty-six hours in the hope of locating the BEF, but uses the single word 'notorious' to describe his view of the ensuing action.

The upshot of these events was that, thanks to aerial reconnaissance, the allies knew exactly where the German First Army was and where it was going, whereas, thanks to the 4th Cavalry Division being out of the picture for several days, von Kluck had only the vaguest idea of the BEF's whereabouts at the end of that period. Indeed, the fog of war was causing problems for a great many people. On 3 September, Moltke issued fresh orders to von Kluck, instructing him to act as flank guard to von Bülow's Second Army. Moltke was obviously unaware that von Kluck was still driving his men hard and for that reason First Army was almost two days' march farther south than Second Army. If Moltke's intention was that Bülow's army should form the spearhead of the German drive, then von Kluck would have to halt for that period. Unable to contact Moltke directly, von Kluck interpreted the former's order to mean that the French were to be driven south-east of Paris, for which purpose his own army was ideally suited. He therefore continued to march south-east, crossing the Marne south-east of Paris, apparently indifferent to the fact that his own right flank was wide open.

On 5 September Joffre opened his counter-offensive. Maunoury's Sixth Army, under the temporary command of General Joseph Gallieni, the military governor of Paris, advanced eastwards from the capital towards the Ourcq, where von Kluck's right flank lay open to attack. Luckily for First Army's commander, the situation was saved by General Hans von Gronau, commanding his right-flank corps. Perversely, von Kluck refused to believe that Gronau was facing anything worse than a spoiling attack, although he did send back another corps to support him. Maunoury had now resumed command of his army and the Battle of the Ourcq raged on for two days. Only then did von Kluck realise that the French clearly meant business and that he was in an extremely dangerous situation. He recrossed the Marne, changed front to the west and launched a furious series of counter-attacks that forced Maunoury onto the defensive on 7 September. The situation was stabilised by Gallieni, who rushed reinforcements up to the front in a fleet of taxicabs, and indeed any other motor vehicle he could lay his hands on, finally halting von Kluck's countermeasures.

Meanwhile, Bülow had continued to march to the south-east, with the result that a thirty-mile gap had opened between him and von Kluck. This was quickly detected by air reconnaissance and promptly exploited by Joffre. The BEF and the French Fifth Army, the latter now commanded by d'Espèrey, simply turned about and began marching north into this, part of the latter driving back Bülow's right wing on the Petit Morin river. Tired as they were, the sudden change from continuous retreat to offensive advance served as a tonic for their morale. The British, normally critical of their allies, discovered that they actually liked Franchet d'Espèrey; he won battles, had a certain style and possessed a name that they quickly changed to Desperate Frankie to demonstrate their approval.

Simultaneously, fighting became general along the entire length of the front. With his armies making little or no gains and actually losing some of the ground they had taken, Moltke's headquarters was in receipt of a constant stream of depressing reports. On 8 September Moltke despatched one of his staff officers, Lieutenant Colonel Richard Hentsch, to travel the length of the front by car, calling at the various army headquarters on the way, and assess the situation for himself. This was a task of enormous responsibility for a middle-ranking officer, but Hentsch clearly enjoyed his superior's confidence. He reached the headquarters of Second Army on the 9th to be told of Franchet d'Espèrey's turning of the army's right flank. Bülow, worried and depressed, issued orders for his army to retreat, orders which Hentsch tacitly approved. The same day Hentsch continued his journey to First Army's headquarters where he found a more positive atmosphere created by local successes. Nevertheless, Hentsch knew that the BEF was moving steadily up the gap and closing in on First Army's rear and, speaking with Moltke's full authority, he ordered von Kluck to withdraw as well. Having been advised of the situation, Moltke issued a general order for a retirement by all the German armies to the line Noyon–Verdun.

This signalled not only the end of the Battle of the Marne, which had resulted in a major strategic victory for the Allies, but also the failure of the Schlieffen plan. There were several reasons for this failure. Of these the most important were that it demanded too much of marching men and their logistic services for the distances involved, that Moltke's reinforcement of his left wing at the expense of his right, contrary to Schlieffen's intentions, contributed to the weakness of the right at the critical moment, and that Paris itself had presented an obstacle to the planned deployment. Three weeks of fighting had cost each side unheard-of casualties, amounting to approximately 500,000 men in killed, wounded and captured. Amid the shock of failure, the German military hierarchy reached the belated conclusion that a family name, no matter how distinguished, was not enough to guarantee victory. On 14 September Moltke was relieved and replaced by General Erich von Falkenhayn.

The Germans' withdrawal to the high ground north of the Aisne was carried out efficiently over a period of five days, at the end of which they began entrenching their position. The Allies followed slowly but their attacks failed to break through these field fortifications. The northern flanks of both armies remained open so that between 15 September and 24 November there followed what became known as The Race to the Sea as each attempted a turning movement on the other until the North Sea Coast was reached.

The decisive action of this phase of the fighting became known as the First Battle of Ypres and was in effect a fight to the death between the BEF, now consisting of I, II, III and IV Corps plus the Cavalry Corps and a contingent of Indian troops, reinforced with the French XI and XVI Corps, now responsible for the defence of a salient around the town, and the German Fourth and Sixth Armies, commanded respectively by Duke Albert of Württemberg and Crown Prince Rupert of Bavaria. Falkenhayn had impressed upon his army commanders that this was the last chance for a breakthrough to the Channel ports, possession of which was of decisive importance and could lead to the BEF being driven out of the war. For that reason, the success of their offensive had to be achieved, whatever the cost. To that end, their troops consisted of an unusual combination of recently raised reserve corps recruited from fiercely patriotic young idealists, including a high percentage of university students, plus a number of Guard regiments – the former lacking the fear taught by experience and the cynicism of those whose tremendous efforts had been nullified by the failure of the Schlieffen Plan, and the latter because their iron discipline would carry them through, just as it had at St Privat.

The battle lasted from 18 October until 24 November. The furious German attacks stretched the BEF to its limits. The line was held by constantly shrinking infantry battalions, reinforced with recalled reservists, by the first Territorial units to reach the front, and by cavalry holding the trenches as infantry. Local situations became so desperate that only the formation of scratch units of cooks, clerks, drivers and headquarters personnel, rushed into the line in the nick of time, prevented a breakthrough.

Yet it was even worse for the Germans. Filled with enthusiasm, the young volunteers marched happily into the attack in their close-ordered formations only to melt away amid the walls of high explosive shell bursts, the blizzard of musketry from the barely seen trench lines ahead, and the rain of shrapnel blasting down at them from above. It took such a very short time for them to learn that it was not an adventure. When the casualty lists were posted in their home towns, the loss of these young men became known as The Massacre of the Innocents.

On 11 November the Prussian Guards regiments were committed in one last frantic attempt to fracture the Allied line. The four regiments of Major General Winckler's Guards Division advanced in line on either side of the Menin Road with the three battalions of each regiment deployed behind each other in column. To the waiting men of the British 3rd Division they emerged from the morning fog 'like ghosts', the sense of eerie unreality heightened by the fact that they were using their parade step, a piece of astonishing bravado that was to have terrible consequences. Some doubted what they were seeing, but reliable accounts speak of them marching 'like automata'. In 4th Guard Grenadier Regiment officers and men began falling in such numbers that the pace was increased. At this critical juncture, with the grenadiers on the point of launching their final assault, a Royal Artillery forward observation officer discovered to his horror that his telephone line to the guns had been severed by shellfire. He ran back until he reached the break, then ordered his battery to fire continuous shrapnel. The grey line staggered, halted, then broke and ran.

The 2nd Guard Grenadier Regiment had taken the road itself as their centre line. It also happened to be the boundary between the British 4th Royal Fusiliers and a French regiment, the 4th Zouaves. To the surprise of the guardsmen, they found the British and French forward trenches abandoned. This had actually become standard practice during the enemy's opening barrage, and as the German advanced beyond they came across their previous tenants, coming forward to re-occupy the trench line, and drove them back into a wood beyond Veldhoek. The leading grenadier battalion charged into the wood but were surrounded and either killed or captured by detachments from several British regiments; although the support trenches were retaken, the original front line trench remained in German hands.

Nearby, the 1st Foot Guard Regiment had sensibly delivered their attack at a trot, rolled over the weakly held fire trench and over-whelmed the three understrength battalions holding the sector. For a moment, it seemed as though they could go all the way to Ypres, directing their advance between Veldhoek and Polygon Wood. The 3rd Foot Guard Regiment, on their right, was acting in the belief that the wood had been cleared by the 54th Reserve Division. This was not the case and, as the regiment passed the southern edge of the wood, it was raked by riflemen of the 1st King's Regiment from their weapon pits among the trees. The 3rd Foot Guard deployed for an assault on the wood from a distance of only fifty yards and at this point all hell broke loose. First Foot Guards had halted to observe the progress of the attack on Polygon Wood and were suddenly brought to a standstill by the fire of two small detachments holding strong-points ahead of them. British artillery firing from Hooge began landing shells on 1st Foot Guard's battalions, which had been dispersed and were running for shelter into Nonne Boschen (Nuns' Wood), between Polygon Wood and the Menin Road. Simultaneously, German guns were firing on Veldhoek and Polygon Wood, while the rattle of rifle and machine-gun fire remained constant. Gradually, quiet returned and slowly the drifting smoke thinned. From their weapon pits in Polygon Wood the 1st Kings saw what seemed to be yet another attack forming up. Strangely, not one of the silent grey figures was moving. A freshet of wind blew a wider gap in the smoke, revealing bodies piled together into a bank where 3rd Foot Guards had formed ranks for their intended attack on the wood. Of the regiment itself, all that remained was a handful of stragglers, including an officer or two, and the reserve battalion, which had not been engaged. First Foot Guard managed to rally just 900 men in Nonne Boschen, lacking almost all of their officers.

With the recovery of the Allied positions lost earlier in the day the First Battle of Ypres ended. The BEF had sustained 58,155 casualties, the French 50,000 and the Germans a shocking 130,000. The German Emperor strongly denied that he had once called the BEF 'a con-temptible little army', a name that its survivors, known to each other and the world as The Old Contemptibles, wore with pride for the rest of their days. For the moment they were, as the saying goes, 'used up', but many of the wounded would return and train the large citizen armies that were forming in the United Kingdom. What the German Emperor did say as he raged hysterically at his generals in the aftermath of defeat during the First Battle of Ypres, was that the British were 'trash and feeble adversaries, unworthy of the steel of the German soldier!' Several regiments of the Prussian Guard, the élite of the Imperial German Army, would not have been inclined to agree with that particular non-combatant's assessment.

One of the future General Heinz Guderian's best remembered sayings was that 'Only movement brings victory'. As far as the Western Front was concerned, there would be no further movement of any note for another three years. Instead, the opposing armies faced each other in siege conditions, each hoping to achieve a breakthrough and restore movement to the battlefield. Such ground as was gained was won at a terrible cost in lives, and turning it into a major breakthrough proved impossible. The principal reason was that even if the trench lines were overrun and a mile or two beyond changed hands, it was never possible for those on the offensive to get their horse-drawn artillery across two lines of trenches, a shell-torn no man's land and a deep tangle of barbed wire before those on the defensive had rushed in reserves to close off such gaps as existed. Both sides increased the strength and methods of their artillery until it became the principal man-killer but achieved little else. The Germans tried poison gas, but that only produced a limited success when the wind was blowing in the right direction. On 21 February 1916 Falkenhayn launched a major offensive against Verdun, recognising that this would be defended to the last as a symbol of French determination. His intention was to bleed the French Army white and compel its surrender. The battle, which cost the French some 542,000 and the German approximately 434,000 casualties, was a bloody, brutal, unscientific killing match that raged on until 18 December.

Simultaneously, between 24 June and 13 November, the British and French launched a major counter-offensive on the Somme sector. It presented similar scenes of industrialised carnage to the fighting at Verdun, with one important difference that will be discussed in the next chapter. The Allies pushed their line forward for approximately eight miles but were unable to secure a breakthrough. The British sustained 418,000 casualties and the French 194,000. The Germans, however, incurred the shocking loss of some 650,000 men, including a high proportion of pre-war officers and NCOs. This loss of experienced junior leaders was particularly serious as it ensured that the Army would never be quite the same again. The regular officer corps was keen to preserve its elite status. Middle class reserve officers did not possess the same standing although they were more numerous. Rather than grant commissions to men from the ranks, the Army created a new class of appointment for promising NCOs. An individual so promoted was known as an *Offizierstellvertreter*, that is, Officer Substitute, giving him the responsibilities of a subaltern but not the status.

Together, the German Army's losses at Verdun and on the Somme cost Falkenhayn his position as Chief of the Imperial General Staff on 29 August. He was appointed commander of the Ninth Army, with which he successfully resisted the Romanian invasion of Transylvania following Romania's declaration of war on Germany and Austria two days earlier. He was replaced by General Paul von Hindenburg and his Chief of Staff, General Erich Ludendorff, the hero of Liège, who decided to cut their losses and pursue a defensive strategy in the west.

CHAPTER 13

# Imperial Endings

During the opening phase of the war the second major element in Count Schlieffen's plan was the need to defend East Prussia with far smaller forces than were employed by the German Army in the west, and to reinforce the former heavily once France had been decisively defeated. This would enable a major offensive campaign to be mounted against Russia which, it was anticipated, would be unable to stand unaided against the combined might of Imperial Germany and the Austro-Hungarian Empire. After all, it was reasoned, it was less than a decade since she had sustained a humiliating defeat, including the loss of her battle fleet, at the hands of Japan, a defeat that had been followed by revolution. This had been brought under control, but unrest continued to rumble on just below the surface, aggravated by government incompetence and harsh policy of repression.

To everyone's surprise, on the outbreak of war Russian mobilisation had taken place at a much faster rate than had been expected, largely because of French urgings. Two armies were quickly deployed against East Prussia, the First, under General Pavel Rennenkampf on the right, and the Second, commanded by General Aleksandr Samsonov, on the left. Rennenkampf had served in China during the Boxer Rebellion and had also taken part in the Russo-Japanese War, commanding the Russian right wing during the critical battle of Mukden. The correspondent of *The Times*, reporting the war, described him as 'a poor leader of men'. Samsonov was the more experienced of the two, having served in the Russo-Turkish War of 1877–78, then against the Boxers, and at Mukden during the Russo-Japanese War. He was described as being energetic and resourceful but lacking in strategic insight. During the last campaign a bitter feud had developed between the two generals, each of whom accused the other of letting him down. This was so severe that they came to blows on a Manchurian

143

railway station and had to be pulled apart. It was symptomatic of contemporary Russian administration that the two had been given neighbouring commands when the chances of one going to the assistance of the other in the event of his encountering trouble were remote, to say the least.

The defence of East Prussia was entrusted to the German Eighth Army, commanded by Colonel General Max von Prittwitz. Like most of his contemporaries, Prittwitz had served in the wars of 1866 and 1870, during which he seems to have attracted neither praise nor stricture. He owed his present appointment to the fact that he was considered to be an expert on Russian and Japanese affairs. Despite this, he was easily unsettled by developing events and his decisions were driven by caution. There were, too, special considerations that would apply to the conduct of warfare on what became known as the Eastern Front. With the exception of railways, the means of communications were difficult. Beyond the Russian frontier few roads were surfaced outside cities and the more important towns. The rest would become mud-wallows in the spring and autumn rains, while any sort of campaigning in the Russian winter involved enormous hardship and difficulties of movement; not for nothing had one of the country's Emperors declared that the best generals in his service were named January and February. Distances, too, were immense, so that it was impossible to create a continuous front from north to south in the manner of the Western Front. Within the spaces between the still considerable defended areas there were still tasks that could be performed by cavalry, notably reconnaissance and raiding. There was always a shortage of barbed wire, particularly in the Russian armies, so that even in the best defended areas aprons never reached the depth and density that they did on the Western Front.

On 17 August 1914, in the area of Stalluponen, the centre of Rennenkampf's advancing army bumped into the German I Corps, commanded by Lieutenant General Hermann von François, an officer of Huguenot descent whose father had been killed during the Franco-German War. Prittwitz, aware that Samsonov's Second Army was advancing to the south, was concerned that François was in danger of being cut off and ordered him to retreat at once. The latter, an independently minded and able commander, replied with a signal to the effect that 'General von François will withdraw when he has defeated the Russians'. This he proceeded to do by launching a surprise attack on Rennenkampf, inflicting 5,000 casualties and taking 3,000 prisoners. Then he obeyed his orders and withdrew to Gumbinnen, some fifteen miles to the west.

Despite his reverse, Rennenkampf pulled his army together and closed up to Gumbinnen. Prittwitz, now on the verge of panic lest Samsonov should appear from the south and trap him, was for withdrawing again but was persuaded by François to mount an attack on Rennenkampf. This went in on 20 August and resulted in a drawn battle, although François did succeed in forcing the Russian right into a five-mile retreat. The failure to secure a decisive victory finally broke the Eighth Army commander's nerve. He made a telephone call to Moltke, on the far side of Germany at Koblenz, informing him that he was withdrawing to the line of the Vistula, which was heavily fortified, and requested sufficient reinforcements to enable him to hold the river line.

Moltke was horrified. Such a course of action would mean abandoning East Prussia and that could not be tolerated for one minute. Prittwitz was dismissed on the spot. His replacement was the elderly General Paul von Hindenburg who was brought out of retirement. Heavily built with cropped hair, he could not have been mistaken for anything other than the Junker that he was and indeed the principal reason for his being returned to duty was his detailed knowledge of the north-eastern corner of the country. As Chief of Staff he was given General Erich Ludendorff, the hero of Liège. The latter was aware that the two Russian armies were actually advancing on diverging axes and what he planned was nothing less than the complete destruction of Samsonov's Second Army. A solitary cavalry division would be left to watch Rennenkampf while, using the German frontier railway system and requisitioned road transport, François's I Corps would be shipped to a position south of Samsonov's troops while the rest of the Eighth Army came down from the north and savaged them from several directions.

The Germans had one priceless advantage in that their opponents, from General Yakov Zhilinski, the commander of the Russian North West Front (Army Group) down to the radio operators working for Rennenkampf and Samsonov, made the vast bulk of their transmissions in clear. The Germans were also guilty of this idiotic lapse in security, but to nothing like the same extent. The fact was, they knew exactly where the Russian formations were, where they were going and, generally, what they intended to do.

No sooner had Prittwitz departed than Lieutenant Colonel Max Hoffmann, the Eighth Army's senior operations staff officer, began preparing his own plans for Samsonov's destruction. His *pince-nez* and round face may have suggested the banker rather than the man of action but he possessed one of the most incisive brains in the Army. Hindenburg and Ludendorff reached the Eighth Army's headquarters in Marienburg on 23 August where Hoffmann presented them with his plans and, as these dovetailed in all major respects with Ludendorff's, demonstrating the uniform thought process of the German Army's General Staff in similar unwelcome situations, Hindenburg let them stand. They were, quite simply, an application of the principles of *Vernichtungverdanke*.

Rennenkampf seemed neither to know nor to care that the Germans were beginning to thin out the troops holding the front opposite him. Very quietly, I, XVII and I Reserve Corps plus one cavalry brigade slipped away to the south until, by 27 August, all that remained facing him were two cavalry brigades. To make matters worse for Samsonov, he was operating in a virtual labyrinth of lakes and woodland that hindered the tactical deployment of his army.

On 26 August his advance guard came into contact with the outposts of the German XX Corps. During the next two days the Russians intensified their pressure, forcing XX Corps to retire on Tannenberg. This apparent success concealed the fact that Samsonov's five corps were marching straight into a trap for by now I Corps lay echeloned on the right around Gilgenburg, XX Corps and 3rd Reserve Division were at Tannenberg, a Landwehr division was at Osterdode and XVII and I Reserve Corps were north-east of Allenstein. Back at North West Front Headquarters, Zhilinski's map table revealed the terrible danger in which the Second Army was now placed. The Front Commander ordered Rennenkampf to go to Samsonov's assistance, but Rennenkampf had no interest in saving his old enemy's bacon and made only a token response.

On 28 August Hindenburg struck. First he mounted a diversionary attack on the Russian left, then smashed into their right wing east of Allenstein with XVII and I Reserve Corps. Two Russian corps, together with Second Army's Headquarters, were driven into Tannenberg forest. To his horror, Samsonov realised that the Germans had penetrated the space between his own army and that of Rennenkampf. In the densely wooded, virtually trackless country of lakes and swamps in which he was entrapped there was no chance of co-ordinating a response, even if his internal communications had been up to the job, which they were not. Disorganised and badly led, his troops were simply shepherded along by the advancing Germans and surrendered in droves.

By 30 August the only remaining exit from the trap was along a narrow causeway of land leading towards Ortelsburg. Those Russians who could were streaming along it in a disorderly mob. Samsonov and what remained in his army were trapped in an area of woods, swamps and wide lakes. Artillery officers, attempting to extract their guns, were forced to abandon them in axle-deep mud. On the following day the tragedy reached its conclusion. In the depths of despair, Samsonov walked away from his headquarters and into the trees, where he took his own life. Only one-fifth of his army was able to straggle along the line of the railway into Ortelsburg. Russian casualties amounted to approximately 120,000 men, including 92,000 taken prisoner. Captured equipment included some 300 guns, a large quantity of machine guns, supply wagons and supplies contained in trains on the Ortelsburg–Allenstein railway. The German Eighth Army sustained approximately 15,000 casualties. At Hoffmann's suggestion, the battle was named Tannenberg to expunge the painful memory of the battle of the same name, fought in 1410, at which the Order of Teutonic Knights had been heavily defeated.

On 31 August Rennenkampf was ordered to stand fast. In the circumstances it was an instruction that simply invited destruction. With his troops now spread across a wide area, First Army's commander chose to ignore it and, abandoning his ambitions relating to the capture of Königsberg, he initiated a withdrawal to the area of the Masurian Lakes with his left anchored near Angerburg.

By 2 September, having been reinforced with the Guard Reserve Corps and XI Corps, recently arrived from the Western Front, the German Eighth Army outnumbered its opponents. With the last fugitives from Samsonov's doomed command now rounded up and packed off to prison camps, Hindenburg could embark on the next phase of operations, which would involve the pursuit and destruction of the enemy's First Army. His intention was to turn Rennenkampf's southern flank and with this in mind he despatched I and XVII Corps to an area near the central point of the Masurian Lakes and sent the 3rd Reserve Division even farther south to Lych, some thirty miles from the southern end of Rennenkampf's line.

On 9 September the Germans began their attack. The Russian
formations holding the northern end of their line were forced out of
their positions but conducted an orderly withdrawal. In the south,
however, the day's fighting resulted in XVII Corps having its left
flank turned. Fortunately, François' I Corps came to their rescue
the following day and it was the Russians who had the worst of the
encounter. Meanwhile, near Lych, the 3rd Reserve Division had
fought a fierce battle against the Russian XXII Corps and forced it
to fall back south-eastward. Its commander signalled Rennenkampf to
the effect that he had no alternative but to retreat. In the north, the
army commander threw in a counter-attack that pushed the German
XX Corps back for several miles. He hoped that this would buy
him sufficient time for him to restore his line but in this he was
disappointed as the German units north and south of the penetration
simply continued their advance. The hitherto successful Russians,
appreciating that they were in danger of being surrounded, withdrew hastily.

By 11 September the Russians had been pushed back to a line
running from Insterburg to Angerburg, but the southern end of this
was coming under such continuous pressure that it was beginning
to resemble a fish-hook. Rennenkampf, realising that he was on the
point of being dangerously outflanked, gave the order for a general
retreat across the Russian frontier, covered by a strong rearguard.
The remnants of his army escaped from the trap by hard marching,
depriving Hindenburg of a complete victory. Finding only empty
roads littered with abandoned equipment ahead of him, he ordered
both his wings to increase the pace of their march to their physical
limit but was forced to a temporary standstill by alarmist rumours of
a Russian counter-attack. By the time the pursuit was resumed the
Russians were half a day's march ahead, passing through Gumbinnen
on 12 September and Stalluponen the following day. Shortly after,
they crossed the border and settled into the frontier defences.

Rennenkampf may have been relieved that he had been able to
bring at least some of his troops home, but the truth was that his First
Army had almost ceased to exist. Its casualties amounted to 125,000
killed and wounded plus a further 45,000 taken prisoner; 150 guns
had also been lost. German losses amounted to 40,000 killed or
wounded. Russia never really recovered from the loss of her First
and Second Armies, which were the best equipped that she had. The

double disaster led to Zhilinski's immediate dismissal and an Allied crisis of confidence in the Russian Army.

The autumn of 1914 saw the creation of Ober Ost, short for *Oberbefehlshaber der gesamten Deutschen Streitkrafte im Osten* (Military Occupation Authority of the German Empire), the first head of which was the newly-promoted Field Marshal Paul von Hindenburg, who retained General Erich Ludendorff as his Chief of Staff. The term Ober Ost referred not just to the field commander, but also to his governing military staff and the districts they controlled, often with a degree of harshness.

Early in 1915 Hindenburg approached Falkenhayn, now Chief of General Staff, with a plan for an offensive that would result in an advance beyond the Vistula and hopefully reduce Russia's capacity to continue fighting. Falkenhayn believed that the war could only be won or lost on the Western Front but finally agreed to sanction the operation. Two German armies, the Eighth under General Otto von Below and the Tenth Colonel General Hermann von Eichhorn, would mount the northern attack in the area of the Masurian Lakes, while in the south the Austro-German South Army under General Alexander von Linsingen would strike through the Carpathian range at Lemberg, while the Austrian Third Army under General Borojevic von Bojna relieved the besieged fortress of Przemysl and General Karl von Pflanzer-Baltin's Austrian Seventh Army advanced on Czernowitz.

In the north Hindenburg was faced by General Baron Thadeus von Sievers's Tenth Army in the area of the Masurian Lakes. On 7 February 1915 it was subjected to a surprise attack by Below's Eighth Army in a blinding snowstorm. The Russians sustained heavy losses and were bundled back some seventy miles in a disorderly retreat that lasted a week. During this General Bulgakov's XX Corps was surrounded by Eichhorn's German Tenth Army in Augustow Forest. It continued to resist valiantly until 21 February when, having exhausted its ammunition and rations, it surrendered. However, the time gained by its stand enabled the Russian Tenth Army to rally and establish a new defensive position. The following day General Pavel Plehve's newly-formed Twelfth Army counter-attacked, bringing the German advance to a halt and put an end to what became known as the Second Battle of the Masurian Lakes.

The Germans sustained 16,200 casualties. Russian losses included 56,000 killed, wounded and missing plus approximately 100,000 men taken prisoner and a large quantity of guns and equipment. To the south German and Austrian forces had fared less well. Linsingen's attempts to break through the Carpathian mountains broke down in freezing snow and blocked passes and Borojevic von Bojna was unable to relieve Przemysl, which surrendered the following month. Pflanzer-Baltin, however, captured Czernowitz and took 60,000 prisoners before being halted by a Russian counter-attack.

The partnership between the German and the Austro-Hungarian Armies was not an easy one. The latter, as one German officer commented unkindly, might waltz well but had been schooled in defeat. Again, the principal reason for its problems was that it was a polyglot army drawn from the many races of the Habsburg Empire in central and eastern Europe. Only the loyalty of the ethnic Germans of Austria itself could be relied upon. Conscripts drawn from one part of the empire would be posted to another far away so that, if the situation arose, they would not have to fight their kin in neighbouring countries. Very few of them were even remotely interested in fighting for the Habsburgs and the Czechs in particular were inclined to desert in huge numbers whenever they could. Again, the Austrians' concept of operational punctuality differed from that of the Germans. For their part, the Austrian view of the German Army was that its commanders were arrogant and lacked an understanding of the problems facing the Austro-Hungarian Empire.

Thus far the Central Powers, as the Austro-German alliance was known, had won battles in the east without actually winning a campaign. That, however, was about to change. In Germany itself, Hindenburg's victories were widely acclaimed while the lack of progress on the Western Front was largely ignored. Emperor William II decided to capitalise on this. Allocating reinforcements to Falkenhayn, he instructed him to assume direct command of the German armies on the Eastern Front. Hindenburg's army group was to maintain pressure on the Russians to the north of Warsaw, while the new German Eleventh Army, under General August von Mackensen, was to mount an offensive farther south in the area between Tarnow and Gorlice with Austrian support.

For this operation, which began with a four-hour bombardment on 2 May, the Central Powers had superior numbers available. The Russian Third Army's sector was ruptured on a twenty-eight-mile front and breaches began to appear in the southern boundary of the huge salient containing much of Russian Poland and Galicia. Przemysl was recaptured on 3 June, Lemberg was occupied on 22 June and during the period 23–27 June bridgeheads were secured across the River Dniestre.

Welcome as this success was, it was little enough compared to what followed. In June another new German army, the Twelfth under General Max von Gallwitz, burst through the northern boundary of the Polish salient and advanced on Warsaw, which was abandoned by the Russians between 4 and 7 August. The entire Russian front inside the salient was falling apart. By 18 August its fragments had been pushed back to the river Bug. One after another the Russian cities in the path of the offensive fell – Brest Litovsk on 25 August, Grodno on 2 September and Vilna on 19 September. Here, torrential autumn rains finally brought an end to the Germans' astonishing 300-mile advance. The Eastern Front now stretched from Riga on the Baltic coast to the eastern end of the Carpathian range. Under the leadership of their commander, the Grand Duke Nicholas, the Russians, with their legendary endurance, had somehow managed to retain the structure, despite being critically short of everything. His reward was to be dismissed and sent to the Caucasus Front, where Russia was at war with the invading Turks. In his place, the Emperor Nicholas II assumed personal command, a disaster that would prove too much for Imperial Russia, despite the professional guidance of his Chief of Staff, General Alexiev. Russian casualties on the Eastern Front during 1915 amounted to two million men, half of them as prisoners of war, while the Central Powers' total loss exceeded one million.

Elsewhere, Italy, hoping to profit from Austria's involvement in other areas, had declared war on her on 23 May 1915, hoping to gain the disputed territories of Trieste and Trentino. To the Central Powers, this opening of another front, albeit one that remained static among the mountains for the time being, was far from welcome and required Germany to provide further support for her ally. In 1914 an Austrian attempt to invade Serbia had ended in humiliating failure. However, on 6 October 1915, Serbia was invaded again by Austria, Germany and her ancient enemy Bulgaria. In command of the invaders was the newly promoted Field Marshal von Mackensen, although the form of the campaign, consisting of converging attacks into the Serbian heartland, had been planned by Falkenhayn. Out-numbered by almost two to one, the Serbs fought hard and although they skilfully avoided being trapped in a double envelopment they were forced into a dismal retreat over snow-covered mountains into Montenegro and Albania. Their losses amounted to 100,000 killed or wounded, 160,000 taken prisoner and 900 guns lost. In addition, Germany was providing support for the Ottoman Empire, although on a lesser scale.

During 1916 the Central Powers enjoyed mixed fortunes on the Eastern Front. In March a Russian offensive in the area of Lake Naroch was defeated with the loss of up to 100,000 killed or wounded and 10,000 men taken prisoner, while German casualties were barely one-fifth of these figures. However, on 4 June the Russian South West Army Group under General Alexei Brusilov, one of the ablest commanders in the Russian Army launched a major offensive on a 300-mile frontage. To achieve maximum surprise, there were no prior concentrations of troops and no preliminary artillery barrages that might have suggested preparations for a major operation were in progress, yet so thorough was the planning that the Austro-German lines were torn apart in two places, routing the Austrian Fourth and Seventh Armies, taking 70,000 prisoners and threatening the important railway junction of Kowel. This, however, was Imperial Russia where personal jealousies and resentments could affect the conduct of operations and in this case neither army group commander on Brusilov's flanks seemed inclined to support his success. On 26 June a counter-stroke by the army group under General Alexander von Linsingen checked the northern sector of the Russian advance. Brusilov was ordered by General Alexiev, Chief of Staff at Imperial Headquarters, to renew his attacks, which he did on 28 July, and made additional gains until forced onto the defensive by ammunition shortages. He was, however, able to mount a third phase to his offensive on 7 August. This took him as far as the Carpathian foothills but by then his troops were exhausted and, by 20 September, the offensive had finally run down. It had cost Russia one million casualties, more even than that huge empire could afford, but the Austrian loss had been greater still and if it had not been for the vast number of German reinforcements streaming across Europe from the Western Front the probability is that the Austro-Hungarian Empire would have been knocked out of the war by the end of the year.

There was another consequence of the offensive, which for Russia was to have most unfortunate results. The Romanian government had been so impressed by the early successes of the Brusilov offensive that, on 27 August, it declared war on Germany and Austria, hoping thereby to acquire Transylvania, to which it believed Romania had a claim. Unfortunately for Romania, too, there had been a number of important changes across the lines. The failure of Falkenhayn's offensive at Verdun had led to his being dismissed as Chief of Imperial General Staff and replaced by Hindenburg, who took Ludendorff with him. The new commander at Ober Ost was Prince Leopold of Bavaria, who was given General Max Hoffmann as his Chief of Staff. This solved a nagging problem in command circles, for Hoffmann had bitterly resented Hindenburg and Ludendorff being given all the credit for the victories of Tannenberg and the Masurian Lakes, for which he believed he had laid the groundwork. One result of these changes was that Falkenhayn, whose abilities as an army commander were not in doubt, was given command of the German Ninth Army on the Eastern Front.

Although there must have been exceptions, the Romanian officer corps was looked upon as decadent, devious and lacking integrity, yet, while as a whole the army was untrained, inexperienced and quite unready for the shock of modern warfare, its rank-and-file consisted of hardy peasant soldiers who settled down quickly and fought with dogged determination. Their generals, however, were no match for Falkenhayn, closing in from the north with his Ninth Army, or Mackensen's Third Bulgarian Army, reinforced with German and Turkish formations, marching north from Salonika. The German armies joined forces at the end of November, inflicting a disastrous defeat on the Romanians at the Battle of the Arges River, 1–4 December. The survivors fled north into Russia, having sustained over 300,000 casualties, including a high proportion of sick and desertions. The Central Powers incurred some 60,000 battle casualties, and about the same number incapacitated by sickness. For Germany, the prize was the acquisition of Romania's grain- and oil-producing areas. Simultaneously, the Russian army was compelled to extend its front southwards into the area known as the Dobruja, where the Danube delta emptied into the Black Sea, which it simply could not afford to do.

On the Eastern Front, therefore, the year 1916 had been one of mixed fortunes for the Central Powers. On 21 November Franz Josef, Emperor of Austria and King of Hungary, died after a reign lasting forty-nine years. During this his life had been filled with personal tragedies, but he had succeeded in preserving the integrity of his empire and was generally liked by his subjects. He was succeeded by his great nephew Karl, who had had comparatively little preparation for the task that lay ahead.

In the event, it was the Russian Empire that collapsed first. From the beginning of the war it was apparent that the greatest number of head wounds had been caused by shrapnel shells bursting overhead. Every first-class army had reduced this major cause of casualties by issuing its soldiers with steel helmets, with the exception of Russia. The sight of Russian troops going into action still wearing their soft caps was, in fact, merely symptomatic of the many shortages revealing that the empire had come to the end of its resources. During the first days of March 1917 shortages of food and fuel caused riots and strikes in Petrograd, as St Petersburg was known during the war. The police were unable to control the situation and the city's military garrison sided with the rioters. The incompetence or indifference of the Romanovs to their people's sacrifice and suffering had finally turned the population against them. When the Emperor left his field headquarters for the capital in the vain hope of retrieving the situation his train was halted and he was denied further progress until he signed an article of abdication that included his heirs. His tragic story, and that of his immediate family, was to end the following year in their mass murder in a Siberian cellar.

In Petrograd a Provisional Government had been formed under the leadership of Alexander Kerensky. Unhappily, it was forced to share power with the Petrograd Soviet and its promise to continue the war against the Central Powers was rendered meaningless by the Soviet's issue of 'General Order No. 1', depriving officers of their disciplinary authority. The immediate results were the collapse of any form of military authority and the murder of many officers. Others, finding that their orders were ignored, simply went home.

Somehow, Kerensky managed to assemble such troops as were still capable of offensive operations and, under Brusilov's direction, the Russian Seventh and Eleventh Armies mounted a fresh offensive in the direction of Lemberg on 1 July, pushing back General Count Felix von Bothmer's composite German-Austrian-Turkish South Army for thirty miles on a 100-mile frontage. Subsidiary operations on Brusilov's flanks mauled two Austrian armies but by 5 July the Russians felt that they had done enough and discipline only held good for defensive tasks. On 19 July Hoffmann counter-attacked with troops drawn from the Western Front. One after another, Russian armies disintegrated to the point that none remained south of the Pripet Marshes. The resulting German advances halted only because of inadequate logistical resources and insufficient reserves.

It was during this period that the German Army developed its own method of breaking the deadlock of trench warfare. Its author was General Oskar von Hutier, who had commanded a division in France during the war's early months before being transferred to the Eastern Front as a corps commander in the German Tenth Army in 1915, taking part in the conquest of Russian-ruled Poland and Lithuania during the next two years. In 1917 he was appointed commander of the German Eighth Army on the Baltic coast at Riga. Here the Russian Twelfth Army, commanded by General Klembovsky, held a bridge-head along the west bank of the river Dvina. Hutier's intention was to eliminate the bridgehead and capture Riga as a prelude to an advance on Petrograd. Klembovsky knew that he was about to be attacked, but he believed that von Hutier would eliminate the bridgehead before attempting a river crossing. He therefore retained his more reliable troops in the bridgehead itself and detailed divisions of doubtful quality to hold the river line. What Hutier actually intended was the precise opposite. His plan was to force a crossing of the river line, then swing north towards the coast, so placing the defenders of the bridgehead and Riga itself inside a trap.

Hutier had seen too many prolonged artillery barrages followed by massed infantry assaults along the entire line produce nothing better than horrific casualties. The alternative method that he had devised consisted of several phases. The first consisted of a com-paratively short artillery bombardment including large calibre high explosive and a high proportion of poison gas shells, the intention being the neutralisation of those holding the front line rather than the destruction of the trench systems. This would be followed by a rolling barrage under cover of which specially selected and trained storm troops formed into assault battalions would infiltrate through previously identified weak points in the enemy's defences, avoiding combat and known strongpoints whenever possible, with the object of capturing or destroying the enemy's command headquarters and artillery control centres. The third phase would see more heavily armed units closing in to destroy those strongpoints that had been by-passed by the storm troops.

The method was first used at Riga on 1 September 1917. Following a five-hour bombardment, a mere noisy disturbance by Western Front standards but sufficient to drench the Russian positions with gas, shatter the occupants' nerves with high explosive and blind them with smoke, the German infantry swarmed across the river, their rapid advance past those positions that were still holding out unnerving the remainder of the defenders, who began streaming away to the east. Within hours Riga was in German hands, together with 9,000 Russian prisoners. Klembovsky, however, was no fool and, seeing the way matters were developing, had already withdrawn the remainder of his troops through Riga and along the coast road to Pskov. There had been comparatively few men killed or wounded on either side. Hutier's immediate reward was a personal visit by his emperor, who awarded him the *Pour le Merité*.

On 24 October the same tactics were employed again, this time by General von Below's Austro-German Fourteenth Army against the Italian Second Army on the Caporetto sector of the Isonzo Front. General Luigi Cadorna, the Italian Commander-in-Chief, had suspected that this sector had been chosen as the target of a major Central Powers offensive and gave instructions for a defence in depth to be prepared. These were ignored, with catastrophic results.

The German bombardment, erupting in the forward positions, disrupted communications with the rear so that formation headquarters were left floundering in a fog of war as dense as that enveloping their choking front-line troops. And then came the storm-troopers, sinister grey groups flitting in groups through the gas zone and on towards the artillery and administrative areas, followed by larger formations that eliminated any centres of resistance that had been by-passed. Regiments began shredding away from the front while those on either side, lacking instructions from a paralysed command system, were forced to conform to the movement. Soon, the whole of the Second Army was straggling rearwards, compelling the retreat of Third Army on its right.

Cadorna had hoped to check the flood of fugitives along the line of the river Tagliamente but the pursuit was as rapid as it was ruthless. Crossings were forced before the Italians could reorganise their shattered forces. Even Second Army's headquarters staff was reduced to the common lot of fugitives, incapable of organising a coherent front from the drifting wrack of its troops. Not until 7 November did the Italians turn and fight again, manning a hastily-dug defence line that followed the southern bank of the river Piave. In less than three weeks they had sustained a staggering 300,000 casualties, lost 2,500 guns and been driven back over seventy miles from their original front line. Had it not been for the arrival of British and French reinforcements despatched urgently from the Western Front, plus the inescapable rule that the power of an attack diminishes in proportion to the distance it has covered, thereby giving the Italian army the time it needed to form a new front, Italy might well have been knocked out of the war.

A point of interest here is the presence of a young officer named Erwin Rommel, commanding a detachment of the Württemberg Mountain Battalion. During the fifty-two hours since the start of the offensive the Rommel Detachment climbed 8,000 feet, descended 3,000 feet, and in the process isolated, defeated or destroyed elements from five Italian regiments, captured 150 officers, 9,000 men, eighty-one guns and numerous transport vehicles. Its own losses amounted to six killed, including one officer mortally wounded, and thirty wounded, including one officer. Rommel had pushed his men hard, but no harder than he pushed himself. He received the *Pour le Merité* and promotion to captain, a rank that he was to hold for the next fifteen years because of the Army's post-war reduction in strength.

# CHAPTER 14

# Land Ironclads and Storm Troopers

For those Germans holding the ruins that had once been the village of Flers, its forward defence trenches and Delville Wood to the south, the morning of 15 September 1916 suggested a fine day to follow with a touch of early ground mist providing the first hint of autumn. Two-and-a-half months earlier the apparently endless Battle of the Somme had begun. For those with previous service on the Verdun sector it mirrored the horrible repetition of its course, although the enemy here were the British and not the French. The British would attack and take an area of the German trench system. Then the Germans would counter-attack and recover it, or not, depending upon circumstances. The heaviest casualties would be sustained during these counter-attacks, especially among the junior officers and experienced regular NCOs who were leading them. Then there was the daily trickle of casualties caused by shellfire and snipers. At night men might be detailed for a patrol or raid on the enemy's trenches, or the enemy would come across in his turn, usually to secure a prisoner, and there would be brief but brutal close-quarter fights for which the chosen weapons were knives, nailed clubs and hatchets. These things were done because they had to be done. The men in the trenches opposite had to be killed if one wanted to stay alive, but because they lived the same kind of animal existence there was a mutual fellow feeling. Hatred rarely came into it; that was the stock in trade of civilian beer hall warriors at home, from whom the real face of war was hidden.

Few of those in Flers and Delville Wood that morning could have guessed that they were about to witness the birth of an altogether new kind of warfare. Ever since the onset of trench warfare in late

1914, the British and French Armies had striven to find a means of breaking the deadlock that was consuming lives by the tens of thousands without any real hope of achieving a decisive result. Various ideas were tried and tested but in the final analysis it came down to designing a vehicle protected against machine-gun and rifle fire by armour plate, capable of being driven across shell-torn ground, crushing the enemy's barbed-wire entanglements and able to inflict serious casualties with its own guns and machine guns. The British and French had each produced designs capable of manu-facture on a large scale. The British had won the race, however, and also produced the better trench crossing design in the shape of a rhombus, a design that has yet to be bettered when it comes to obstacle crossing. It was manufactured in great secrecy under the pretence that the vehicles were mobile water cisterns, or tanks, for use on the Eastern Front and the name tank has stuck ever since; alternative names that were suggested and rejected as being too obvious were 'landship' and 'mobile fort'. There had been tremendous pressure for them to be committed to action and eventually Field Marshal Haig had decided to employ the comparatively few that were available against objectives on the Somme sector rather than wait until they could be employed *en masse*. This was a mistake, and also one which forfeited the element of surprise.

In Flers the usual morning exchange of artillery fire had taken place when, shortly after 05:30, there came the sound of sustained machine-gun and rifle fire from the direction of Delville Wood, punctuated by the periodic detonations of a larger weapon. An SOS rocket hissed skywards from among the shattered tree stumps that now constituted the wood. Promptly, shells from the German supporting battery tore overhead with a sound like ripping cloth, then came the crump of explosions from beyond the rise separating the village from the wood. It was impossible to see what effect they had, but now a new sound was added to the battle. It resembled that of an aircraft engine, but it rose and fell unevenly and from time to time was accompanied by an odd clattering noise. After a while this was followed by the ferocious yelling of men closing their enemies with the bayonet. There followed comparative silence as a few fugitives from the out-post crested the rise, running hard for the village. They were badly shaken and their stumbling words told a strange tale. They had been attacked by a strange vehicle that crossed their trenches and rolled over their wire, scything through their comrades with its multiple machine guns. They had fired everything they had at it without harming it in the least. Then the British infantry had broken out from behind it, the steel of their bayonets reflecting the red of the early morning sky. They had escaped, but none of their comrades had been so lucky.

The tank was a Mark I male commanded by Captain H. W. Mortimore. We do not know the names of the rest of his crew, which is sad as they had taken part in an incident that marked the beginning of a new phase in the conduct of warfare. Many years later Mortimore discussed the action with the late Major John Foley of the Royal Tank Regiment. He said that he was twenty-three at the time, but that with the exception of his sergeant, who was a little older, the remainder of the crew were barely out of their teens. He added that, despite none of them having been in action before, their performance was first class.

His account of the action was recorded in John Foley's book *The Boilerplate War*:

> We met up with the KOYLI [King's Own Yorkshire Light Infantry] all right and set off for Delville Wood, with the infantry coming along behind me along an old communication trench. I saw lots of flashes coming from the edge of the wood – I think they were machine guns but there was such an awful din going on I couldn't make out whether or not they were firing at me.
>
> I gave the order to open fire with one of the 6-pounders, but there was so much shelling coming down in the target area that I couldn't see whether ours was doing any good or not. Anyway, I think we must have helped, because the next thing I saw was the company of KOYLI with fixed bayonets charging into the wood.
>
> I managed to get astride one of the German trenches in front of the wood and opened fire with the Hotchkiss machine guns. There were some Germans in the dugouts and I shall never forget the looks on their faces when they emerged. The KOYLI established themselves securely in the wood just before zero hour for the main attack. My orders were to advance east at zero hour and join in the main battle, so we started off but hadn't gone 300 yards before we got a direct hit on the starboard sponson. I don't know whether it

was just a lucky shot by an enemy battery or whether in fact I was being fired on over open sights. Anyway, they knocked out my starboard sponson, killing two of the crew, and broke my track. So there we were stuck in the middle of nowhere with one sponson out of action and one track shattered. Anyway, we were able to bring a certain amount of fire to bear on the enemy trenches, which we did. After a little while our own infantry came past us, so we had to stop firing and wait for someone to come up and give us a hand to salvage the tank.

The attack on Delville Wood was a preliminary to the main attack on Flers village, which commenced at 06:20 and was delivered by New Zealand infantry, spearheaded by tanks from the same battalion as *D.1*. The ensuing battle was witnessed by a German newspaper correspondent whose account was recorded by Bryan Cooper in his two fine books *The Ironclads of Cambrai* and *Tank Battles of World War I*:

> When the German outposts crept out of their dugouts in the mist of the morning and stretched their necks to look for the English, their blood was chilled in their veins. Mysterious monsters were crawling towards them over the craters, stunned as if an earthquake had burst around them, they all rubbed their eyes, fascinated by the fabulous creatures . . .
>
> One stared and stared as if one had lost the power of one's limbs. The monsters approached slowly, hobbling, rolling and rocking, but they approached. Nothing impeded them; a supernatural force seemed to impel them on. Someone in the trenches said 'The devil is coming,' and the word passed along the line like wildfire.
>
> Suddenly tongues of flame leapt out of the armoured sides of the iron caterpillars. Shells whistled over our heads and the sound of machine-gun fire filled the air. The mysterious creature had yielded its secret as the English infantry rolled up in waves behind the 'devil's' coaches.

It must be emphasised that the shock, horror and fear induced by the first tank attack were purely local in their impact. It would be a very long time before every German soldier who took his place in the front line could expect to even see a tank. Yet, despite their limited employment thus far, Haig was to comment of their employment during the Battle of the Somme, 'Whenever the tanks advanced we took our objectives, and when they did not advance we failed to take our objectives'. There had been too few of them to make any difference to the overall outcome of the battle, but Haig, now convinced of their value, asked that an additional 1,000 should be built to an improved design. It was in this area that the German High Command made a most serious error of judgement. Its senior automotive engineers carried out detailed examinations of tanks that had bogged down or been knocked out inside their lines and the conclusion they reached was that they were costly, incorporated numerous mechanical faults and were unreliable. In the circumstances their recommendation was that the German Army should not embark upon a tank production programme. This conclusion took no note of the possibility that British and French designers were fully aware of these shortcomings and were already working to eliminate them in the next generation of tanks, which were actually on the point of production.

The Battle of the Somme, described by an officer of the Guard Reserve Division as 'the muddy grave of the German Army', is usually said to have ended on 18 November 1916. The British sustained 418,000 casualties, the French 194,000 and the Germans 650,000. In February 1917 the Germans abandoned their remaining positions and withdrew some twenty miles to the stronger defences of the Hindenburg Line, which was also more economic to hold in terms of manpower.

On 9 April 1917 the British First and Third Armies, commanded respectively by Generals H. S. Horne and Sir Edmund Allenby, launched an offensive on the Arras sector, preceded by a heavy bombardment and gas attack. On the first day Canadian troops took and held Vimy Ridge, but thereafter the rate of advance decreased. The offensive finally ran down on 15 April. The British sustained 84,000 casualties during the Battle of Arras while German losses were approximately 75,000. The battle had been designed as a preliminary phase to a major French offensive, subsequently named after the bombastic General Robert Nivelle, who claimed that his methods held the key to success in trench warfare and foolishly made confident promises of victory in public. His offensive began on 16 April and quickly degenerated into a disastrous failure. Five days later it was all over and the French had sustained almost 120,000 casualties. German losses were far lower despite the fact that they included some 21,000 men taken prisoner.

The French Army had sustained greater losses in earlier battles, but after everything its men had endured, the empty promise of victories was too much to bear. Starting on 29 April, widespread mutinies broke out along the line. The best that could be expected of the troops was that they would hold their ground if attacked; for the moment, further offensive operations were out of the question. The government, severely shaken by the scale of the mutinies, replaced Nivelle with General Henri Pétain, who gradually succeeded in talking the men round with a combination of understanding, tact, firmness and the application of justice. By 20 May the mutiny was over. Incredibly, thanks to the efficiency of French counter-intelligence agencies, all news of the mutiny was suppressed.

By now an unexpected and almost informal metamorphosis had taken place in the top level of the German High Command. Ludendorff, now holding the rank of First Quartermaster-General, was *de facto* commander of land operations, but courteously referred his decisions to Hindenburg, the army commander, for approval. As nominal Commander-in-Chief the Emperor was treated with respect and duly informed of changes in situation as they occurred, but he was completely out of his depth and was rarely consulted save on routine matters. Ludendorff knew nothing of the French mutinies until they were almost over, and by then his reserves had been transferred to the northern sector in response to the British attacks at Arras.

On the British sector, Haig was keen to begin a major offensive in the Ypres salient, but appreciated that first the dominant Messines Ridge had to be secured. Tunnelling companies succeeded in placing one million pounds of high explosive beneath the German defences on the ridge without being detected. A prolonged bombardment of the ridge convinced its defenders that nothing unusual was contemplated then, on 7 June, the giant mines were detonated, blasting a huge gap in the German lines. In a meticulously planned attack, General Sir Herbert Plumer's Second Army swarmed forward and took the position at the cost of 17,000 casualties. German losses amounted to 18,000 killed and wounded, plus 7,500 men taken prisoners.

Haig's offensive, sometimes referred to as the Third Battle of Ypres but more often as Passchendaele, began on 31 July. Years of shellfire had destroyed the drainage system of the countryside over which the battle was fought so that heavy rain in August, and again later in the offensive, turned the whole area into a bog in which men vanished and tanks sank up to their roofs after covering a few yards. On 6 November the capture of Passchendaele ridge and village, a mere seven miles from Ypres, concluded the offensive. British losses included 80,000 killed and missing, 230,000 wounded and 14,000 taken prisoner; the French sustained some 50,000 casualties; and 50,000 Germans were killed or reported missing, 113,000 were wounded and 37,000 taken prisoner. The name Passchendaele has since come to epitomise the misery and dreadful waste of trench warfare on the Western Front.

Curiously, one branch of the British service that benefited from the experience of Passchendaele was the recently formed Tank Corps. Understandably, its commander, Brigadier General Hugh Elles, and his Chief of Staff, Major J. F. C. Fuller, were angry that their vehicles, which should have been regarded as the Army's priceless asset, had simply been wasted by being driven into a bog. They made strong representations to higher authority that the Tank Corps should be allowed to show what it could achieve by fighting together on good, firm going. To conceal the enormous importance of the undertaking it was simply referred to as a 'tank raid' and was to take place on the unspoiled chalk downland of the Cambrai sector. Here, the defences of the Hindenburg Line were intact, but Fuller devised methods by which the tanks could overcome them without too much difficulty. The leading wave would carry huge brushwood fascines on their roofs. When the tanks reached the enemy line, the fascines would be shaken into the trenches. The tanks would then cross them, turn right and engage those holding the trenches. In this way, successive trench lines would be overcome. More tanks would head deep into the enemy's rear areas while others, fitted with grapnels, would haul away the enemy's barbed-wire aprons, enabling the infantry to follow through.

The original plan for a 'tank raid' was developed into a more ambitious operation intended to achieve a major breakthrough. The forces involved were General Sir Julian Byng's Third Army of nineteen divisions, with the assault spearheaded by 378 tanks of the Tank Corps, led by Elles. In the line opposite was the German Second Army, initially with six divisions, under General Georg von der Marwitz. Following a brief bombardment, the attack went in shortly after first light on 20 November. A huge gap was torn in the German defences with comparative ease, completely justifying the Tank Corps' ideas on how its vehicles should be used. Only in two areas was there little cause for satisfaction. First, the British Cavalry Corps was to have exploited beyond the line of the breakthrough but arrived too late to achieve anything worthwhile since, in the fading light, the Germans had rushed in sufficient reinforcements to enable them to seal off the penetration. Second, on the Flesquières sector the commander of the British 51st Highland Division rejected the battle drill devised by the Tank Corps and substituted his own, with unfortunate consequences. Nevertheless, a remarkable success had been achieved overall and, for the only time during the war, the church bells in the United Kingdom were rung in celebration of a victory.

Then, on 30 November, when all but a handful of tanks in need of heavy repair had been withdrawn, the unthinkable happened. The Germans counter-attacked with totally unexpected speed and vigour. The British strongpoints were quickly by-passed to be surrounded and forced to surrender by follow-up units. The storm troopers swept on across the ground so recently captured by the initial British assault until half of it, and a little more besides, was lost until their counter-offensive ran down on 3 December. Taken together, the two phases of the Battle of Cambrai cost the British approximately 44,000 casualties and the Germans approximately 53,000.

The Germans, of course, were using the infiltration tactics devised by von Hutier that had proved so successful at Riga and Caporetto. The United States had declared war on Germany on 6 April 1917, but the belief of the German High Command was that the war could be ended before the tiny American regular army could be expanded to many times its original size, equipped, trained and shipped to Europe. Now that Russia had been defeated and rendered impotent, this could be achieved by transferring troops from the defunct Eastern Front. Hutier, who had been ordered to the Western Front, oversaw the creation of storm troop battalions formed from the pick of the army, which would be used to spearhead the major offensive that would be mounted in the spring of 1918. This would require special preparation by the artillery, and involved a remarkable partnership between Hutier and Colonel Georg Bruchmüller, a professional artilleryman. Bruchmüller had entered the Prussian Artillery in 1885 and although much of his service was spent in the Foot Artillery, his principal interest lay in heavier guns, howitzers and mortars. Between 1901 and 1902 he commanded a battery in the Demonstration Battalion of the Royal Prussian Foot Artillery at the Jutebog artillery range, where he was influenced by the ideas of one of the instructors,

Captain Arthur Bilse, a specialist in heavy artillery. Bilse became a general but was killed in action on 1 January 1916.

Prior to the war, Bruchmüller was injured in a riding accident and forced to retire. He was recalled in 1914 and the long break in his active career explains the fact of his middle rank status while he was working with von Hutier. His first appointment on recall was as divisional artillery commander in the 86th Infantry Division. His belief was that batteries should register their targets by survey rather than with ranging rounds which could divulge the location of the guns to an observer. He also believed that supporting attacks with an unexpected concentration of accurate fire on registered targets would produce better results than protracted bombardments across an area. Additional tenets were that fire should be applied to the entire depth of the enemy's position rather than just his forward defences, while advancing infantry should have the support of a rolling barrage.

Perhaps the most telling of all his innovations was the use of artillery to inflict paralysis on the enemy's command system. Individual batteries of field, medium and heavy guns would receive a fire plan incorporating a timetable. The first stage of the paralysis phase involved surprise concentrations hitting headquarters, telephone exchanges, command posts, enemy batteries and infantry positions and included a high proportion of gas shells. The second stage required the reinforcement of batteries already engaged in counter-battery work. The third would involve continued fire on those forward enemy infantry positions still holding out and the employment of the heaviest weapons against long range targets. Secrecy in preparation was considered to be a major element in achieving success.

Bruchmüller had commanded von Hutier's artillery during the attack on Riga and had reached the Western Front in time to participate in the Cambrai counter-stroke, being rewarded with the *Pour le Merité* so rapid had been the success of his methods at Riga, Caporetto and Cambrai. Of those on the receiving end of his programmes, only the most senior artillery officers can have understood what had happened. There cannot have been many of them and of those who survived some would have been thinking over the subject in prison camps.

During the winter of 1917–18 both sides prepared for the opening battles of the following year. Hutier's storm troop battalions assembled and trained hard, their volunteers confident that, having gone through the selection process, they were the best soldiers in the Imperial Army. Bruchmüller began assembling his 'travelling circus' of guns and their supporting elements that would move up and down the front in accordance with requirements. Across the lines, although they did not know it, the British were adjusting their positions in a manner that would actually favour a German offensive.

In addition to these developments, there was now an agreement in the upper echelons of the Imperial Army that it did need tanks. Some damaged British vehicles were recovered from various battlefields and repaired but the consensus was that Germany must be seen to be capable of designing and manufacturing her own tanks. The task was given to a committee which went by the codename *Allgemeine Kriegs-department 7 Abteilung Verkehrswesen*, shortened to A7V, standing for General War Department 7, Traffic Section. Following trials, its first battleworthy tank, also named A7V, was completed on 1 October 1917. A total of 100 were ordered but only twenty had been completed by the time the war ended. It officially entered service on 27 February 1918 when it was demonstrated to the Emperor. It consisted of an armour-plated box with underslung tracks and was armed with one Russian 57mm gun in the bow and six Spandau or Maxim machine guns distributed around the hull. Within an incredible eighteen crewmen attempted to perform their duties in supreme discomfort. German tanks, whether A7Vs or captured British Mark IVs, were only committed in small numbers, rarely more than once a month. Their method of employment was severely limited by the A7V's almost total inability to cross trenches. In action, they would motor up to the edge of an allied trench and engage those within.

By the beginning of 1918 Ludendorff had reached the conclusion that Great Britain had become the dominant partner in the Allied alliance. Because of the previous year's mutinies, he believed that if the French were beaten into surrender, the British would continue to fight, that the reverse did not apply and that the next major offensive must be designed to inflict a major defeat on the British and separate them from their Allies. Codenamed MICHAEL, the offensive would begin with a massive assault on the Arras–Cambrai–St Quentin sector. The strategic objective would be the communications centre of Amiens, and a mere twenty miles beyond were the glittering prizes of the Somme estuary and the sea. If only the sea could be reached, the Western Front would be ripped apart and the British armies confined to a coastal enclave, fighting for their very survival. It was an attractive strategy and one which would form the basis of a plan devised by the future Field Marshal von Manstein some twenty-two years later.

In addition to von Hutier and Bruchmüller, Ludendorff's team now included General von Below, the victor of Caporetto. Along a forty-mile stretch of front no less than sixty-seven divisions of the German Seventeenth, Second and Eighteenth Armies had been concentrated against just thirty-three belonging to the British Fifth and Third Armies. In great secrecy the German artillery had assembled 4,010 field guns against only 1,710, and 2,588 medium and heavy pieces were ranged against the 976 available to the British.

By this phase of the war, British manpower reserves were seriously run down. This was reflected in the layout of the defences that would bear the brunt of Ludendorff's offensive. It contained three elements: a Forward Zone, consisting of little more than a series of fortified outposts; a Battle Zone trench system manned by about one-third of the defenders, some two or three miles behind the Forward Zone; and a Rear Zone trench system, housing the reserves, some four to eight miles beyond the Battle Zone. Every aspect of this disastrous system played right into Ludendorff's hands. The Forward Zone provided the storm troops with the very gaps through which they would seek to infiltrate; the Battle Zone was within range of the German artillery yet lacked dug-outs in which the troops could shelter during bombardment; and in places the Rear Zone had not even been dug, its location being marked by a line of spit-locked turf. Added to this was the fact that each nine-battalion division was badly below strength, battalions consisting of 500 effectives in contrast to the 1,000 with which they had gone to war. In the circumstances the outcome of the German offensive's opening phase was never in doubt.

At 04:40 on 21 March approximately 7,000 German guns fired the opening salvo of the war's most concentrated bombardment, creating an atmospheric disturbance so severe that when the 2,500 British guns replied there was no appreciable increase in the level of noise. Bruchmüller's preparation continued from 04:40 until 09:40, with one thirty-minute break at 06:40 to rest the gunners, and produced the required results. The storm troopers' H-Hour was 09:40. Their rapid advance was assisted by a natural mist and they encountered almost no resistance in the shattered wreckage of the British Forward Zone. In fact their progress was so rapid that they were forced to send up their green signal rockets to obtain an acceleration of the rolling barrage. Behind them came the Battle Groups, isolating and subduing any small pockets of stubborn defenders, and behind them in turn came the main weight of the attackers. At noon the *Schlachtstaffeln* (Battle Squadrons) of the Imperial German Air Service arrived over the battlefield to provide the ground troops with air support.

Stubborn resistance was encountered from the remnants of broken units and *ad hoc* groups of men formed on the spot from cooks, clerks, batmen, signallers, drivers and even regimental tailors and barbers who would normally have been considered too old for the front line. Artillerymen struggled desperately, but not always successfully, to get their guns away. The lucky ones were able to withdraw themselves, but others, more quickly surrounded, were never heard from again. Occasionally a tank or two would inflict casualties and cause a delay, but the attackers always worked round them. By nightfall a forty-mile gap had been torn in the line and the British Fifth Army was on the verge of disintegration.

Within four days all the ground that had changed hands during the Somme battle was once again in German hands. The crisis reached such desperate proportions that on 26 March the Allies appointed General Ferdinand Foch as Supreme Commander. Fully aware of the strategic significance of Amiens he immediately despatched British and French divisions into the danger area. On 5 April the line was stabilised at Villers-Bretonneux, just ten miles east of Amiens. This resulted partly from Foch's countermeasures and partly from the inescapable law that the further an offensive's spearhead travelled the less impetus it possessed. The storm troopers might well have advanced forty miles in a week, but now they were on the verge of exhaustion and had lost many more comrades than had been anticipated, caused by the stubborn defence, the ground attacks mounted by the British Royal Air Force, and their encounters with tanks.

At this point another factor played a decisive factor in the battle. On 28 March German air reconnaissance aircraft reported that the country between Albert and Amiens was clear of Allied troops, yet for some unknown reason the storm troopers refused to proceed beyond Albert. A staff officer sent up to investigate found them staggering about, drunk beyond reason, wearing top hats and other looted clothing, and well beyond the control of their officers. They had discovered an Allied stores depot, stuffed with many items that the British naval blockade had made almost a memory in Germany itself, including alcohol and tobacco in all their forms, tea, coffee, luxury foodstuffs and even such mundane items as boot blacking. It took time to restore order and by then the drive and enthusiasm of the early days was lacking. The advance slowed and finally stopped as Allied resistance hardened.

Although the Allied supply depots had blunted the advance on Amiens, it would have been possible for Ludendorff to have captured Amiens at one point. The reason he did not do so stemmed from a decision taken as early as 23 March. Instead of maintaining the westward advance of his three armies he dispersed their effort, ordering the Seventeenth and Eighteenth Armies to turn respectively to the north-west and south-west while in the centre the Second Army continued along its original axis. Ludendorff's first offensive, MICHAEL, had failed and although further offensives would follow, none were as promising. The British had sustained 178,000 casualties and the French 77,000, figures which included a total of over 90,000 men captured, plus 1,000 guns lost. German losses were almost as serious, totalling some 250,000 casualties.

On 9 April Ludendorff launched his second offensive, codenamed GEORGETTE. It was mounted on a twelve-mile sector of the front extending from the Ypres salient southwards to the la Bassée Canal. It was still the First Quartermaster General's belief that if the British were defeated the French would surrender and his intention now was to unhinge the British left flank by taking the strategic railway junction of Hazebrouck. The offensive, which officially ended on 30 April, recaptured all the ground lost during the Battle of Passchendaele and Messines Ridge as well as inflicting 82,000 British casualties. His own losses, however, amounted to 98,000 men and further depleted the ranks of the storm troop battalions, which were of far higher quality than the rest of the German army.

Despite the disappointing end of MICHAEL, Ludendorff had certainly not lost interest in capturing Amiens. On 19 April four A7Vs and five captured British Mark IVs had spearheaded a successful attack on the St Quentin sector while, on the 24th, a total of thirteen A7Vs and captured Mark IVs led a major attack at Villers-Bretonneux, on the principal road into the city. This resulted in the first tank-versus-tank action in history. Unfortunately for the Germans, their tanks were spread across a wide area and unable to provide their infantry with support when it was needed. The result was that two British female (i.e. armed only with machine guns) Mark IVs were forced to retire damaged while one A7V was captured after overturning in a sandpit and another was abandoned by its crew after being hit but was recovered after dark. Both fell victim to a British Mark I male (i.e. armed with 6-pounder guns and machine guns), commanded by Second Lieutenant Francis Mitchell, which also flayed the advancing German infantry with case shot. A few hundred yards to the south-west was the village of Cachy, near which two battalions of storm troopers were resting in a hollow. They were spotted by a British reconnaissance aircraft, the pilot of which re-crossed his own lines and dropped a message to a British tank company lying some distance to the rear, suggesting that if they hurried they would catch the enemy in the open. The company was equipped with Whippet light tanks, intended for use with cavalry, and its commander, Captain Thomas Price, seized the opportunity immediately. In line abreast, forty yards apart, his seven Whippets charged into the hollow from the north, taking the storm troopers completely by surprise. Those who sought cover in shell holes from the rattling machine guns were pursued and crushed. At the end of their run the tanks turned and combed the hollow again, their tracks now covered with blood and human remains. Both German battalions were completely dispersed with the loss of some 400 men killed or wounded. One Whippet, ignoring Price's instruction to stay off the skyline, was knocked out and three were damaged – at the time it was thought by artillery, although it was subsequently confirmed that the four had come within range of a solitary A7V that had remained in the area. The attack on Villers-Bretonneux was abandoned.

Ludendorff's Third Offensive, codenamed BLÜCHER but some-times known as the Third Battle of the Aisne, was launched on 27 May and continued until 6 June. Its objective was a thirty-mile sector of front stretching from Noyon eastwards along the Chemin des Dames. This was held by General Jacques Duchesne's French Sixth Army, consisting of thirteen French and four British divisions, the latter having been sent there for a rest after enduring the GEORGETTE offensive. The attack was delivered by the German Seventh and First Armies, commanded respectively by General von Bohn and General Fritz von Below. Following the limited success of his first two offensives, Ludendorff's thoughts had altered somewhat. He still intended to separate the British from the French, but his amended plan was to force the French to withdraw their reserves from Flanders prior to launching a final and decisive offensive against the British.

Although the Germans won a great tactical victory that took them across the Aisne and on to the Marne, the cost to both sides being comparable to those of the two earlier offensives, the final results were counter-productive. Ludendorff allowed himself to be diverted from his original objective by the prospect of a drive on Paris, leaving himself with too few troops to man the extended line formed by the new salient.

Painfully aware of this shortcoming, Ludendorff mounted a fourth offensive, codenamed GNEISENAU but also known as the Battle of Noyon-Montdidier, on 9 June. Two German armies were involved, the Eighteenth under General Oskar von Hutier and the Seventh under General Max von Bohn. Eight A7Vs were divided between three infantry divisions but achieved little because the Germans had not yet learned the benefit of concentrating their tanks. Two were knocked out, two broke down and two were knocked out but recovered later. Two days later the French counter-attacked with four divisions, spearheaded by forty-eight Schneider and ninety-six St Chamond medium tanks. Twelve British armoured cars were available to exploit a breakthrough yet, despite recovering some of the ground lost during the opening hours of the offensive, the Germans managed to hold their line intact and they were not employed. By 13 June the offensive was over, each side having sustained 35,000 casualties while the French also lost seventy of their tanks.

Ludendorff possessed just sufficient assets for one final throw of the dice. He gave his fifth offensive the codename MARNESCHUTZ-RHEIMS, but it is also known variously to military historians as the Second Battle of the Marne and the Fourth Battle of Champagne. His intention was to cross the Marne and achieve the isolation of Rheims by converging thrusts to the east and west of the city. He had four armies available for the task: General von Eben's Ninth; General Max von Bohn's Seventh; General Bruno von Mudra's First; and General von Karl Einem's First. To the west of Rheims, five A7Vs were allocated to three infantry divisions, while to the east of the city fifteen captured Mark IVs, plus five more in reserve, were allocated to two infantry divisions and one dismounted cavalry division.

Facing them were five French armies: General Henri Gouraud's Fourth; General Henri Berthelot's Fifth; General Jean Degoutte's Sixth; General Antoine de Mistry's Ninth; and General Charles Mangin's Tenth, incorporating strong American, British and Italian elements. Available for their support were no fewer than 746 tanks, mainly light Renault FTs. In terms of comparative strength, fifty-two German divisions were facing forty-four French, eight American, four British and two Italian divisions. In artillery the Germans had a clear superiority, deploying 609 heavy guns against 408 and 1,047 field batteries against 360. The Allies, however, possessed a major advantage in that they could field 223 tanks, mainly light Renault FTs, against the Germans' twenty-five listed above.

This was a battle that Ludendorff had to win. The numerical superiority of the German armies, achieved by the transfer of formations from the former Eastern Front, had been diluted by the serious casualties incurred during the four previous offensives. It was true that large numbers of German troops were still active in Eastern Europe. However, they had to be retained there by Ober Ost because of the generally unsettled state of the area and the threat posed by agitators from Bolshevik Russia. It was also true that American troops had entered the conflict on the Western Front and would continue to do so in ever-increasing numbers. At home, the British blockade was causing severe food and other shortages that were destroying civilian morale.

The battle opened on 15 July. The thrust east of Rheims was blunted the same day, but to the west of the city those defending the south bank of the Marne were forced to endure one of Bruchmüller's firestorms lasting three hours. When this lifted the storm troopers swarmed across the river on anything that would float and began to assemble twelve temporary bridges. By evening they had secured a bridgehead on either side of the village of Dormans, four miles deep and nine miles wide. This survived a major bombing raid by no fewer than 225 French aircraft, but the arrival of British and American troops to support the French halted further progress on 17 July. Two days later the Allies went over to the offensive and, with one brief operational pause, continued to push the Germans back until 6 August, when the battle finally ran down. It had cost the Germans 139,000 killed or wounded, plus 29,367 men captured. In addition, 793 guns, 3,000 machine guns and thirteen tanks had been lost and most of the ground taken during earlier offensives was once more in Allied hands. The Allied losses amounted to approximately 133,000 killed or wounded, plus 102 tanks disabled, many of which were repairable. The Second Battle of the Marne proved to be as much a turning point in the war as had the First, for from that point onwards the German Army was forced to fight a defensive war.

General Ferdinand Foch, the architect of the victory, was rewarded with the baton of a Marshal of France.

Ludendorff's five major offensives had cost the German Army in excess of half a million casualties, plus huge quantities of equipment. The blow dealt by his failure in the Second Battle of the Marne also, however, inflicted devastating damage to the Army's morale. He had described the battle as the *Friedensturm*, implying that a decisive victory would bring peace. The troops had given their best, as they had in the earlier offensives, but their reward had been defeat. Naturally, they felt that all their sacrifice and effort had been for nothing and their will to continue fighting was severely damaged, the more so as dreadful reports of starvation at home reached them. Remarkably, even as his most recent offensive ran down, he was planning a sixth offensive that would, once more, be directed against the British in the north. Within two days, all his dreams would be shattered.

Behind the British lines at Amiens all was hustle and bustle as preparations were made for a concentrated tank attack that would dwarf that at Cambrai the previous year. The intention was not simply to remove the threat to Amiens but also to achieve a breakthrough and force a German withdrawal. The troops involved were drawn from Sir Henry Rawlinson's Fourth Army, including the Australian and Canadian Corps, with a total of thirteen divisions, the Cavalry Corps with three divisions and the Tank Corps. The last consisted of 324 Mark Vs, a much improved medium tank requiring only one man to drive it, ninety-six Whippet light tanks, forty-two tanks in reserve, 120 supply tanks, twenty-two tracked gun carriers and an armoured car battalion. A diversionary operation would be mounted on the right flank by General Eugene Debeney's French First Army.

The Royal Air Force had achieved complete air superiority, thereby denying German intruders from examining preparations for the attack. As the tanks came forwards in their hundreds to move into their hides after dark the sound of their tracks was drowned by low-flying bombers droning up and down the lines. For the attack itself a large number of squadrons had been detailed for ground support and some of these had the specific task of dealing with the enemy artillery batteries that lay in the path of the tanks.

Across no man's land on a thirteen-mile frontage were two German armies, the Second under General George von der Marwitz and the Eighteenth under General Oskar von Hutier. The former had ten divisions in the line and four in reserve, while the latter had eleven in the line and four in reserve. Very few of these formations were still considered to be battleworthy, while the morale of the remainder was low. The reasons for this resulted partly from weariness with a war that had no apparent end, and partly because divisions had been stripped of their best soldiers to form the storm troop battalions. The men were tired and jittery; they reported the presence of tanks that did not exist so often that Army staff tended to ignore all such reports.

The constant droning of aircraft was unsettling, too. At 04:00 on 8 August the droning continued as usual, but now it was masking the distinctive sound of engines and tracks as the tanks began moving forward to their start lines. At 04:20 they passed through the infantry and took the lead. Simultaneously, the fire of 3,500 guns blasted forth. One third of their shells dropped as a rolling barrage in front of the attack while the remainder crashed onto known German battery positions.

The battlefield was cloaked in a dense mist but now the sound of roaring engines and rattling tracks could only mean one thing. The defenders, already shaken by the barrage, found the approaching noise more terrifying than if the tanks had been visible. SOS rockets hissed upwards, but it was too late. The huge shapes were bursting through the mist, crushing their way through the wire and towering over the parapets. Those who resisted were swept away in a blast of 6-pounder case shot and machine-gun fire. Some men bolted but the majority surrendered on the spot. The tanks rolled on, but not all Germans ran or surrendered. The artillery had always maintained a pride in their calling and they stuck to their guns until the last minute. Some measure of their effort can be judged by the fact that they knocked out no fewer than 109 tanks, a quarter of those engaged.

It was not enough to stop the advance. By mid-morning the tanks had broken through the trench system and were moving across open country. The cavalry divisions began to pass through, their regimental officers desperate to justify the continuing existence of their arm. Sadly, the opportunity was wasted while they waited for specific orders from their Corps Headquarters, which was lagging behind the advance. Near Harbonnières they made one charge that captured a supply column, but most of their time was spent rounding up the thousands of the enemy who had been left behind by the tanks' advance. Long before dusk they began retiring whence they had come to feed and water their mounts, insisting on taking both Whippet battalions with them. The outranked Tank Corps Headquarters' understandable fury at this dog-in-a-manger attitude might not have been justified if cavalry and Whippets had shown themselves to be compatible. The fact was that they were not. When there was little or no opposition the horsemen galloped ahead, leaving the much slower light tanks behind. However, a single machine gun was enough to halt the troopers' progress and they had perforce to wait for the Whippets to arrive and deal with the problem. Then off they would canter until brought up sharply by the next machine gun. Just what might have been achieved if both Whippet regiments had been let loose was demonstrated by Lieutenant Clement Arnold's Whippet 'Musical Box'. Arnold managed to shake off the dead hand of his immediate cavalry superior and for the next ten hours earned himself and his tank immortality by creating mayhem in the German rear areas until knocked out at point-blank range. The lesson was repeated by the British armoured cars, some of which penetrated so far into enemy territory that they captured a corps headquarters intact while its occupants were packing their bags.

Be that as it may, a hole seven-and-a-half miles deep had been punched through the German lines, a hole that was only filled for the time being by rushing in troops from all over the front. Total German casualties exceeded 75,000, including 29,873 prisoners. Coming as it did on the heels of his reverse during the Second Battle of the Marne, the defeat plunged Ludendorff into the depths of despair. What troubled him most was the fact that the huge number of prisoners indicated the extent to which the Army was affected by war weariness; furthermore the high percentage of officers who had surrendered clearly suggested a belief among the officer corps that there was no further point in continuing the war. He described 8 August as 'The Black Day of the German Army' and indicated to Hindenburg that he intended advising the Emperor that as victory was no longer possible the war must be ended.

British losses included 22,000 killed wounded and missing, but of the 109 tanks disabled many were repairable. The battle initiated a slow but sustained Allied advance along the front that continued for the remainder of the war. Elsewhere, one by one, each of Germany's allies accepted defeat and requested an armistice – Bulgaria on 29 September, Turkey on 30 October, and Austria-Hungary on 3 November. Germany herself had requested an armistice as early as 6 October but the continued presence of Ludendorff, regarded by some as a military dictator, was not acceptable to President Woodrow Wilson of the United States. Under pressure Ludendorff resigned on 27 October, being replaced by General William Groener. On 29 October a mutiny of the High Seas Fleet was followed by further mutinies, revolts and disorders across Germany, many of them inspired by pro-Bolshevik agitators. At this stage there was very little violence, the local reins of power simply being taken over by soldiers' and workmens' councils.

Throughout Germany little sympathy remained for the institution of monarchy. The country was desperate for peace but it was felt that the Allies held the Emperor responsible for starting the war and that they would never negotiate with Germany as long as he sat upon its throne, in addition to which there was little personal respect remaining for him. The same was true to a lesser extent of those German monarchs who had supported him. The first indication of permanent change took place on 8 November in Bavaria, where the head of the ruling Wittelsbach dynasty was courteously informed by Kurt Eisner, leader of the local soldiers' and workmen's council, that the monarchy had been abolished, news which was received with philosophic acceptance by the king himself.

The following day, no doubt inspired by the news, huge crowds of soldiers and workmen marched through the streets of Berlin, singing republican songs. Some windows were smashed, a few shots were fired, but the Imperial Palace was occupied without difficulty and everywhere the symbols of monarchy were torn down. The local area commander, General von Linsingen, had taken the precaution of concentrating a large number of machine guns in the city, but the sympathy of his troops, and notably that of the Garde, lay with the marchers and they were never used. Linsingen was left with no alternative save to resign.

Some days earlier the Emperor had left Berlin for the Army's Main Headquarters at Spa in Belgium. His mind seemed to be quite divorced from what was taking place around him. Hindenburg found himself physically unable to brief his sovereign on the continuing story of defeat and retreat. William, unable to grasp the awful reality of what was taking place, remarked that he would return to Germany, riding at the head of his undefeated armies. He was told that none of the army commanders would find this acceptable and was horrified when, at his request, they each confirmed this view. Groener tartly suggested that perhaps His Majesty should seek death among his soldiers. The idea was dismissed on the grounds that he was more likely to fall into the hands of disaffected troops, with consequences that could not even be guessed at. When news of events in Berlin and Bavaria reached the Headquarters, Hindenburg advised the Emperor that unless he abdicated the outcome would be a civil war. On learning that his favoured Garde regiments had joined the revolutionaries, William accepted the reality of the situation but because of the Crown Prince's reservations he announced that he would abdicate as Emperor but not as King of Prussia. Such a course would have been a political impossibility, but at 14:00 on 10 November the Emperor signed the necessary document. However, when an official tried to read its content to Berlin over the telephone, he was interrupted and told that the document:

> was too late to be of any use. The Chancellor [Prince Max of Baden] has already put out a telegram through the news agency to say that the Emperor and Crown Prince have abdicated, and that he himself has become Regent and Herr Fritz Ebert Chancellor.

There was little more to be said. William left for what would become a lifelong exile in Holland. His former Empress was still in Berlin but joined him after Hindenburg had despatched 'loyal' troops to see her to safety.

The Armistice took effect at 11:00 on 11 November 1918. Under its provisions Germany was required to:

> Immediately evacuate all occupied territory, plus Alsace-Lorraine.
>
> Evacuation by all forms of German military presence of the west bank of the Rhine, and also of bridgeheads on the east bank of the Rhine at Mainz, Coblenz and Cologne, these bridgeheads to be as much as thirty kilometres radius.
>
> Repatriation of all Allied prisoners of war, without immediate reciprocity and repatriation of all civilians of Allied nations.
>
> Surrender, in good condition, of the following materials of war:
> 2,500 heavy guns
> 2,500 field guns

25,000 machine guns
3,000 trench mortars
1,700 aeroplanes, including all night-bombing machines in the possession of the German forces
All German submarines

The internment in British ports with only German care and maintenance parties on board, of the following German naval vessels:
6 battle-cruisers
10 battleships
8 light cruisers including two minelayers
50 destroyers of the most modern types

The human cost to Germany had been horrific. Some eleven million men had been mobilised of whom 1,808,546 had been killed in action while a further 4,247,143 had been wounded. In addition, 760,000 civilians had lost their lives as a direct consequence of the war.

The Allies, too, had sustained terrible losses and in their view Germany's war guilt had earned her punishment and humiliation, the precise nature of which would become apparent during the negotiation of a peace treaty and the setting of the reparations she would be required to pay. It was a short-sighted policy that would sow some of the seeds for an even more terrible war.

# CHAPTER 15

# Poisoned Decades

For the moment Germany remained quiet, despite the fact the entire structure of the country had undergone an irreversible change. Yet, as John Buchan was to comment:

> Orderly as was the first stage of Germany's revolution, and strenuous as were the efforts made to provide administrative continuity, on one side the revulsion was complete. The old absolutism was gone and monarchy within the confines of Germany had become a farce – hated in some regions, in all despised as an empty survival. For centuries the pretensions of German kinglets had made sport for Europe. Now these kinglets had disappeared, leaving no trace behind them. In Bavaria, Saxony, Württemberg, the Mecklenburgs, Hesse, Brunswick and Baden, the dynasties fell with scarcely a protesting voice. And with them fell the men who had been the pillars of the thrones, the great nobles and the industrial magnates who had risen to power by courtiership.

In 1919 Germany and Austria, the latter now reduced to a small central European republic, also abolished their respective aristocracies, although their members were permitted to retain a version of their titles.

Contrary to the expectations of 1914, only one section of the German Army had marched home in triumph, that of General Paul von Lettow-Vorbeck, who had successfully fought a guerrilla campaign in German East Africa (then known as Tanga, later Tanganyika and now Tanzania) and only surrendered after the Armistice had been signed. With them marched a tiny group of naval officers and seamen, the last survivors of the light cruiser SMS *Königsberg*, which had tied down a considerable portion of the Royal Navy in the Indian Ocean.

It was during this period that the revolution dissolved into violence between Left and Right. The most prominent groups of the former, strongly influenced by Bolshevik dogma, were known as Spartacists, named after the slave leader who had rebelled against the might of the Roman Empire. In some areas it was not uncommon for serving officers to be spat upon or have their epaulettes ripped off, such was the contempt for the vanished Establishment. The Right was spear-headed by *Freikorps*, acting independently of the Army but usually containing a high percentage of ex-officers. For a while a state of virtual civil war existed in the capital and other parts of the country, forcing the government to remove itself to the quieter country town of Weimar. Early in 1919 the *Freikorps* were incorporated into a central command structure, although their loyalties lay to their own unit commanders rather than to an elected government. Better trained and equipped than their opponents, they emerged the victors in Germany itself and went on to the Baltic provinces of the former Russian Empire where the German minority was struggling to keep the Bolsheviks at bay.

On 28 June 1919 the Allies concluded a peace treaty with Germany at Versailles. As the price of Germany being granted an armistice she had already been required to hand over 5,000 locomotives, 150,000 wagons and 5,000 motor lorries in good working order, together with all the necessary spares. This, drastically reducing as it did the flow of foodstuffs, fuel, manufactured goods and raw materials, would, taken together with reparations set at the colossal figure of £66 billion, ensure that her economic recovery would be delayed for many years. Simultaneously, she was stripped of her colonies and humiliated in every way possible, being forbidden military aircraft, heavy artillery, and fighting vehicles of every kind save for a few unarmed armoured personnel carriers. The Great General Staff was to be disbanded, the number of cadet academies drastically cut back and the size of the Army reduced from 400,000 to 100,000 men. The feeling of most Germans was that the treaty left them *Heerlos, Wehrlos und Ehrlos* – disarmed, defenceless and dishonoured. Many men left the Army voluntarily once the civil war was over, but some 15,000 officers and a proportionately higher number of senior NCOs who had neither intention nor reason to resign were discharged. Many of these men had actually fought the revolutionaries on behalf of the same government that was now consigning them to the scrap heap. Their sense of betrayal was also aggravated when it became obvious that the better jobs in the new regular Army, the Reichsheer, were going to men who had remained safely in barracks along with the rump of the old army. Those who had thus been abandoned became natural recruits for the infant Nazi (National Socialist) Party, bringing organisation and discipline to its gangs of uniformed street thugs, the SA (*Sturm Abteilungen*), so that the latter easily defeated their less regimented enemies of the Iron Front, which included both Socialist and Communist private armies. Naturally, in the 1920s the ex-service members of the SA could not have been expected to foresee the direction history was to take, but their victory was a major factor in Hitler's rise to power, and once an evil of that magnitude had been unchained the tragedy could only pursue its course.

The officer selected by the government to command the Reichsheer was Colonel General Hans von Seeckt who, it will be remembered, had no qualms about dispersing mourners by force when order was in danger of breaking down at Berlin Cathedral during the funeral of Emperor William I. By 1914 he was serving as a corps chief of staff in von Kluck's First Army and was able to witness the reasons for the failure of the Schlieffen Plan at first hand. He had come to admire the quality of the British Expeditionary Force, remaining a convinced advocate of the small professional army in preference to the *levée en masse*. In 1915 he served on the staff of General von Mackensen and played a major part in the defeat inflicted on the Russians at Gorlice-Tarnow. He went on to take part in the second invasion of Serbia and continued to serve on the Eastern Front for the remainder of the war.

The Allies were determined that Seeckt was not going to become a twentieth century Scharnhorst, employing conscription to create large reserves for the Reichsheer. Instead, the Army's strength was set at 100,000 men who would engage for a fixed term of twelve years. Seeckt's intention was to create an army of instructors of above average ability so that when the time came for the Versailles Treaty to be abrogated it could be expanded quickly to the desired level. For the moment it numbered 4,000 officers and 96,000 other ranks, serving in eighty-one cavalry squadrons and twenty-one infantry regiments, organised into three cavalry and seven infantry divisions. The value of tradition was particularly emphasised, each squadron or company of the Reichsheer assuming the traditions, honours and customs of a regiment in the old Imperial Army.

A great deal of clandestine activity took place with the object of circumventing the Allied Control Commission, which was supposed to oversee the implementation of the Versailles Treaty's provisions. Aspects of tank technology and design were shared in secret with Sweden and the Soviet Union, the latter being on the point of launching a huge tank manufacturing programme. So-called motoring and gliding clubs provided preliminary training for mechanised troops and the future Luftwaffe's air crews, while unit and divisional orders of battle were steadily brought up to date in the light of technical advances. Military attachés throughout the world supplied details of significant developments in their field. The writings of Major General J. F. C. Fuller and Basil Liddell Hart attracted the attention not only of those officers who saw the potential of mechanised warfare, but also of those who had been schooled in the traditions of von Moltke the Elder and von Schlieffen, citing the similarity in the basic thought processes expressed by Fuller in his famous Plan 1919, which was to provide a basis for the future *Blitzkrieg* or 'Lightning War' technique.

Such activities were to be expected, but there were other agencies that operated in a far darker world, revealing the shape of things to come. They operated under the control of an organisation known as *Sondergruppe R* (Special Group R) that was responsible for the murder of Germans suspected of being informers for the Allied Control Commission. When the German Supreme Court tried a man suspected of such a murder, Seeckt wrote a secret letter to its President admitting that the organisation formed part of his department but arguing that such murders were justified by the struggle against the Versailles Treaty and that his court should acquit the defendant.

With the creation of an independent Poland, Germany had lost territory, notably the 'Polish Corridor' dividing East Prussia from the rest of Germany by a wide strip of land permitting Poland access to the Baltic coast at Gdansk (Danzig). Seeckt took the view that the 1914 common Russo-German frontier in the east should be restored:

> The existence of Poland is intolerable and incompatible with Germany's interests. She must disappear and will do so through her own inner weakness and through Russia – with our help ... A French advance through Germany to the help of Poland would make nonsense from the military point of view.

His words were prophetic and would become reality in less than twenty years.

Seeckt was loyal to Germany, but not necessarily to the republic. In 1926 this conflict led to his making the most serious mistake of his career. Prince William Hohenzollern, the grandson of the former Emperor, requested and received his permission to attend that year's army manoeuvres. To his horror, the prince turned up wearing the uniform of the now defunct First Foot Guards. This was too much for the government and Seeckt was forced to resign. The only other important post he was to hold was as head of the German military mission to China in 1933, but his earlier work had ensured that Germany would go to war in 1939 with the world's most efficient army.

The international effects of the financial earthquake caused by the Wall Street crash of 1929 caused the German economy to go into recession the following year, producing mass unemployment. Prior to this, Adolf Hitler's Nazi Party had attracted little attention from the electorate, but as a result of the 1930 Reichstag elections its influence as a political force expanded steadily. Field Marshal von Hindenburg, who had been elected President in 1925, reluctantly appointed Hitler as Chancellor on 30 January 1933. Less than a month later the Reichstag burned down in mysterious circumstances. Hitler succeeded in pinning blame on the communists, claiming that the destruction of the building was intended by them to disrupt a new election. Hindenburg outlawed the communist party and, the SA having intimidated the remaining opposition, the Nazis won the election by a wide margin.

By 1934 the SA had risen to a strength of 400,000 and considered itself to be the rival of the Reichsheer, towards which it maintained a hostile and highly provocative attitude. Hitler was well aware that, if it chose to, it could unseat him and took what he considered to be suitable precautions. During the night of 30 June, subsequently known as 'The Night of the Long Knives', the SA leadership throughout Germany, plus anyone against whom the Chancellor bore a grudge, including two generals, a total of seventy-seven persons, was murdered by members of his own bodyguard, the SS (*Schutzstaffeln*), and of the security service, the SD (*Sicherheitsdienst*). Addressing the Reichstag, he emphasised that these killings had been necessary to protect the integrity of the German Army and preserve it as the non-political instrument of the nation.

The ageing Field Marshal Hindenburg was now failing and clearly did not fully understand what Hitler had done, for he sent him a congratulatory telegram. When he died on 2 August Hitler promptly combined the offices of President and Chancellor in one title, that of Führer (Leader). The armed services were immediately ordered to swear the soldier's oath of unconditional loyalty and obedience, not to their country or its constitution, but to Adolf Hitler, 'The Führer of the German Reich and Commander-in-Chief of the Wehrmacht.' This was a very different matter from swearing loyalty to a monarch, which the majority of senior officers had once done, and many accepted it with serious reservations since its effect was to make the Army, Navy and Air Force the property of a politician. Nevertheless, having once taken the oath, most officers considered themselves honour-bound by it, and in the long term this was to have terrible consequences for Germany. As a sop to their pride Hitler restored the officer's right to wear his sword in public.

At this period Hitler's popularity was at its height. He had his position as *de facto* dictator ratified by plebiscite so that it could not be challenged legally. Possessed of a strange, magnetic personality, facets of which appealed to many men, his speeches contained everything their audiences wanted to hear. He reminded them that in the fifty years prior to 1914 Germany had become a great empire, honoured throughout the world for her undoubted achievements in so many fields. All that had been destroyed during the war when the Army was stabbed in the back by those within the country's financial and commercial infrastructure, which contained a large Jewish element. This was nonsense, of course, but the story had been put about for years by Ludendorff and other officers who were anxious to restore their own and the Army's reputation and it was rarely questioned. These great wrongs, he promised, would be put to rights. Perhaps Hitler's speeches would have made a lesser impression had they not been delivered at huge rallies orchestrated by his brilliant publicist, Dr Josef Goebbels, who also staged parades intended to convey the strength and popularity of the Nazi Party, which also formed popular youth movements. Such was Goebbels' control of the media, including the press, radio and the cinema, that the impression given was that Germany was on the verge of a new golden era.

On 16 March 1935 Hitler repudiated the restrictive clauses of the Treaty of Versailles and made it clear that Germany would re-arm as she thought fit. Conscription was introduced with the object of the Army's being able to fight a full-scale defensive war by 1939 and an offensive war by 1943. The 100,000-strong Reichsheer lost its title and was submerged under the flood of conscripts as its units were split and split again, amoeba-like, to form fresh regiments which, in turn, would produce their own offspring. Inevitably, this seriously diluted the quality of units so that it was several years before the lost ground was recovered. The new Army resembled neither the Reichsheer nor the Imperial Army, for it was intended for short wars rather than the sort of protracted struggle that had taken place between 1914 and 1918. It was, in fact, an army that was being re-armed in breadth but not in depth, most of the modern equipment being issued to the armoured and motorised formations that would form its cutting edge, while the rest continued to rely on the horse as a prime mover.

On 7 March 1936 Hitler ordered his troops to re-occupy the Rhineland. France, lacking the support of the United Kingdom, declined to respond with force. Subsequent evidence confirmed that, had she done so, German generals would have deposed Hitler and withdrawn from the Rhineland. Hitler had simply been confirming his belief that the former Allies no longer possessed the stomach for fighting. Later that year he consolidated his position by establishing an alliance with Italy. However, it was not until 5 November 1937 that he made known his full intentions at a secret meeting with the heads of his armed forces and his foreign minister. Germany's territorial frontiers would be expanded to achieve the necessary *Lebensraum* (living space) for its population. First, Austria and Czechoslovakia would be seized by force of arms, then Poland and finally Russia. This programme would commence in 1938 and be completed by 1943.

Austria was occupied without difficulty on 12–13 March 1938 as was the Sudetenland (actually part of Czechoslovakia but containing a three-million strong German population) between 7 and 29 September. War between the remains of Czechoslovakia and Germany seemed probable when the latter claimed yet more territory. British Prime Minister Neville Chamberlain flew to Munich for talks with Hitler in the hope of de-fusing the situation. He returned home believing that he had secured 'peace for our time'. In the event, Hitler had simply used him to buy time and annexed the provinces of Bohemia and Moravia the following March, leaving Slovakia nominally independent. This was an extremely important development for, without the acquisition of the Czech armaments industry, it would have been impossible for

Germany to mount a major campaign, the reason being that most of the German tank fleet consisted of light PzKw Is and IIs, armed only with machine guns, while the PzKw IIIs and IVs, though classed as medium tanks, were too few in number to take on a first-class army, like that of France. However, the Czech PzKw 35(t) and PzKw 38(t), though lacking certain features, were classed as mediums and their possession almost filled the gap. In terms of equipment the infantry fared rather better. The old Maxim-type medium machine gun was replaced by the MG34 light machine gun with a rate of fire of 800–900 rounds per minute, which would be replaced in turn by the MG42, capable of firing 1,200 rounds per minute. Section leaders and their equivalent were armed with the MP38 or MP40 machine carbines, each of which had a rate of fire of 500 rounds per minute. A German infantry platoon therefore possessed a higher combined output of fire than that of similarly sized sub-units in many armies.

Simultaneously, the Luftwaffe had been developed into an efficient tactical air force, capable of providing the ground troops with frequently decisive support. Its bombers, notably the Junkers Ju87 dive-bomber and Junkers Ju88 fighter-bomber, Heinkel He111 and Dornier Do17 level bombers, received protection against enemy fighter from the excellent Messerschmitt Bf109 fighter. The major mistake made by those responsible for the Luftwaffe's equipment was the failure to develop a long-range heavy bomber that could be employed in strategic roles. Both the re-constituted Army and the Luftwaffe saw active service during the Spanish Civil War on the side of the Nationalists from 1937 onwards. This provided a proving ground for equipment and enabled the evaluation of tactical methods that could be applied elsewhere.

The tank had restored mobility to the battlefield and with that came the opportunity to renew the traditional German concept of *Vernichtungsgedanke*, the Annihilation Battle, in which the enemy was isolated, surrounded and destroyed if he did not surrender. Most armies tended to fight their wars at two levels – the strategic, related to the conduct of a campaign, and tactical, the local means by which success can be obtained. The German Army also fought its battles at what became known as the operative level, employing corps-sized formations, and was adept at forming battle groups from different arms for specific tasks. It had long become expert in the use of 'saddle orders', involving instructions passed to formation commanders on the move, usually by a staff officer or a general's aide, this process being further accelerated by the widespread use of radios.

Hitler was determined to tighten his hold on the Army to the limit, even if it involved employing the grubbiest of methods. When his widowed Minister of War, General von Blomberg, married for the second time, rumours began to circulate immediately that the new Frau von Blomberg had an interesting past, a situation regarded so askance in Prussian military circles that the minister had no alternative but to resign, his function being assumed by the Führer himself. Likewise, the rumour mill put it about that the Commander-in-Chief, General von Fritsch, was a practising homosexual and he, too, had to resign. His replacement was General Walther von Brauchitsch, a capable and intelligent artillery officer whose task, by tradition, required that he must never shrink from speaking honestly and, if necessary, with brutal frankness to the Head of State if, in his opinion, the situation warranted it. Sadly, he was not the man to carry such a heavy responsibility for he was completely dominated by Hitler, whose wild, uncontrolled rages could shatter his nerves for hours at a time. Next to go was General Ludwig Beck, the Chief of General Staff, whose open criticism of the Nazi hierarchy made his removal inevitable. It was ironic that his replacement, Colonel General Franz Halder, a Bavarian and a Catholic, despised Hitler so much that he was already involved in a conspiracy to assassinate him.

The Army's upper levels of command were now dominated by artillerymen who were products of the Imperial Army. They included General von Brauchitsch, Colonel Generals Halder and Fritz Fromm, respectively the Chief of Army Equipment and commander of the Replacement Army, and the future Field Marshal Wilhelm Keitel, Colonel General Alfred Jodl and General Walter Warlimont of the Armed Forces Supreme Command (OKW). That so many artillerymen had risen to the heights of their profession stemmed not from the intellectual standards demanded by their arm as much as from the fact that the artillery sustained proportionately fewer casualties in the First World War than either the infantry or the cavalry.

During the coming war many other general officers who were products of the Imperial Army would achieve greatness. Field Marshal Erich von Manstein, the greatest of them all, had served in the Foot Guards, and so had General Hans-Jürgen von Arnim. Field Marshals Erwin Rommel and Walter Model were infantrymen, as were Generals Hermann Balck, Heinrich Eberbach, Fritz-Hubert Graser, Josef Harpe,

Gotthard Heinrici, Hermann Hoth, Hans Hube, Walther Nehring, Georg Reinhardt, Rudolf Schmidt, Georg Stumme and Wilhelm Ritter von Thoma. Field Marshal Ewald von Kleist was a hussar, and so were General Eberhard von Mackensen, Hasso von Manteuffel and Gustav Ritter von Vaerst. General Ludwig Crüwell, Leo Geyr von Schweppenberg and Erich Hoepner were all dragoons.

# CHAPTER 16

# The Blitzkrieg Years

Hitler had absorbed Austria and most of Czechoslovakia into a Greater Germany without the slightest difficulty, and in March 1939 issued a series of non-negotiable demands to the Polish government regarding the return of the Polish Corridor and Danzig to Germany. In addition to these being firmly rejected, the British and French governments informed him that they fully intended to support the Polish stance. This, and subsequent warnings, gave Hitler pause for thought but, following due consideration, he reached the conclusion that while the Western Allies had commenced a process of re-armament, this had not gone far enough to pose a threat and that in any event neither the United Kingdom nor France was in a position to provide practical assistance for Poland in the event of a German invasion. Their implied threat, he believed, was an empty one and would fade once Poland had been occupied.

He did, however, take the precaution of negotiating a secret non-aggression pact with the Soviet Union while he mobilised a quarter-of-a-million reservists for 'refresher' training. On 1 September he launched a full-scale invasion of Poland. The plan of attack had been devised by von Brauchitsch and, predictably, consisted of a double envelopment, the inner jaws closing on Warsaw and the outer jaws on Brest-Litovsk. The southern arm of the pincers was formed by Field Marshal von Rundstedt's Army Group A, while the northern arm consisted of Army Group B under Field Marshal Fedor von Bock. The Luftwaffe, commanded by Reichsmarshall Hermann Göring, an ardent Nazi given to wearing ornamental uniforms of his own design, quickly established dominance over the outnumbered Polish Air Force. For two days the Poles resisted fiercely before commencing their retreat, harassed all the while by continuous, nerve-shattering dive-bomber attacks. The German armoured formations broke through the cordon of Polish armies deployed along the frontier, and accelerated into the enemy's hinterland, disrupting his command structure and logistic network.

On 2 September the United Kingdom and France served ultimata on Germany, requiring her to withdraw from Poland. These were ignored and the following day they both declared war on Germany. Hitler's bluff had been called and, to his chagrin, he was now faced with a major war, the outcome of which was by no means certain. Meanwhile, the Poles fought on without any real hope of relief. Moreover, they lived in an age when treachery was common currency. On 16 September the Red Army rolled across the country's eastern frontier, announcing blandly that it had intervened to stop the fighting, in the Poles' best interests. Despite this, Warsaw held out until 27 September and isolated Polish groups fought on until 6 October. A considerable number escaped across the Romanian border and continued the fight against Germany elsewhere.

The one-and-a-half million-strong Polish Army had been effectively destroyed in the first ten days' fighting. The cost to Germany was 8,000 men killed, 32,000 wounded and 3,400 missing. The tenacity of Polish resistance is reflected in German tank losses – some 400 vehicles knocked out, including an admitted loss of 218 totally destroyed.

Among those fighting alongside the German Army in Poland were members of a comparatively new organisation, the Waffen SS – Armed SS (Schutzstaffeln) – which had its roots in Hitler's personal bodyguard, the Leibstandarte SS Adolf Hitler, and differed from the Allgemeine (General) SS, which ran the concentration camps and worked closely with the Gestapo. These organisations formed part of the empire of terror run by Reichsführer-SS Heinrich Himmler, one of the most powerful and dangerous men in the Third Reich. The Waffen SS was exclusively Nazi in its origins and outlook and, by the end of its career, consisted of numerous divisions recruited from like-minded individuals in many European countries. It showed no mercy to its enemies, whether military or civilian, and committed some of the war's worst atrocities. It was never part of the Army, by which it was disliked.

Months passed following the conquest of Poland without anything more than small-scale local actions taking place on the Western Front. A curious lethargy seemed to take possession of the British and French armies, quiescent behind their defences, notably the hugely expensive Maginot Line. They seemed to be relying on the same policy of blockade and economic strangulation that had borne fruit in the First World War but that, as then, would have taken years to produce results.

Meanwhile, the focus of events had shifted to Scandinavia. Germany was heavily dependent on supplies of Swedish iron ore to support her war effort. Much of this passed through the northern port of Narvik and then down the long Norwegian coast to Germany. Matters came to a head when, on 16 February 1940, the British destroyer HMS *Cossack* intercepted the German pocket battleship *Graf Spee*'s supply ship *Altmark* and captured her. Norwegian protests ceased when it was learned that the German ship was armed, engaged in naval operations and had British prisoners aboard. From this point on, Hitler was determined to take possession of the Norwegian coastline while Winston Churchill, then First Lord of the Admiralty, was equally determined to deny the route to German shipping.

It was, however, Denmark that was first to feel the full consequences of Hitler's interest in the area. On 9 April German troops stormed across the Danish frontier and into the Jutland peninsula. Simultaneously, an infantry battalion, concealed in the holds of a merchant ship in Copenhagen harbour, came ashore to make prisoners of the Danish king and government. Fortunately, this entirely illegal attack on a small, non-combatant country was executed with very little bloodshed.

Between 8 and 10 April a series of clashes took place off the Norwegian coast between British and German warships, the latter escorting an invasion convoy. The Germans had the worse of the encounter although their convoy reached its objective. More German warships were lost to Norwegian gunboats and coastal defences when they tried to fight their way up Oslo Fjord and, in actions between 10 and 13 April, an entire flotilla of ten German destroyers was sunk by HMS *Warspite* and her accompanying destroyers at Narvik. However, all of the invasion forces' initial objectives were seized by airborne and airlanding troops who were reinforced by a major airlift, enabling the seaborne convoys to put their troops and equipment ashore, including a small armoured detachment.

Having consolidated their positions, the invaders spread out across the country, overcoming the resistance of the tiny Norwegian Army and its supporting militia. Simultaneously, Luftwaffe squadrons flew in and began operating from captured airfields. The British and French reaction was to land troops in the north of the country but, faced with the Luftwaffe's complete air superiority, they were unable to fight effectively. Some were evacuated at the beginning of May, taking the Norwegian king and his government with them. They did, however, manage to force the German garrison out of Narvik after a protracted struggle, but even this success was short-lived as they had to be evacuated in turn because of catastrophic events in Western Europe.

There, the continued passivity of the Allies behind the Maginot Line resulted in several changes of view at OKW. There was relief that they had not launched a spoiling attack during the Polish War, or for some time afterwards, as a large proportion of the German tank fleet was either undergoing repair or awaiting replacement, a critical consideration as it was already outnumbered by that of the French. There was also bewilderment at there being no indication that the Allies intended taking the initiative, possibly because they were worried that Germany might launch a mechanised version of the old Schlieffen Plan through Belgium and were keeping sufficient troops available to meet such an eventuality, considered by many to offer a reasonable prospect of success. In fact, both OKW and OKH (*Oberkommando des Heeres* – Army General Headquarters) were of the opinion that such a course of action was too obvious and were actively studying alternatives. Independently, Lieutenant General Erich von Manstein, a nephew of the recently deceased Field Marshal Paul von Hindenburg, was considering a revolutionary plan of his own that would destroy a major portion of the Allied strength and eliminate their numerical superiority in armour. At the time he was serving as Chief of Staff to Colonel General Gerd von Rundstedt, the Commander-in-Chief of Army Group A, whose headquarters were at Koblenz. Having verified with Lieutenant General Heinz Guderian of the *Panzertruppen* that the Ardennes Forest was nothing like as tankproof as the French and Belgians believed, Manstein sat down to complete the details of his plan. Its essence was that of an apparent repetition of the Schlieffen Plan, involving an invasion of the Low Countries, to draw the best Allied armies north into Belgium. A concentration of German armour, having passed through the Ardennes, would then cross the Meuse and carve a forty-mile-wide corridor across northern France to the coast. The effect of this would be that those Allied armies to the north of the corridor would be isolated, deprived of supplies and reinforcements, and finally forced to surrender. To the south of the corridor, the rump of the Allied armies, now seriously outnumbered and lacking most of their armour, would be forced into a general retreat until they either surrendered or requested an armistice. The genius of the plan lay not merely in its simplicity, but in its attention to detail.

Having obtained von Rundstedt's approval, Manstein submitted his plan, named *Sichelschnitt* (Sickle Cut) to OKH on 31 October. It was ignored. He submitted it again three times in November, twice in December, and once in January 1940. On the last occasion the memorandum was supported by a note from von Rundstedt, requesting that it be shown to the Führer. However, neither Brauchitsch nor Halder were inclined to approach Hitler with a plan lacking their confidence. Manstein was regarded as an importunate nuisance and he was sent to command a corps in Stettin, far removed from any area of influence.

Nevertheless, one of his former colleagues, Lieutenant Colonel von Tresckow, mentioned the *Sichelschnitt* concept to a personal friend, Colonel Schmundt, who was Hitler's adjutant, while the latter was making a routine visit to Koblenz. Knowing that Hitler had himself expressed interest in the Somme estuary as a strategic objective, Schmundt advised him of Manstein's plan when he returned to Berlin. Manstein was ordered to present himself and discussed his ideas at length in Hitler's study. He found the Führer 'surprisingly quick to grasp the points which our Army Group had been advocating for many months past, and he entirely agreed with what I had to say'. Manstein then returned to Stettin while Hitler, modestly claiming the plan as his own, ordered Brauchitsch and Halder to prepare fresh directives based on *Sichelschnitt*. These were subjected to the test of war games and found to be viable.

The opening date for the German offensive was set as 10 May. On the eve of this the balance of the respective combatants stood as follows. Germany had mobilised two-and-a-half million men deployed in ten panzer divisions, nine motorized divisions and 104 infantry divisions. These were organised in three army groups – in the north, General Fedor von Bock's Army Group B, containing two armies, held a line from the North Sea to Aachen; in the centre, and concentrated in an area between Aachen and Strasbourg, was von Rundstedt's Army Group A, consisting of four armies and a panzer group containing most of Germany's 2,574 tanks. In support were 3,500 combat aircraft. The Allied armies were deployed along the French borders from Calais to Switzerland. They possessed 100 divisions of which nine were British, one was Polish and thirteen were fortress troops manning the Maginot Line. The Allies possessed 3,609 tanks, of which some were better armed and armoured than their opponents. The French possessed three armoured divisions but lacked a corps headquarters to control them, several light armoured divisions and numerous independent tank battalions allocated to infantry divisions. The French Armée de l'Air possessed 1,400 combat aircraft and the Royal Air Force contingent about 290 aircraft. In the neutral Low Countries, the Belgian and Dutch armies could field, respectively, 600,000 and 400,000 men although in neither case were the troops fully trained or equipped with up to date weapons.

At 05:35 on 10 May Army Group B flooded across the Belgian frontier. The Belgians had intended to fight along the line of the Albert canal but were soon forced to withdraw when their flank was exposed by a spectacular glider-borne attack which resulted in the surrender of the allegedly impregnable Fort Eban Emael, dominating the junction of the canal with the river Meuse. Simultaneously in Holland, airfields and bridges had been secured by paratroop and airlanding operations, including one involving 120 paratroopers and assault engineers being landed by a dozen floatplanes on the Maas in the centre of Rotterdam to secure a vital bridge. Other important locations were secured by special forces, often referred to as Brandenburgers, wearing Dutch or Belgian uniforms and armed with the appropriate weapons. Fighting was severe and the cost of laying an airborne carpet across Holland was heavy, especially in the number of Junkers Ju52 transports destroyed in the air or wrecked on landing. Fortunately for those involved, they were relieved by the 9th Panzer Division, which had driven straight across Holland and broken through to them on 12 May before turning north towards Rotterdam. The effect of this was to isolate the Dutch Army before the Allies could reach it. The army's commander, General Henri Winkelman, was warned that if he did not surrender the Luftwaffe would destroy Holland's cities, just as it had destroyed Warsaw the previous year. To emphasise the point, bombing turned the business centre of Rotterdam into an inferno while negotiations were still taking place. The Queen of the Netherlands and her government had already escaped by sea to England and Winkelman surrendered unconditionally on 14 May.

As soon as the German offensive had begun General Maurice Gamelin, the Allied Commander-in-Chief, had ordered his western-most armies north into Belgium in accord with the contingency plan that had made allowance for the Germans attempting to repeat the Schlieffen Plan in mechanised form. Ultimately, some thirty-five Allied divisions had entered the trap prepared for them by von Manstein's plan. In the meantime, General Erich Hoepner's XVI Panzer Corps had crossed the Maastricht Appendix and then motored across Belgium until it reached the Gembloux Gap. There, on 12 and 13 May, it fought a fierce encounter battle with General Prioux's I Cavalry Corps, con-sisting of two light armoured divisions (*Divisions Légère Méchanique*). Technically, the majority of French tanks were superior to those of the Germans save in one particular, namely one-man turrets that required the tank commander not only to control his vehicle's movements but also to act as his own gunner and loader. The result was hasty and often inaccurate gun-laying and loading the wrong ammunition, e.g., high explosive instead of armour-piercing when a 'hard' target was being engaged. Dive-bombing provided a further distraction for the French crews. Each side lost over one hundred tanks and both claimed a victory. Prioux's regiments withdrew having fulfilled their mission of screening the French First Army's deployment along the river Dyle. This left the battlefield in German hands, permitting recovery of many damaged tanks. Hoepner may have been dis-appointed by the check he had received, but the scale of the fighting convinced Gamelin that the epicentre of the coming battle would be in central Belgium when the real threat was actually unfolding else-where. Because of this, the French 1st and 2nd Armoured Divisions were despatched north into the trap.

Meanwhile, on Army Group A's front, Panzer Group Kleist was moving steadily through the Ardennes towards the Meuse. By the evening of 12 May its three panzer corps had closed up to the river on a forty-mile front running from Dinard in the north to Sedan in the south. Opposite them, and straddling the boundary between the French Second and Ninth Armies, were four Class B Reserve divisions composed of middle-aged reservists. It had never been Gamelin's intention that these men should bear the brunt of the battle and their sector was actually expected to remain a quiet stretch of the line. Within hours it would become an inferno of bursting explosives.

From 09:00 the following morning until 15.00 that afternoon an entire Air Fleet of Luftwaffe bombers battered the chosen crossing sites.

As the aircraft droned away, motor rifle troops began crossing in their assault boats only to meet determined resistance and sustain serious casualties. Energetic action by the German divisional commanders assembled tanks, anti-tank and anti-aircraft guns on their own bank to suppress centres of resistance opposite. By dusk, footings had been gained on the enemy bank, but it seemed as though much hard fighting would be required to turn these into bridgeheads. Then, quite unexpectedly, the French 55th Division bolted at about 18:00, followed by the neighbouring 71st Division. Suddenly, a yawning gap had opened between the two French armies. The originator of this disastrous panic was a shell-shocked artillery officer who claimed to have seen German tanks on his own bank of the river; the tanks he had seen were French and they were moving up to support their infantry. Immediately the French resistance faded, German engineers worked frantically to put their bridges in place.

During the next two days Army Group A's six panzer divisions crossed the Meuse bridgeheads and began the drive to the Channel coast. At first Gamelin and his senior commanders reacted calmly. It was decided to commit the three French armoured divisions in a converging attack designed to seal off the huge penetration – the 1st from the north, the 2nd from the west and the 3rd from the south. The flaw in the plan was that each would be operating independently under local command, thereby forfeiting the obvious advantages of co-ordinating their counter-stroke.

The morning of 15 May found the 1st Armoured Division (*Division Cuirassée*) replenishing its fuel in close leaguer near Flavion. It had run its tanks dry the previous day trying to reach the battlefield over roads clogged with refugees and the tangle of panic-stricken units trying to escape from the front. The French armoured divisions were armed with the formidable Char B2, a thirty-two-ton vehicle protected by 60mm armour, armed with a 75mm gun in the front plate, a 47mm gun in the turret and two machine guns. The 7th Panzer Division, under the command of Major General Erwin Rommel, came across the scene shortly after moving out of its bridgehead. The Char B2 was a feared opponent known to the Germans as the *Kolosse* but at this stage Rommel was more interested in covering miles to the west than starting a stand-up fight with such a formidable enemy. He called up the dive-bombers to occupy their attention then swung away to by-pass the threat. Following behind him was the 5th Panzer Division, which arrived as the French had begun to deploy out after the bombing. The second major tank battle of the campaign now took place. The French claimed to have knocked out approximately 100 of their opponents who were shocked to discover that their own 37mm guns made no impression on the Char B2's armour. Despite this, the German crews quickly learned that the French tank's vulnerable points were its exposed tracks and its prominent radiator louvres, which were clearly visible on the sides of the hull. These were taken as aiming marks and a growing tally of kills was slowly notched up. The French began to give ground, losing yet more of their vehicles destroyed by their own crews, having been abandoned because of mechanical failure or fuel shortage. At last light the 1st Armoured Division broke contact, shedding yet more vehicles as it withdrew during the night until by dawn on the 16th this once mighty formation had been reduced to just seventeen tanks.

Had it not been subjected to astoundingly bad staff work, compounded by order, counter-order and general disorder, the 2nd Armoured Division would probably have shared the fate of the 1st, as its original axis of advance would have taken it straight into the path of Lieutenant General Hans Reinhardt's XLI Panzer Corps. At one stage its major elements found themselves simultaneously travelling in opposite directions. At 17:00 on 14 May Reinhardt's tanks overran part of the divisional artillery. The remaining wheeled vehicles took refuge south of the Aisne, leaving the tanks north of the river. The division was never able to re-assemble and was therefore removed from the French order of battle with a minimum of effort on the Germans' part. Its tanks, however, attached themselves to the nearest infantry formations and fought, without their supply and technical echelons, under their command for as long as they were able.

On the same day Guderian's XIX Panzer Corps was counter-attacked by French armour near Sedan. The attack was beaten off but heavy casualties were caused by a 'friendly fire' incident when a dive-bomber formation attacked a German concentration at Chemery. As a result of this, Guderian left the 10th Panzer Division and the motorised infantry regiment *Grossdeutschland* behind to hold the high ground at Stonne, protecting the southern shoulder of the bridge-head, while he set off westwards the following day with the 1st and 2nd Panzer Divisions.

The 3rd Armoured Division entered the general area at about 16:00 on 14 May and was in a position to mount an attack. Now, incredible as it may seem, the counter-attack was cancelled by the corps commander concerned, a General Flavigny, who deployed the division's tanks as an eight-mile-long line of static pillboxes along the southern edge of the German penetration. The division re-assembled the following morning but was then committed to several days of mutually destructive attritional fighting against 10th Panzer and *Grossdeutschland* at Stonne.

By 16 May the French were fully aware that they had sustained a major defeat although they were still unable to read the battle correctly. Some officers thought that the German armour would wheel south behind the Maginot Line, others that Paris was its objective. Few guessed its real destination and, even if they had, all the available reserves had marched north into Belgium. However, something had to be done and Prime Minister Reynaud replaced Gamelin as Commander-in-Chief with General Maxime Weygand.

On 17 May Guderian's XIX Panzer Corps was attacked at Laon by the French 4th Armoured Division, commanded by Major General Charles de Gaulle. The division was not yet fully formed or equipped and was easily driven off by units of 1st Panzer Division. For most of the time, however, the German armoured formations in what became known as the Panzer Corridor simply motored along, finding the crowds of refugees and French soldiers wishing to surrender more of a hindrance than anything else. Fuel tanks were replenished from French service stations or captured airfields to which the Luftwaffe delivered supplies. At the higher levels of command there had always been a nagging fear that the Army's panzer spearheads would be cut off by counter-attacks cutting through the corridor behind them, but the campaign was developing just as von Manstein said it would. On 20 May Guderian reached the sea, having also secured useful bridgeheads over the Somme at Péronne, Amiens and Abbeville. The campaign seemed all but over.

Then, on 21 May, a dramatic change took place. Weygand had proposed that the panzer corridor should be severed by converging thrusts from north and south. The southern thrust never really developed, but near Arras the British 50th Division and 1 Army Tank Brigade, the latter equipped with small but heavily armoured Matilda infantry tanks, broke into 7th Panzer Division's line of march behind its armoured spearhead, inflicting serious loss on its two motor rifle regiments. The division's 37mm anti-tank guns were useless but by concentrating the entire resources of his artillery, including his 88mm anti-aircraft guns, Rommel was able to halt the counter-attack. His own Panzer Regiment 25, returning to the battlefield, ran into an anti-tank ambush and was attacked in turn by the remnants of the French 3rd Light Armoured Division, receiving a rougher handling than Rommel chose to admit. Although the British withdrew that night, he had obviously been shaken by the encounter as his report contained the wildly exaggerated claim that he had been attacked by 'hundreds' of tanks.

Alarm bells rang all the way up from Rundstedt's Army Group A headquarters to OKH and OKW. It seemed that the worst fears of Brauchitsch, Halder, Keitel, Jodl and even the Führer himself for the security of the panzer corridor were being realised. Reinhardt's XLI Panzer Corps, echeloned to the right-rear of Guderian's XIX and closer to the coast than Hoth's XV, was immediately ordered back along the corridor towards Arras in case the situation deteriorated further and for the next twenty-four hours the final northward slice of Manstein's sickle remained suspended. When it was resumed it was against much tougher opposition, especially at Boulogne and Calais but on 27 May King Leopold of the Belgians, accepting that further resistance was pointless, ordered his troops to surrender. The effect of this was to leave the British left flank wide open to German attack. The position of the British Expeditionary Force and the trapped French divisions had become untenable.

Despite this, Vice Admiral Bertram Ramsay, RN, the Flag Officer Dover, achieved the astonishing feat of assembling over 1,000 vessels with which to evacuate the troops from Dunkirk. His armada included destroyers and smaller warships, cross-channel ferries, pleasure steamers, coasters, trawlers and craft as small as cabin cruisers manned by their civilian owners. Their losses were heavy but between 28 May and 4 June no fewer than 338,000 men, including 112,000 French and Belgian soldiers, were evacuated although all their heavy weapons and vehicles had to be left behind.

Just why two German army groups failed to overrun the con-tracting Allied perimeter caused furious arguments among senior commanders. Hitler had halted the drive of the panzer divisions as early as 24 May, leaving the final phase to be completed by von Bock's infantry and the Luftwaffe, which Göring had begged to be allowed to administer the *coup de grace*. Yet Hitler's decision, influenced by Rundstedt, was the correct one. The greater part of France still had to be conquered and in some cases panzer formations' tank strength had fallen below fifty per cent. Time had to be allowed for broken down vehicles to catch up and for those still with their units to catch up on their maintenance. Even if the remaining German armour had been launched at the Dunkirk perimeter, it would soon have become entangled among the marshland, canals and other water obstacles bordering the area.

The Luftwaffe's performance in the final act of this drama was disappointing. Those on the beaches who were being strafed and bombed daily were not inclined to support such a view, yet for every German sortie that attacked those trying to find shelter among the dunes or the shipping offshore others were intercepted by RAF fighter aircraft flying from airfields in England. Luftwaffe records show 156 aircraft destroyed during the Dunkirk period, while an equivalent number will have returned to base in a 'severely damaged' or 'damaged' condition. RAF records show a loss of 106 aircraft during the battle.

The next phase of the Battle of France began on 5 June. The front line lay along what had been the southern edge of what had been the panzer corridor, now known to the French as the Weygand Line. France had been severely traumatised by the events of the past three weeks but, somehow, Weygand had managed to inject something of the spirit of 1914 into his countrymen. He constructed a defensive zone several miles deep, based on towns, villages and woods rather than a continuously held line. Wherever possible, these zones were mutually supporting, while the areas between were turned into artillery killing grounds. The army still possessed a few tanks, but their numbers were few in comparison with their opponents and in quality they did not compare with the hundreds of fine machines squandered in Belgium and north-east France.

At first, incredibly tough resistance ensured that the Germans made little progress. Von Kleist's panzer group was so seriously checked that it had to be moved to a less obstinate sector further east. However, as the backbone of the French defence consisted of artillery, the Luftwaffe made this their special target. Once the artillery had been silenced and the French tanks destroyed, the panzer formations flooded through into what was now effectively empty space. It was apparent that France could not hope to win and on 10 June Italy, hoping for a share of the spoils, declared war on her and invaded the south of the country. Paris, having been declared an open city on 13 June, was entered by a token force of infantry the following day. Dijon and Lyons fell while, farther east, Guderian's panzer group created the very situation envisaged by the long-dead Count Schlieffen, trapping several French armies against the Swiss frontier and the Maginot Line while the latter was coming under simultaneous attack by von Leeb's Army Group C. The effect was to create a huge pocket from which no fewer than half a million men marched into captivity.

France's position was now hopeless. On 17 June Prime Minister Renaud resigned and Marshal Henri Pétain took his place. An armistice was requested and granted on 25 June, the terms specifying that three-fifths of France would pass into German control and all French troops were to be disarmed. The negotiations took place in the same railway carriage in the Forest of Compiègne in which the 1918 armistice was signed. General Huntziger led the French delegation and negotiated directly with Hitler.

The German Army had reached the peak of its achievements. Prior to the recent campaign it had defeated Poland, Denmark and Norway. Now, it had added Holland, Belgium, France and the United Kingdom to the list. More successes would follow, but in the long term they would turn to ashes. The first such failure would take place shortly after the fall of France. When Winston Churchill, now Prime Minister of the United Kingdom, failed to react to Hitler's peace feelers, the Führer declared that he would make preparations for a landing on the British coast. No such landing could be made unless the Luftwaffe succeeded in winning air superiority over the Channel and southern England, and when it turned to bombing cities the only result was to harden the British public's resolve. Grand Admiral Raeder, the Commander-in-Chief of the Kriegsmarine, also informed Hitler that crossing the Channel was a very different matter from a river crossing. There were tidal considerations that reduced the suitable landing periods to a number of tactical 'time windows' that might be further reduced by unfavourable barometric pressure, wind strength and light conditions. Most important of all, the Kriegsmarine's losses during the invasion of Norway had been so heavy that it no longer possessed the resources to escort an invasion convoy. Although some preparatory steps had been taken in respect of the projected invasion, such as the development of deep wading tanks and the concentration of barges in some of the Channel ports, the Führer's enthusiasm for a cross-Channel invasion began to wane with the coming of autumn and in due course the operation was postponed indefinitely.

Despite having signed a non-aggression pact with Stalin during the war with Poland, Hitler's hatred of Communism and the Soviet Union was boundless. 'All we have to do is kick in the front door and the whole rotten structure will come tumbling down,' he had once remarked. He was, however, not ready to act in 1940 and was busy arranging alliances and political support among the nations of south-east Europe. He brought Hungary, Romania and Bulgaria under his control by political means and guaranteed the support of Yugoslavia by ensuring that the country was governed by a pro-German faction. However, a major problem was beginning to surface in the shape of his fellow dictator Benito Mussolini, who was annoyed when Hitler occupied Romania without bothering to mention it to him. In a fit of pique he announced that he was going to 'occupy' Greece. This wild piece of optimism came to nought when the Greeks chased the invading Italians back into Albania. At the same time a tiny British force of little more than two divisions had trounced then utterly destroyed a 250,000-strong Italian army in North Africa. It was apparent to Hitler that unless he intervened, Mussolini faced a similar crushing defeat in the Balkans and would be swept from power in Rome. He therefore issued instructions for the planning of a German invasion of Greece from Bulgaria under the code name of Operation MARITA.

His plans required a sharp revision when, during the early hours of 27 March 1941, the Balkan apple cart was well and truly overturned by a *coup* in which anti-German elements seized power in Yugoslavia. Hitler's furious and illogical reaction was that the new government in Belgrade represented a threat not only to MARITA but also to BARBAROSSA, his code name for the projected invasion of the Soviet Union. It said much about his mental state when he screamed orders to the effect that Yugoslavia was to be 'beaten down with merciless brutality in a lighting operation', which he predictably named PUNISHMENT.

Neither Greece nor Yugoslavia was capable of offering serious resistance, Greece because so much of her strength was already deployed against the Italians, and Yugoslavia because her army was poorly armed and fragmented by racial, religious and political differences. For example, Yugoslavs of Austro-German descent would almost certainly welcome the invaders, while the Croats had not the slightest intention of fighting for a country that treated them as second-rate citizens. Both countries placed too much faith in their mountains' ability to hold back armour. Operations MARITA and PUNISHMENT began on 3 April and were completed on 28 April 1941. The same combination of armoured spearheads and the destruction of stubborn knots of resistance by dive-bombers that had produced such excellent results in western Europe was used. There was actually very little fighting and Major General von Mellenthin, serving as a staff officer in the German Second Army, remarked that its advance was 'virtually a military parade'. That a sledgehammer had been used to crack a nut was confirmed by the fact that 345 Yugoslav soldiers marched into captivity while total German casualties amounted to just 558.

The Greeks, reinforced by a British corps shipped across from North Africa, put up a much tougher fight, although when the fighting against the Italians is taken into account their losses came to 70,000 killed or wounded and 270,000 captured. The British corps' loss came to 12,000 from all causes and, although eighty per cent of its personnel were evacuated by sea, all heavy equipment had to be abandoned.

The Greek tragedy had one more act to run. Some of those evacuated from the mainland were landed on Crete. Others arrived until the island's garrison had grown to 32,000 Commonwealth and 10,000 Greek troops. Heavy equipment included just sixteen 25-pounder field guns, sixty anti-aircraft weapons and twenty-one worn-out Matilda tanks. Little or no air cover was available. Having secured control of the mainland Balkans the Germans already intended to secure the island to prevent its airfields being used against targets in Europe and to use them themselves for attacks against British targets in the Middle East. It was to be invaded using parachute and airlanding troops, plus a division of mountain troops, a total of 23,000. Heavy weapons would be delivered by sea once a beachhead had been secured and, as usual, the Luftwaffe's dive-bombers would serve as flying artillery.

The landings began on 20 May. The airborne troops met ferocious resistance, sustaining unexpectedly heavy casualties, but managed to secure an airfield after thirty-six hours, enabling reinforcements to be flown in although the Royal Navy sank or dispersed the convoys carrying reinforcements and heavy weapons. The cost in transport aircraft was prohibitive but the constant bombing attacks and poor communications made a coherent defence impossible. On 27 May, General B. C. Freyberg, commanding the Allied garrison, ordered an evacuation through Sfakia on the south coast and Heraklion in the north. From then until 1 June over 18,000 men were evacuated through these ports although nine British warships were sunk and more damaged, mainly by the Luftwaffe. The Allies sustained 17,320 casualties, including 12,000 taken prisoner. The German casualties amounted to 7,000 killed or wounded, while losses in aircraft were heavier than had been allowed for. Hitler, horrified by the personnel casualties of his airborne troops (approximately fifty per cent) forbade any further operations of this kind and consigned them to the role of élite infantry. In the event, possession of the island paid few dividends and a garrison was required to hold down the population.

It can be argued that Hitler's Balkan forays were a major contributory factor in his losing the war. The start of Operation BARBAROSSA, his projected invasion of the Soviet Union, had to be postponed for five weeks. Given that the lack of surfaced roads in Russia limited the full scope of mechanised warfare to the period between the spring thaw and the winter rains, it can be seen that much of this priceless time had been lost already. An optimist might have claimed that the remainder would suffice, to which a realist would comment that there was absolutely no margin for error. Again, the tanks that had taken part in Operations MARITA and PUNISHMENT required three weeks of heavy maintenance before they were fit to take the field again. Even so, the effects of wear and tear on tracked vehicles are cumulative.

The Soviet Army, like that of the Tsar before it, was huge and could call on apparently limitless manpower reserves if it had to. Most of its senior officers had been butchered by Stalin during his purges of the 1930s. The survivors were too frightened to argue with the all-powerful Party apparatchiks who ran the country. The Party gave the orders and the soldiers carried them out, supervised by commissars who reported regularly on their loyalty. If the soldiers failed, that was their fault because the Party was never wrong, so ran the dogma. Furthermore, in Soviet armoured regiments the only tanks fitted with radios were those of the commanding officer and his company commanders, making communication, command and control all but impossible. This was the least desirable situation, for an army crippled by fear and internal paralysis was to meet an enemy grown skilled in fighting fast-moving mechanised campaigns.

On the eve of BARBAROSSA, Germany possessed seventeen panzer divisions in the line and two in reserve. Between them, they possessed a total of 3,332 tanks of which the majority, even at this stage, were light tanks or ageing Czech stock. The intention of BARBAROSSA was that these should spearhead the drive to the operation's final objective, a line running south from Archangel to Astrakhan on the Volga. This, it was said, would place targets in Europe beyond the range of the Soviet Air Force and, in Hitler's opinion, ensure the death of communism on the wind-steppes in inner Asia. Little further proof is needed that the lunatics were running the asylum.

BARBAROSSA began at 03:15 on 22 June 1941. The Luftwaffe's four air fleets achieved complete surprise, destroying 1,489 Soviet aircraft on the ground and 322 more in the air during the first day's fighting. By the end of the first week the figure had risen to an incredible 4,990. On the ground, three army groups were involved in the invasion, the largest being Field Marshal von Rundstedt's Army Group South, consisting of fifty-two infantry divisions, including a major contri-bution from Germany's Romanian, Hungarian and Italian allies. The army group would be spearheaded by five panzer divisions of Panzer Group I under von Kleist. Army Group Centre, under Field Marshal Fedor von Bock, consisted of forty-two infantry divisions and nine panzer divisions, the latter being divided between Panzer Group II (Guderian) and Panzer Group III (Hoth). Army Group North, com-manded by Field Marshal Wilhelm Ritter von Leeb, was the smallest of the three as it was responsible for a comparatively narrow sector of front, although this would involve a difficult run through the Baltic States. It consisted of seven infantry divisions and Panzer Group IV (Hoepner) of three panzer divisions.

Army Group South encountered the most serious resistance, being opposed by the enemy's South West Front, a Soviet Front equating to a western army group. The Front was commanded by Colonel General Mikhail Kirponos, who had performed well during Russia's war against Finland. He had six mechanised corps available and it says much for his abilities that by 25 June they were converging on four of Panzer Group I's divisions. Unfortunately for Kirponos, the Luftwaffe pounced on his columns and seriously wrote down his strength. Despite this, a fierce but untidy tank battle raged for the next four days, at the end of which Kirponos was forced to extract what remained of his corps and retreat on Kiev, shedding tanks by the hour because of breakdowns or lack of fuel. The Germans had been astonished at the many different types of tank in the Soviet service. Some were useless multi-turreted monsters that their opponents called *Kinderschrecke*, meaning things to frighten children. Others were out-dated and of little use, but two types, the T-34 and the KV (Klimenti Voroshilov) caused very serious concern. The T-34 combined the three essential elements in tank design, firepower, protection and mobility, so well in its design that at one stage it was suggested that it should be copied for the German Army, a suggestion that was dismissed at once as it reflected badly on German abilities. The KV's strength lay in its armour, which could only be penetrated by German tank guns with a flank or rear shot at close quarters. Very quickly, the panzer regiments learned to whittle away the enemy's older types while the divisional medium artillery and 88mm anti-aircraft guns, with the Luftwaffe's assistance, dealt with the T-34s and KVs.

Army Group Centre was opposed by West Front. This was commanded by General D. G. Pavlov, who had served in Spain during the Spanish Civil War and was regarded by Stalin as the Soviet Union's leading expert on armoured warfare. He had three mechanised corps at his disposal but quickly demonstrated that he had no instinct for the game. Guderian and Hoth carved swathes through his confused troops with their panzer groups so that by 27 June they were 200 miles east of their start lines and their spearheads were closing to form two major pockets, one at Bialystok and the other at Minsk. As the German infantry divisions came up the pockets were surrounded, sealed off and gradually crushed. When the last of the defenders surrendered on 3 July 290,000 men marched into captivity, abandoning masses of equipment, including 2,585 tanks and 1,449 guns. Stalin summoned Pavlov to Moscow and had him shot on the spot.

Pavlov's replacement was Marshal Semyen Timoshenko who immediately attempted to construct a defence line along the upper reaches of the Dniepr and Dvina rivers. It availed him little for by 10 July Guderian was across the Dniepr near Mogilev and Hoth had crossed the Dvina at Vitebsk. Several days' hard fighting were required before the two panzer groups could break out of their bridgeheads and drive on through the rear areas of Timoshenko's armies, but Smolensk fell on 16 July. The following day the armoured jaws came close to shutting on a huge pocket containing elements of twenty-five Soviet divisions, although Timoshenko managed to withdraw several battered units through the corridor that remained open to the east but, as the German infantry marched up, the walls of the pocket became more substantial. Finally, the escape corridor was closed and those trapped within surrendered on 5 August. This time the haul included 250,000 prisoners, 2,000 tanks and a comparable number of guns. For the moment, the coup concluded offensive operations on Army Group Centre's sector.

Simultaneously, Army Group North, led by Hoepner's Panzer Group IV, had been making good progress against Colonel General F. I. Kuznetsov's North West Front. This was the more remarkable because during its advance on Leningrad through the Baltic States, the going was as bad as anywhere in Russia, consisting of forest and swamp that confined the advance to two corridors between the coast, Lake Peipus and Lake Ilmen. Not long after crossing the frontier, Reinhardt's XLI Panzer Corps was heavily counter-attacked by two Soviet mechanised corps. Luftwaffe assistance enabled Reinhardt to gain the upper hand while, simultaneously, von Manstein's LVI Panzer Corps skirted the southern edge of the battle and headed directly for Dvinsk, covering 200 miles in four days and securing the town's bridges by *coup de main*. Kuznetsov had now been replaced by Marshal Klimenti Voroshilov who mounted a major counter-attack with newly-arrived troops, temporarily isolating Manstein's corps for three days. Elsewhere, Army Group North's advance guard crossed the Luga on 8 August. Novgorod fell a week later and by the end of the month Leningrad was cut off from the rest of Russia, remaining a prisoner of the Wehrmacht and the Finnish Army on the Karelian isthmus for the next 900 days. Some 20,000 survivors of North West Front, trapped between the Luga and the developing siege lines, laid down their arms. Von Leeb's Army Group North had fulfilled its brief, the only army group to do so.

A slim chance remained that BARBAROSSA would obtain its objectives, but that was destroyed by Hitler himself when he issued his Directive No. 33 on 19 July. The directive re-defined the entire strategy of the campaign. The drive on Moscow, initially the primary objective, was to be suspended. Hoth was to be sent north and, in conjunction with Hoepner, was to sever communications between Moscow and Leningrad. Guderian was to go south and assist von Rundstedt in his conquest of the Ukraine. These completely pointless orders ran quite contrary to the fundamental military principle of maintenance of the objective throughout any operation. In this case only the capture of Moscow could guarantee a German victory and in deployments to that end every effort should have been made. The enormity of the error so shocked the Army's senior officers that many, including Brauchitsch, Halder, Jodl, von Bock, von Rundstedt, Guderian and Hoth, either protested strongly in person or formally through their superiors. The attitude of the former lance corporal to his generals was one of inverted snobbery. They did not, he sneered, have the slightest understanding of the economic or political aspects of war and he refused to alter his decision.

That kind of stupidity also existed on the Soviet side of the lines. Kirponos, having conducted a skilful withdrawal from the frontier and avoided the kind of disasters that had destroyed Pavlov farther north, found himself paralysed by an order from Stalin to the effect that he must hold Kiev at all costs. The result was that when Guderian's panzer group, driving south-west from Smolensk in obedience to the Führer's *diktat*, encountered von Kleist's advance guard moving north at a village named Lokhvitsa, some hundred miles east of Kiev, a gigantic pocket was formed enclosing most of South West Front. At first the Russians were unaware of their danger, and by the time they realised what had happened Rundstedt had enclosed them in an iron ring. Kirponos died leading one of several attempts to break out. The last resistance crumbled away on 26 September, yielding no fewer than 665,000 prisoners, 900 tanks and 3,719 guns.

Hitler basked in the glory of a victory he believed that he had created, but wiser heads knew that his decision had cost him the campaign. He now declared that the emphasis of the advance must be returned to Moscow as soon as possible. Unfortunately, it took time to unscramble his earlier re-deployment so that it was not until early October that Guderian and Hoth, both furious at the additional wear caused to their tanks, returned to their earlier axes of advance, to be joined by Hoepner. For a little while longer all went well. Hoth and Hoepner closed off one pocket at Viazma while a second was sealed off at Bryansk by Guderian and Kluge, yielding a further 663,000 prisoners, 1,242 tanks and 5,412 guns.

Then came the rains, showers at first, followed by torrential downpours. The bottom fell out of the roads and movement became impossible. On 4 December German infantry entered Moscow's south-eastern suburbs but were quickly driven out. Then fresh Russian divisions from Siberia, properly clad against what would become unbelievable cold, counter-attacked along the front, forcing local retreats. The opinion of senior German officers was that a withdrawal was necessary. Brauchitsch, now seriously ill, put their views to Hitler who screamed that he was 'a strawhead – a vain, cowardly wretch', then dismissed him and appointed himself as the Army's new Commander-in-Chief. He warned the three army groups that no further withdrawals would be tolerated. The troops stayed under cover from the weather in the more important villages and towns along the principal road and rail links and quickly devised ways of keeping themselves alive and healthy and their weapons in working order, but about half the horses that had begun the campaign died from a combination of overwork and exposure. Fortunately, the Luftwaffe managed to deliver sufficient supplies to keep most of the men alive.

When it came to establishing a balance sheet, BARBAROSSA had failed in its object of destroying the Soviet Union although it had inflicted serious damage on its armed services. Nine major and thirteen smaller pockets had yielded approximately three million prisoners, equating to 150 divisions, plus 14,287 tanks and 25,212 guns. No record exists of Russian dead and wounded. The Soviet Union was able to continue fighting because her considerable armaments industry had been shipped east of the Urals, beyond the range of the Luftwaffe's bombers. Germany and her allies had sustained approximately 800,000 casualties and lost 2,300 tanks through various causes.

Hitler's treatment of Brauchitsch was bitterly resented by the Army's senior commanders. These highly skilled professionals were the very men who for two years had won one outstanding victory after another for the Führer, whose opinion of them he had just made plain. Rundstedt and Leeb asked to be relieved of their commands rather than act contrary to their judgement, and their requests were granted. Bock left on sick leave, handing over Army Group Centre to von Kluge. Neither Guderian nor Hoepner could tolerate Kluge who, having been the recipient of some frank speaking, reported them to Hitler; both were dismissed at once. Further departures and dismissals followed until almost all the major formation commanders had been replaced.

Whenever possible Dr Josef Goebbels, Hitler's publicity and propaganda expert, saw to it that the troops' shivering in worse winter conditions than even the oldest Russians could remember, that their diet of news covered events elsewhere that suggested the war was still going Germany's way. In particular, the news from Libya suggested that Lieutenant General Erwin Rommel's Afrika Korps were teaching the British a thing or two about armoured warfare. The

Afrika Korps, never more than four divisions strong because the Royal Navy's control of the Mediterranean meant that more could not be supported, had been sent to Libya early in the year when the Italians were on the verge of collapse. Nominally, Rommel was under Italian command, but he seemed to be telling them how to run a war. He had chased off a British force of worn-out tanks from their position on the border between Tripolitania and Cyrenaica and pursued them all the way to the Egyptian frontier, save for the port of Tobruk, which he besieged. He had beaten off two British attempts to break through his frontier defences, and had recently inflicted heavy losses on a third before being forced to abandon the siege of Tobruk and retire briefly into Tripolitania. Reinforced, he had returned to the attack and now the two armies faced each other on a line running south from Gazala on the Mediterranean coast.

Even allowing for the fact that Dr Goebbels' news bulletins and press releases frequently painted a wildly optimistic picture of events, those senior officers who knew Rommel best were divided in their opinion. Some considered him to be a brilliant opportunist who produced results; others that he was a gambler and that one day he would gamble once too often.

# CHAPTER 17

# Gotterdammerung

In 1942 the German Army's attempts to make good its shortage of main battle tanks began to take shape. First, anti-tank guns protected by armoured shields were fitted to obsolete and captured tank chassis, the advantage being that the limitation in the size of guns imposed by fitting them to enclosed turrets did not apply. Secondly, it was possible to up-gun the assault guns, growing numbers of which had been entering service with the artillery since the 1940 campaign in France. Thirdly, a new generation of tanks was in the process of design and construction. This included the PzKw V Panther, better protected and armed with the most powerful 75mm tank gun in service, and the PzKw VI Tiger E, heavily armoured and armed with an even more powerful 88mm gun, an expensive and time-consuming tank to build, as well as being unable to cross some bridges.

Having stabilised the front during the winter and built up their depleted tank strength, the Soviet Army felt strong enough to mount an offensive in the spring of 1942. The object of this was the re-capture of the city of Kharkov, two tank corps and thirteen tank brigades being assembled for the task, a total of 1,200 tanks and 640,000 men under the command of Marshal Timoshenko. The offensive began on 12 May and punched a hole varying in depth between fourteen and twenty miles through the sector of front held by General Paulus' Sixth Army. Timoshenko was fully aware that Army Group Kleist had assembled around Kramatorsk, some miles below the southern shoulder of the pocket, yet to Stalin he was dismissive of the potential danger it presented, as was his senior political officer, Nikita Khrushchev.

For once, Hitler and his Chief of Staff, Colonel General Franz Halder, were in complete agreement. They had been planning an offensive of their own, codenamed FREDERICUS, and they simply decided to activate it at once. On 17 May Kleist, possessing a local superiority of 4.4 to one in tanks, 1.3 to one in infantry and 1.7 to one in artillery weapons, smashed through the southern wall of the Russian salient. Timoshenko still failed to read the situation correctly and sent back a single tank brigade to deal with the threat. However, once the enormity of what had taken place became clear to him, both tank corps followed in rapid succession. The following day, recognising that he had entered a trap, he asked Stalin for permission to cancel the drive on Kharkov. Stalin refused then, too late, changed his mind on 19 May, for Paulus' Sixth Army, attacking south from Balakleya, had already broken through the northern wall of the salient. The encircled Russians fought hard but in vain. When the guns fell silent, losses among the numerous Soviet officers killed included the deputy commander of South West Front and the commanders of the Soviet Sixth and Ninth Armies. In addition, every Soviet armoured formation inside the salient was wiped out and 250,000 prisoners began their journey to German prison camps. Worse still, the Red Army's fragile self-confidence, painstakingly nursed during the previous six months, had received a shattering blow.

In April Hitler announced his intention of seizing the oilfields of Maikop, Grozny and Baku in the Caucasus, commenting modestly to Halder that their capture represented a master-stroke of economic warfare that would cripple the Soviet Union's ability to fight. He did, however, accept the point made by OKH that the vulnerable left flank of the deep penetration should be protected by a defensive front along the Don from Voronezh to Stalingrad on the Volga. The only other activity along the entire front would be in the siege lines surrounding Leningrad, a city which Hitler detested because it had spawned Bolshevism. Now he developed a fixation centred on destroying the industrial capacity of Stalingrad, another city he loathed because it bore the name of his arch enemy. So, just as he had the previous year, Hitler failed to maintain an objective; he could have Stalingrad or he could have the Caucasus oil but not both. Unfortunately for him and for Germany, he wanted both without the means to acquire them and could therefore have neither. His decision was to result in the slow but steady destruction of himself and the evil apparatus he had created.

For these joint ventures, Army Group South was to be split in two. Army Group A, under Field Marshal Sigmund List, was to make the deep penetration into the Caucasus while Army Group B, under Field

Marshal Fedor von Bock, returned from sick leave, acted as flank guard and established the proposed defensive front along the axis Voronezh–Stalingrad. A deception plan had convinced the Russian *Stavka* (General Headquarters) that Moscow was the objective, but when a set of genuine plans were found on the body of a staff officer in a wrecked German aircraft, Bryansk and South West Fronts deployed some 1,200 tanks in the path of Army Group B. From 28 June and on into July a sprawling tank battle took place, during which two Russian generals continued to shout orders at each other until an unfortunate adjudication made matters worse by placing the armour under one and the rest of the troops under the other, an arrangement others on the net found unacceptable. Add to this the clumsy handling of the Soviet armour and its defeat was a certainty. Hitler was furious when its survivors escaped across the Don, arguing that von Bock should not only have used his own armour more aggressively to duplicate the enormous captures of the previous year, but also that he was taking far too long to capture Voronezh. For his part, Bock had the temerity to criticise an OKH directive and was instantly dismissed for his trouble, his place being taken by von Weichs.

Once more, Hitler intervened disastrously. Hoth's Fourth Panzer Army was to have led the advance on Stalingrad, but on 17 July the Führer decided that it should drive south along the Don and assist von Kleist's First Panzer Army to secure crossings prior to the great battle of encirclement in which he intended to crush the Soviet South Front against the coast. No such battle ever took place as South Front was retreating out of the trap as fast as it could march, leaving long stretches of the river undefended. Thus, while Kleist's engineers remained unmolested as they completed their bridges, his men sunbathed and swam. Suddenly, Hoth's army arrived and huge traffic jams developed as the roads became clogged with the tens of thousands of vehicles belonging to two panzer armies, ensuring that neither could be properly supplied. To the north Sixth Army was stalled at Kalach when Fourth Panzer Army should have been there to batter a way through for it. Not until the end of July did the situation start to clarify itself. Army Group A moved off into the Caucasus and Fourth Panzer Army reverted to Army Group B. However, the closer Sixth Army got to Stalingrad, the tougher the Russian resistance became until, by the end of the third week of August, no further progress could be made. Commanded by General Vasili Chuikov, the city's defenders were the Soviet Sixty-second Army. Some might claim that it was breaking every rule in the book by fighting a battle of mutual extermination amid acres of industrial ruins, to say nothing of the broad river at its back. In fact, nightly, that river was used to ship in reinforcements, ammunition and supplies, and evacuate wounded. Army Group B had fulfilled its brief by reaching the Volga but Hitler would not be satisfied until he possessed the ruins of the city. All of Paulus' Sixth Army, and much of Fourth Panzer Army as well, were committed to a ferocious struggle that also absorbed reserves and supplies originally destined for Army Group A. This terrible battle, a Second World War re-enactment of Verdun, took place in a landscape of rubble mountains and gutted buildings.

Meanwhile, Army Group A was driving ever deeper into the Caucasus. On 9 August the First Panzer Army reached the Maikop oilfield; on 25 August Mozdok was captured; and on 6 September Novorossysk, the last Russian naval base on the Black Sea, fell. Ostensibly, the total defeat of the Soviet Union seemed imminent and in such circumstances the physical possession of Stalingrad had little relevance.

Others thought differently. When a determined attempt to storm the city in September failed, Halder advised Hitler that the Sixth Army was itself in terrible danger of being encircled as its flanks were covered by the over-extended and under-equipped Third Romanian Army to the north and the equally stretched Fourth Romanian Army to the south. He was immediately relieved because of his apparent failure to appreciate the Führer's genius and was replaced by General Kurt Zeitzler, a staff officer of exceptional ability who had distinguished himself during the Polish and French campaigns and while serving as Kleist's Chief of Staff during BARBAROSSA. Manstein, whose Eleventh Army had cleared the Crimea and taken Sebastopol, had a poor opinion of the Romanians' soldierly qualities and believed that Hitler's fixation on Stalingrad must be apparent to the Russians and that they would soon turn it to their own advantage.

And that is exactly what happened. The decisive operation, code-name URANUS, was planned by Marshals Georgi Zhukov and Alexander Vasilevski and commenced at 07:30 on 19 November. Following a hurricane bombardment, General Nikolai Vatutin's South West Front smashed its way through the Third Romanian Army, leaving five of the latter's divisions surrounded. Hardly had the implications of this sunk in at OKW than, the following morning,

General Andrei Yeremenko's Stalingrad Front overwhelmed or brushed aside the Fourth Romanian Army's resistance. Neither snow nor anything the Romanians could do prevented a broad sweep by the T-34s spearheading the advance of both Fronts, which effected a junction at Kalach on 23 November.

Sixth Army and part of Fourth Panzer Army were now completely surrounded. Paulus requested permission to break out and was supported in this by Weichs and Zeitzler. Hitler may have granted his request had not the braggart Göring intervened, promising to supply everything Paulus needed by air. This groundless boast was to have terrible consequences, for Paulus' daily requirements were put at 600 tons whereas the Luftwaffe's total lift capacity was half of that. In the event, the daily deliveries averaged less than 100 tons, although the aircraft used were able to evacuate some of the wounded.

Hitler asked Manstein, now a field marshal, to take charge of relief operations. With difficulty he managed to scramble together some thirteen divisions which he placed under Hoth's tactical command. Hoth's task involved fighting his way through seventy-five miles of enemy-held territory while the besieged garrison would break out towards him. Starting on 12 December he achieved the impossible by reaching a point just thirty-five miles from the Stalingrad perimeter, but Russian reinforcements had been rushed into his path and he could go no further. Manstein authorised Paulus to start his breakout, but the latter chose to obey a recent Führer directive to hold his positions. There was nothing more Manstein could do for him. Stalingrad was doomed and the overall situation continued to deteriorate. On 16 December the Russians launched a further offensive, Operation SATURN, using the South West and Voronezh Fronts. After three days' fighting the Italian Eighth Army was destroyed and Soviet armour was streaming out to the west.

As if this was not bad enough, these developments threatened to isolate Army Group A in the Caucasus unless Manstein's primary task had become holding open an escape corridor through which most of Kleist's troops could be withdrawn. This was no easy matter and involved a series of mobile operations in response to constant Russian attacks. Nevertheless, the First Panzer Army was able to stream unmolested through Rostov while the Seventeenth Army, its running mate in Army Group A, retired into the Kuban peninsula, from which it was evacuated by sea to the Crimea. Army Groups A and B were then combined as a new Army Group South under Manstein.

On 2 February 1943 Paulus, newly created field marshal in the hope that this would encourage him to keep fighting, surrendered. Stalingrad had claimed the lives of some 120,000 German soldiers and their allies. Another 90,000 were marched off into Russian prison camps, of whom only 5,000 saw Germany again, years after the war had ended. Material losses included 3,500 tanks and self-propelled mountings, 3,000 aircraft, 12,000 guns and mortars and 75,000 vehicles. Hitler ordered a period of national mourning, during which solemn music was played on the radio, and frankly admitted responsibility for the disaster, coupled with an angry statement that Paulus had not expressed gratitude for his recent promotion by failing to take his own life, the surrender of a German field marshal being something inconceivable.

Manstein flew to Hitler's headquarters on 6 February. The Führer was still shaken by the Stalingrad disaster but was sufficiently in awe of Manstein to agree, albeit reluctantly, to his suggestion that, in the general interest, Rostov and the Don Basin should be abandoned and that a new defensive shoulder should be established on the line of the river Mius, behind which Army Group South could re-organise and re-deploy.

Part of Manstein's genius lay in his ability to predict an opponent's intentions, usually well in advance. Golikov's Voronezh Front and Vatutin's South West Front were continuing their drive across southern Russia and their final objectives were becoming more apparent with every day that passed. Golikov was heading for Kharkov while Vatutin would soon swing south along the left bank of the Dniepr and isolate Army Group South in a huge pocket with the sea at its back. However, the Red Army's logistic infrastructure was its Achilles' heel and Manstein was prepared to delay his counter-stroke, the German Army's last successful application of *Vernichtungsgedanke*, until both Fronts had all but exhausted their supplies. Only then would the First Panzer Army, now commanded by General Eberhard von Mackensen, strike northwards into the Russians' flank, driving South West Front back across the Donets. Both panzer armies would then drive into the flank of Voronezh Front and recover Kharkov if it had fallen into Golikov's hands. The offensive would continue in a northerly direction, eliminating those Russian forces remaining in the Kursk area and effecting a junction with Colonel General Rudolf

Schmidt's Second Panzer Army, which would be committed by Army Group Centre at the appropriate time

Golikov captured Kharkov on 16 February. Hitler flew to Manstein's headquarters in Zaporezh the following day, demanding to know what was going on. Manstein explained the details to him, pointing out that he had achieved a local superiority in tanks of seven to one while the Luftwaffe could deploy three times as many aircraft as the Red Air Force. Unable to add anything, Hitler left on 19 February. The following day, with Vatutin's tanks just twenty miles from Zaporezh, Manstein gave the orders for the offensive to begin.

In excellent tank country Mackensen's panzer regiments crashed through the flank of Vatutin's Front. Thanks to a critical ammunition shortage, resistance was brief and columns stalled for want of fuel were ridden over. By the end of the month those who could had escaped across the Donets, leaving behind 615 tanks, 400 guns 23,000 dead and 9,000 prisoners. Golikov despatched a major part of his armoured strength to help his neighbour, only to have it reduced to wreckage by the Luftwaffe's ground attack wings. In desperation he struggled to establish a coherent defence south of Kharkov but was almost immediately overrun by Hoth. Kharkov was isolated on 11 March and in German hands once more four days later. In total, Voronezh Front lost 600 tanks, 500 guns and 40,000 men. Only the spring rains, creating as they did a world of deep, clinging mud, prevented Manstein taking all of his objectives. One very important reason for the completeness of Manstein's victory was the fact that the planning for his counter-offensive took place in his own head-quarters. Had it taken place in OKW, the Russians would have been aware of the most important details, thanks to the informant of the Lucy spy ring. The informant's identity remains one of the war's unsolved mysteries, but his presence at OKW suggests considerable seniority.

If the victory provided cause for celebrations in Berlin, they were tempered by the news from North Africa, where the previous year's successes had been reversed. During the night of 26–27 May 1942 Rommel had attempted to turn the British defence line at Gazala by driving round its southern end. He had much the worse of the next day's fighting, having under-estimated the potential of the recently-arrived Grant medium tanks, and was pinned back against his own minefields. Thanks to a serious lapse in the standard of British generalship, he was left unmolested. However, having expended his water, he was on the point of asking for terms when his Italian allies broke through the minefield with fresh supplies. Having fended off un-coordinated attacks he broke out and defeated the British armour in detail, going on to capture the port of Tobruk and a huge quantity of supplies and war material, being rewarded with his field marshal's baton.

At this point his gambling instinct came to the fore. He pursued the retreating British Eighth Army into Egypt until further progress was halted at El Alamein, some sixty miles from Alexandria. Lack of fuel and hard fighting prevented further progress and a fresh commander, Lieutenant General Bernard Montgomery, arrived to take over the Eighth Army, restoring its morale and re-establishing orthodoxy to its methods. This became painfully apparent when, having accumulated just sufficient fuel to attempt a breakthrough, Rommel attempted to turn Montgomery's position at Alam Halfa and was decisively repelled with heavy loss.

Rommel and his army were now effectively prisoners of their earlier success. The stores captured at Tobruk had all been consumed and the Royal Air Force, having achieved complete air superiority, was making delivery through the ports of Benghazi, Derna, Tobruk and Bardia virtually impossible. The only safe port was Tripoli, one thousand miles distant, so that the quantity of fuel reaching the front was barely enough to take care of day-to-day administration. To advance further was impossible, yet to retreat would result in the sort of mobile warfare the Axis army simply could not afford.

Montgomery was well aware of this and, now that his armour possessed a numerical superiority over that available to Rommel, he intended to fight a 'crumbling' battle, attacking first in one place and then another, forcing Rommel to consume his priceless fuel until he was left impotent. The Second Battle of Alamein began during the evening of 23 October and lasted until 4 November on which date Rommel managed to extricate the remnants of his mobile units, having been delayed for twenty-four hours by a meaningless Führer order to stand fast. When, on 8 November, the Anglo-American First Army landed in Algeria and Morocco, Rommel's sole remaining option was to retreat through Libya to Tunisia, a distance of 1,500 miles, fighting rearguard actions only when they became essential. In Tunisia he could buy time behind the defences of the Mareth Line, originally built by the French to keep out the Italians.

If Rommel hoped that his men might be evacuated from Tunisia to Europe he was sadly mistaken. Hitler and Mussolini intended to turn Tunisia into an Axis redoubt and immediately despatched an extra panzer division, a Tiger heavy tank battalion and whatever infantry formations were to hand, including a penal battalion. Some of these reinforcements were flown across in huge Gotha gliders. In command was Colonel General Hans-Jürgen von Arnim, a former Footguard officer who had commanded a panzer division and then a panzer corps in Russia.

An Allied attempt to seize Tunis by *coup de main* failed and a stalemate ensued during the winter months. In the north, von Arnim's command was designated the Fifth Panzer Army on 23 February. Between 14 and 22 February 1943 Rommel, worried by the possibility of an Allied thrust into the rear of the Mareth position, mounted a major attack on the inexperienced US II Corps, broke through the Kasserine Pass and repelled a piecemeal counter-attack by the US 1st Armored Division, inflicting serious loss. The arrival of British and American reinforcements in the area halted his further progress and he withdrew to Mareth.

On 26 February it was the turn of von Arnim's Fifth Panzer Army. Several British positions in northern Tunisia were attacked and some ground was gained despite stubborn resistance that cost much of the German armour. On 6 March Rommel mounted a major attack on the Eighth Army's position at Medenine with all three panzer divisions. The British kept their anti-tank guns concealed until the German armour was in point-blank range before opening fire. Concurrently, artillery concentrations battered the stalled attackers who were forced to retire, leaving fifty of their precious tanks on the battlefield. Rommel may have been impulsive but he was a realist and could see that the isolated Tunisian campaign was leading nowhere. He flew to Hitler's headquarters and demanded the evacuation of the troops involved. His request was dismissed and he was sent on indefinite sick leave. Von Arnim assumed overall command in Tunisia, General Gustav von Vaerst taking over the Fifth Panzer Army in the north of the country while General Giovanni Messe commanded those in the south, which, from 23 February, became known as First Italian Army.

Following a week's hard fighting, Montgomery manoeuvred the First Italian Army out of the Mareth Line on 26 March, forcing it back to its next defensive position, the Wadi Akarit. While this battle was being fought Lieutenant General George S. Patton's US

II Corps strove to cut Messe's lines of communication with a drive at Maknassy but was blocked by the 10th Panzer Division and a Tiger company, losing forty-four tanks. Tenth Panzer then launched a counter-attack against the US 1st Infantry Division at El Guettar but was brought up short by a minefield and forced to retire after coming under fire from the 899th Tank Destroyer Battalion and concentrated artillery.

The defences of the Wadi Akarit were stormed by the Eighth Army on 6 April. Later that month Fondouk Pass fell to the British IX Corps. The Axis armies were now confined to an enclave in the north-eastern corner of Tunisia, making their last stand on the range of hills that marked the inland limit of the coastal plain. This could have led to protracted fighting had it not been for the ability of the British Churchill tanks to crawl up the slopes of features that Axis commanders considered tankproof. On the 28th a composite battle group containing elements of every German and Italian unit present managed to recapture the key feature of Djebel Bou Aoukaz and hold it briefly after a fierce struggle with 24 Guards Brigade, but this was the last hurrah of an army that had been fought to its limit. Shortly after, the British 6th and 7th Armoured Divisions were streaming out of the Medjerda valley onto the coastal plain and on towards Tunis; simultaneously, the US II Corps, having been re-deployed to the northern end of the Allied line, had also broken through and was heading for Bizerta.

Von Arnim surrendered on 12 May. Some 275,000 prisoners, including numerous senior officers, were taken, and in these terms the disaster, which also cost Germany three panzer divisions, was comparable to that of Stalingrad, three months earlier. The fortunes of war, it seemed, had begun to turn slowly against Germany.

The Allies wasted no time in following up their victory and on 10 July invaded the island of Sicily. Those German units present fought hard but their efforts were undermined by their Italian allies who were war weary and unwilling to continue fighting. The Germans were therefore compelled to make a tactical withdrawal that ended with an expertly executed evacuation across the Straits of Messina the following month.

Mussolini was ejected from office on 24 July and his successor, Marshal Badoglio, opened secret negotiations with the Allies with a view to their granting an armistice. This was granted on 3 September, to be announced five days later. In the meantime Hitler, suspicious and concerned for the safety of German troops in Italy, began moving reinforcements into northern Italy with the intention of disarming the Italians. Simultaneously, Field Marshal Albert Kesselring, believed that the Allies were planning an early invasion and that this would probably take place at Salerno. On 3 September elements of the Eighth Army made a diversionary landing at Reggio Calabria on the toe of Italy, followed by a second landing at Taranto on 9 September, timed to coincide with the landing of General Mark Clark's Anglo-American Fifth Army at Salerno. Kesselring reacted immediately, deploying six divisions around the Salerno beachhead, every detail of which was visible to the German artillery on the surrounding hills. Only naval gunfire and air support, coupled with hurried reinforcement, prevented the collapse of the defence. However, when the leading units of the Eighth Army reached the southern edge of the beachhead, Kesselring began withdrawing northwards on 18 September. Meanwhile, the Italian Army had been disarmed quickly and efficiently, with a minimum of fighting. Most Italians simply went home or joined a partisan unit in the hills.

The Fifth Army now advanced west of the Apennines, taking Naples on 1 October, only to be checked on 8 October by the swollen river Volturno, all the bridges across which had been demolished. The Eighth Army advanced east of the Apennines, taking the huge air base at Foggia on 27 September and on 3 October reached Termoli on the Adriatic. The pattern of the war in Italy was now set. Both to the east and west of the Apennines ridges descended to the sea, with steep-sided river valleys between. A further amphibious operation, intended to unhinge the formidable Gustav Line, involving a landing at Anzio, came dangerously close to disaster because of timidity on the part of the general concerned. For the Allies, therefore, each ridge and major adjoining feature such as Monte Cassino, had to be taken in turn, a costly and time-consuming process. In this context the Germans were masters of creating superbly camouflaged defensive zones, latterly including such unpleasant surprises as Panther turrets, set into a concrete base and projecting just inches above the ground, as well as ingenious booby-traps of every type. They were, too, experts in the art of demolition and were capable of rendering a route unuseable for long periods. This, of course, was not tank country, tanks being used by both sides for infantry support, supplementary artillery, harassing fire and long-range sniping.

There were unpleasant surprises for the Germans too. Eastern Front veterans who later fought in Italy or the West, were horrified by the volume, accuracy, flexibility and rapid response of the British and American artillery, which was able to switch its fire around the battlefield in a manner hitherto unknown. In addition, Allied ground-attack squadrons were always waiting to pounce with cannon fire, bombs and rockets.

For Germany, Italy was a secondary theatre of war, yet when asked why they defended their positions with such tenacity German prisoners usually gave one of two reasons. The first was that by doing so they were removing the need to transfer units from the Eastern Front, and thereby helping to keep the Russians out of their home-land, and the second, given after the D Day landings in Normandy, was that by tying down Allied troops in Italy they were preventing their transfer to France. That the German armies in Italy were the first to surrender in 1945 was simply an acknowledgement that there was no longer any point in fighting.

Following von Manstein's successful riposte in the spring of 1943, there was general acceptance among Germany's military hierarchy that the destruction of the Soviet Union was no longer possible. Against this, it was thought that if the Red Army could be sufficiently weakened by another major defeat, it might be possible to negotiate some sort of peace, based on the *status quo ante bellum*.

On 3 May Hitler convened a conference to discuss the situation on the Russian Front. Present were his OKW staff, General Zeitzler, the Chief of Army General Staff, Field Marshals von Manstein and von Kluge, commanding respectively Army Groups South and Centre, General Model, commander of the Ninth Army, General Heinz Guderian, Inspector General of Armoured Troops since 1 March, and Albert Speer, Minister of Production. Hitler presented a plan produced for him by Zeitzler. Its object was the salient centred on Kursk, measuring one hundred miles across and seventy deep, which had remained in the German line when the spring thaw brought Manstein's counter-offensive to a halt. This would be eliminated by converging attacks directed through the salient's flanks by Army Groups South and Centre, trapping so many Soviet divisions that the Red Army would be decisively weakened.

Opinions differed sharply. Manstein felt that the plan might have worked in April, although at the present time he had serious reservations about it. Zeitzler believed that the Tigers and the new

Panthers would guarantee success. Guderian was more realistic, commenting that the Panther's teething troubles had yet to be cured and, whatever the outcome of the battle, tank losses would inevitably be heavy at a time when reserves should be built up to meet the anticipated Allied landings in France. Speer supported this view. Model pointed out that the objective was so obvious that the Russians were already fortifying the walls of the salient in depth and were also concentrating their armour in suitable counter-attack zones. Model had been well briefed, but he had no idea of the full extent of the salient's defences, for the Lucy spy ring had kept the Russians fully informed regarding German intentions. Ultimately, the salient's walls would be protected by three fortified zones totalling forty-five miles in depth, covered by 20,000 guns, one-third of them anti-tank weapons, and corseted by minefields laid to a density of 2,500 anti-personnel and 2,200 anti-tank mines per mile of front.

Despite the serious objections that had been expressed, Zeitzler's plan was accepted by the conference and activated as Operation ZITADELLE. If the result was failure the consequences for Germany would be catastrophic; a week after the conference Hitler told Guderian that his stomach churned every time he thought of them, suggesting that he was aware that a gamble had been taken when a cautious calculation of risk was required. For what would become the largest tank battle in history, the Germans deployed 2,700 tanks and assault guns, 10,000 artillery weapons, 2,500 aircraft and 900,000 men. Apart from a two-to-one advantage in artillery, Russian strength was not greatly superior to that of their opponents, consisting of 3,300 tanks and assault guns, 2,650 aircraft and 1,337,000 men. These resources were deployed in three Fronts, the northern half of the salient being held by Marshal Konstantin Rokossovsky's Central Front and the southern half by Voronezh Front, now commanded by Vatutin following Golikov's removal after the disasters of February, while in the immediate rear lay General Ivan Koniev's Reserve or Steppe Front.

ZITADELLE began on 5 July. Fears regarding the Panther's premature commitment to action were fully justified. Breakdowns, mainly engine fires and transmission failures, littered the routes between the railheads and operational assembly areas. Further break-downs and battle casualties during the first day's fighting reduced the number of Panthers available to Fourth Panzer Army from a theoretical 200 to a mere forty. As the battle progressed it quickly developed into a brutal contest of attrition in which scientific general-ship had no part to play. It reached a climax on 12 July when the Fourth Panzer Army, with 700 tanks, clashed with the Russian Fifth Guards Tank Army, with 850. To counter superior German gunnery the Russians closed to murderously close range and even resorted to ramming during a mêlée that raged around the village of Prokhorovka. Ultimately, the Russians pulled back, leaving behind over 400 of their number; the Fourth Panzer Army lost about 300 tanks including seventy Tigers. While ZITADELLE was in progress the Allies landed in Sicily. Hitler informed his senior commanders that Italy was on the verge of collapse and that the Eastern Front would have to be stripped of troops to support her. Simultaneously, the Russians commenced a counter-offensive into the Orel salient – a mirror image of the Kursk salient lying immediately to its north – employing General Vasili Sokolovsky's West Front and Lieutenant General M. M. Popov's Bryansk Front. The Second Panzer Army was so badly mauled in the process that Manstein reluctantly transferred several panzer divisions to Kluge so that Model's Ninth Army could be adequately protected. ZITADELLE had run its course and on 17 July Hitler acknowledged the fact. Two immediate results were apparent. First, each side had lost over 1,500 tanks, but this was less serious for the Russians whose output of war material was far greater than Germany's, and who could in any case recover many of their tank casualties from the battlefield, which remained in their possession. In the circumstances, Germany would never be able to create a comparable armoured strike force again. Secondly, an equally intense air battle had been fought over the entire operational area without a clear-cut result. This so depressed the Luftwaffe's Chief of Air Staff, Colonel General Jeschonnek, that he took his own life. He had always been a dedicated advocate of close tactical air support and in this connection would be sorely missed as under his successor, General Günther Korten, the Luftwaffe's priority became the defence of the homeland against the growing offensives being mounted by the RAF's Bomber Command and the US Eighth Air Force from Britain and the US Fifteenth Air Force from bases in Italy. The steady withdrawal of Luftwaffe units meant that in future the German ground troops would be forced to operate with ever decreasing air support. Nor was that all, for large numbers of 88mm anti-aircraft guns were either withdrawn from the front or retained in the homeland for its defence and, as this weapon had few equals in the anti-tank role, the ground troops' protection against armoured attack was reduced proportionately.

Every German general who knew his business knew that with the failure of ZITADELLE the strategic initiative had now passed irrevocably to the Russians. As von Manstein wrote of this period in his book *Lost Victories*:

> Henceforth, Army Group South found itself waging a defensive struggle which could not be anything more than a system of improvisations and stop-gaps. To maintain oneself in the field and in so doing wear down the enemy's offensive capacity to the utmost, became the whole essence of this struggle.

Despite Manstein's expertise in conducting a mobile defence, Hitler ordered him to stand firm at Khakov. When, on 3 August, a Russian breakthrough threatened to isolate and destroy much of his army group, he ignored Hitler's instructions and by use of skilful counter-attacks, fell back in good order to the Dneipr. Unexpectedly, although it was sustaining heavy losses, the Red Army maintained its offensive throughout the autumn. When it finally ran down in November, it had pushed Kleist's Army Group Centre back to the edge of the Pripet Marshes, recaptured Smolensk and Kiev, obtained a bridge-head over the Dniepr and cut off the German Seventeenth Army in the Crimea.

As soon as the ground had frozen hard, the Red Army continued its offensive in the area of the Pripet Marshes and along the Dniepr, forcing Manstein to give ground. In the north General Georg Lindemann's Eighteenth Army was forced to abandon the siege of Leningrad by the Soviet Leningrad and Volkhov Fronts, narrowly escaping encirclement by the Second Baltic Front as it withdrew. These developments forced General von Küchler to institute a general withdrawal by his Army Group North. On 31 January Küchler was replaced by General Walther Model, who halted the Soviet drive on 1 March 1944 along the line Narva–Pskov–Polotsk, an achievement that earned him promotion to field marshal.

Near Korsun, on Army Group South's sector, two German corps were isolated between 29 January and 17 February by the First and Second Ukrainian Fronts, commanded respectively by Zhukov and Koniev. Manstein's relief attempt stalled in a blizzard then bogged down in the subsequent thaw. Some 30,000 men of the trapped formations managed to fight their way out. Soviet estimates of German casualties at approximately 75,000 are believed to be excessive. The Russians continued their advance, crossing the Bug and Dnister rivers.

From 10 March General Hans Hube's First Panzer Army began operating behind the Russians' lines, supplied by air and working under Manstein's instructions. Hube disrupted the enemy's lines of communication and then made his way out using a method known as the 'travelling pocket' in which the flanks and rear fought defensively while the front cleared the way ahead. On 16 April his troops began entering friendly lines, having destroyed no less than 337 Soviet tanks and forty-two self-propelled guns during its remarkable journey. On 20 April Hube was awarded the Diamonds to his Knights' Cross, only one of twenty-seven such awards made during the Second World War, but was killed in an air crash on his way to receive the decoration.

Manstein and Kleist were summoned to Hitler's presence on 30 March. The Führer awarded them both the Swords to their Knights' Crosses, thanked them for their services and then dismissed them. Manstein was convinced that the reasons for his dismissal included his ability to win an argument with Hitler, whose cronies Göring, Himmler and Keitel all resented his attitude of professional independence. Kleist was being punished because he was permitting his army group to give ground, albeit under tremendous pressure from Koniev's and General Rodion Malinovsky's Ukrainian Fronts.

During the middle of June there was talk among senior German commanders of Allied landings in France, although if one believed the news as retailed by Dr Goebbels' propaganda apparatus, the invaders were being pinned down at the water's edge. Of more local interest was the fact that partisan groups, many of them formed from Soviet soldiers left behind by German advances in the war's early years, had virtually paralysed the rear communications of Army Group Centre. General Ernst Busch, the army group's commander, deduced that his sector was about to become the target of the enemy's next major offensive. He requested Hitler's permission to withdraw behind the river Berezina so that the Russian blow would simply strike empty space. He also suggested holding a forward outpost line while the majority of his troops remained out of artillery range in their main position some twelve miles behind. This, he argued, would dislocate the carefully phased Russian timetable and create such disorder and confusion among the attacking echelons that a prompt counter-stroke would be rewarded with handsome dividends. Hitler was not remotely interested and ordered Busch to stand and fight in his present positions.

Opposing Army Group Centre were General Ivan Bagramyan's First Baltic Front, General I. D. Chernyakovsky's Third Belorussian Front and Marshal Konstantin Rokossovsky's First Belorussian Front. The two sides were evenly matched only in terms of manpower. In other respects, the Russians possessed 28,600 guns against 10,000, and 5,300 aircraft against 1,300. In the critical area of armour the Russians could field 4,000 tanks while the Germans could only produce 900. The Russians had also up-gunned the T-34 with an 85mm gun housed in a larger turret and possessed a recently introduced heavy tank, the IS (Iosef Stalin), heavily armoured and armed with a 122mm gun. In the area of assault guns and tank destroyers the Germans possessed a slight advantage.

The Soviet offensive was codenamed BAGRATION and commenced on 22 June, the third anniversary of BARBAROSSA. Supported by a mass of artillery, deployed on an estimated frontage of 400 guns per mile, the Russians rolled forward on a 350-mile frontage along the axis Smolensk–Minsk–Warsaw. Those German formations not immediately swamped by the flood of armour found themselves harried or pinned down by swarms of ground-attack aircraft. One after another, Soviet objectives were isolated by double envelopments. Vitebsk was cut off on 27 June, Mogilev the following day, Bobryusk on the 29th and Minsk on 3 July. No less than forty Russian tank brigades and numerous cavalry mechanised groups were in full cry across what had been eastern Poland, reaching Wilno on 13 July, Lublin on the 23rd and Brest-Litovsk on the 28th. When the offensive finally ran down as it closed up to the Vistula, it had advanced 450 miles in four weeks and torn a 250-miles gap in the German line. The Russians claimed the destruction of twenty-five divisions, 158,000 Germans captured, 381,000 killed or wounded, and the destruction or capture of 2,000 armoured vehicles, 10,000 guns and 57,000 motor vehicles. Whether or not these figures are inflated, the fact was that Army Group Centre had been dealt a mortal blow.

On 6 June 1944, having taken part in the largest amphibious operation in history, British, Canadian and United States forces landed on the coast of Normandy. An Allied landing had been expected and Hitler believed that it would take place in the Pas de Calais. An elaborate deception plan had so convinced him that he was right that he retained the panzer divisions intended to defeat the invasion in that area. While the rest of the Channel coast had been heavily fortified since the conquest of France, its details were well known and the British Army had developed a series of armoured vehicles that could deal with every aspect of the defence and so save the infantry countless casualties Administratively, these vehicles belonged to the 79th Armoured Division but operationally they served in teams, the composition of which varied in accordance with the nature of the task in hand. The vehicles included amphibious tanks, bridge-layers, fascine carriers for use in filling anti-tank ditches, mine clearers, mat-layers for crossing shingle, demolition devices and were later joined by several regiments of flame-throwing tanks.

Altogether, there were fifty-four German divisions in France, including ten panzer divisions. The quality of the infantry divisions varied as many were understrength and the loyalty of some soldiers, notably former Polish and Russian prisoners of war a high proportion of whom spoke little or no German, was doubtful. When the time came, those Poles who could wasted no time joining their country-men fighting with the British; the Polish Armoured Division served with First Canadian Army. The position of Commander-in-Chief West was held by von Rundstedt, who exercised theoretical control over Rommel's Army Group B (Seventh and Fifteenth Armies) and Colonel General Johannes Blaskowitz's Army Group G (First and Nineteenth Armies) in southern France. Rommel's view was that any landing should be met and defeated at the water's edge. As Guderian comments, both he and von Rundstedt held a quite contrary view:

> Our opinion was that it all depended on our making ready adequate reserves of panzer and panzergrenadier divisions; these must be stationed far enough inland from the so-called Atlantic Wall so that they could be switched easily to the main invasion front once it had been recognised.

By midnight on 6 June some 75,000 British and Canadian and 57,500 American troops, commanded at this stage by General Sir Bernard Montgomery, had been landed. Work commenced immediately to link the five beachheads and by 12 June this task had been completed, presenting the enemy with a solid fifty-mile front. However, although the Normandy landings had achieved complete surprise, there was a price to pay inland. Much of Normandy was covered by a type of country known as *bocage*, consisting of small fields and narrow lanes separated by hedges planted in deep earthen banks. This type of landscape was poor tank country and favoured the defence, with the result that Allied infantry casualties were heavy. The Allies' strategic aims were to draw the German armour onto the British sector while the Americans prepared to break out of the southern end of the line. Montgomery achieved this by mounting a series of potentially dangerous armoured operations, notably EPSOM and GOODWOOD, in the Caen area, where the going was more open. These were halted with heavy loss by the concentrated fire of German tanks, assault guns, tank destroyers and anti-tank guns, shooting from concealed positions. They did, however, achieve their object, for such was the combined industrial capacity of the Allies that the loss of four or five tanks to the enemy's one did not matter unduly since these could be replaced at once.

Against this, the German armies in Normandy were being bled white by a combination of naval gunfire support, precision air strikes and concentrated artillery fire. On 1 July Rundstedt held a telephone conversation with Keitel at OKW. The prevailing situations in Russia and France had left Keitel completely at a loss. 'What shall we do? What shall we do?' he kept repeating. Rundstedt's response was sharp and to the point: 'Make peace you fools! What else can you do?' That was not the answer Keitel or Hitler wanted or expected to hear. The following day a Colonel Heinrich Borgmann arrived at Rundstedt's Paris Headquarters. He handed the field marshal the Oak Leaves to his Knight's Cross and a letter of dismissal and informed him that Field Marshal von Kluge would be taking his place. Notwithstanding the appalling situations that were developing, Hitler issued another of his 'no withdrawal' *diktats*. On 17 July the command situation deteriorated further when a prowling Allied fighter-bomber pounced on Rommel's staff car. Seriously injured, Rommel was evacuated to Germany and von Kluge added his duties to his own. For many months, senior German generals had been fully aware that Hitler was leading Germany to a terrible defeat. Several plots had been hatched without result but on 20 July a bomb was planted in the briefing room of the Führer's headquarters in East Prussia. The explosion injured but did not kill him and he exacted an unbelievably savage revenge on the conspirators.

On 25 July the Americans commenced their breakout, codenamed Operation COBRA. It began with the US Army Air Forces carpet bombing a corridor through the German lines with 4,200 tons of high explosive, highly effective although some 500 Americans were killed or wounded by 'short' bombing. Following this, General Omar Bradley's First Army fought its way through the gap to Coutances on 28 July and its armoured spearhead reached Avranches on the 31st. The following day, General George S. Patton's Third Army, the presence of which had been kept a close secret, passed through the Avranches gap. During the next fortnight his armour cleared the enemy from Brittany then swung south to the Loire before turning east. Simultaneously, his infantry headed for le Mans. Even Hitler could see that if the American First and Third Armies turned north those German formations confronting the bridgehead would be doomed. He ordered Kluge to assemble eight panzer divisions for a counter-stroke. Kluge, the professional, suggested that these should form a shield behind which the rest of the army could withdraw across the Seine. This sensible idea was dismissed out of hand. Instead, Hitler ordered a large-scale counter-attack through Mortain to Avranches, the effect of which would isolate Patton's army which would cease to be a threat once its supplies had been consumed. This alternative was chosen entirely from the map without any consideration of what conditions might be like at the front, particularly as regards air superiority. The move was predicted by the Allies and on 30 July the British Second Army reacted with Operation BLUECOAT, an offensive directed at Mont Pinçon and the Vire river. This ensured that those German troops hoping to join the build-up for the Mortain counter-attack had much farther to travel and probably would not arrive in time. The fact was that any sort of travel in daylight hours attracted the attention of Allied ground-attack aircraft. Thus, Kluge was only able to concentrate four panzer divisions possessing a total of 185 tanks and assault guns.

The counter-attack commenced early on the morning of 7 August, aided by poor flying conditions. The 2nd Panzer Division managed to advance seven miles but was then fought to a standstill by the US 3rd Armored Division. Mortain was captured but from the nearby Hill 317 the Americans were able to direct artillery concentrations onto the stalled columns. By noon the sky had cleared and the RAF's deadly Typhoons arrived in swarms, bombing and strafing at will. By 9 August the counter-attack force was back where it had started.

Meanwhile, between 8 and 16 August the First Canadian Army had fought its way steadily down the Caen–Falaise road and driven in the right flank of the German beachhead defence in two operations,

TOTALIZE and TRACTABLE, while on 10 August Patton's army had begun to swing north. Under pressure from the British and Canadians in the north and from the Americans in the west and south, three major German formations, the Seventh Army, Fifth Panzer Army and Panzer Group Eberbach, were pinned inside a pocket twenty-five miles long by fifteen wide. This continued to shrink steadily so that by the evening of the 17th the only escape was via a six-mile gap through which fugitives, motor vehicles of every kind, horse-drawn transport and artillery sought safety to the east, battered the while by the Allied air forces and artillery. When the gap was closed on the 21st only 40,000 of an estimated 100,000 men in the trap had managed to escape. On 15 August von Kluge was forced to shelter in a ditch during a sustained air attack and was therefore absent from his headquarters for some hours. Hitler, by now suspicious of everyone and everything, believed that he had been discussing terms with the Allies and dismissed him. The field marshal had been a luke-warm conspirator in the July bomb plot and, being reasonably certain that the Gestapo was aware of the fact, took his own life. A new front had been opened when Lieutenant General Alexander Patch's Seventh Army landed on the south coast of France, conducting an expert advance up the Rhône Valley to the Vosges Mountains. Patch's command contained a French element that was expanded to become the First French Army. From 3 September the command structure of the Allied armies changed somewhat. General Dwight D. Eisenhower, the Supreme Commander, arrived in France and Montgomery ceded control of the ground forces; he now commanded 21 Army Group in the North, Bradley 12 Army Group in the Centre and General Jacob M. Devers commanded the new 6 Army Group at the southern end of the line. With the remaining Germans in France bottled up in the Channel ports or retiring into the Low Countries or behind the crumbling fortifications of the Siegfried Line, Hitler attempted to restore some logic to the situation by reinstating von Rundstedt as Commander-in-Chief West on 5 September.

In September Eisenhower accepted Montgomery's plan to drop three airborne divisions behind the German lines to secure bridges over the Maas at Eindhoven, the Waal at Nijmegen and the Rhine at Arnhem. The British Second Army would then advance along this 'airborne carpet', relieving each of the airborne divisions in turn, and then outflank the northern end of the Siegfried Line. The Allies were successful at Eindhoven and Nijmegen but the Arnhem end of the operation was a gallant failure, largely because of the rapid reaction of German armoured troops recovering from their ordeal in Normandy. However, in October and November, the Scheldt Estuary was cleared in a series of amphibious operations that relieved the Allies' supply problem.

The re-formed German armies fought hard to hold the Siegfried Line and prevent the Allies closing up to the left bank of the Rhine. Their stand enabled Hitler to accumulate sufficient reserves to mount a counter-offensive in which he hoped to destroy all the Allied armies north of a line Antwerp–Brussels–Bastogne with an armoured thrust through the Ardennes. Success would depend on the capture of Bastogne, St Vith and the Allied fuel supplies, none of which could be relied on. 'This damn thing's not got a leg to stand on!' was von Rundstedt's comment when he looked through the plans.

The Americans, in whose sector the Ardennes lay, regarded it as a quiet sector in which recently arrived formations were introduced to life in the line. The landscape was blanketed by rain, fog and snow and visibility was reduced and air activity impossible. Tactical surprise was therefore complete. On 16 December two American divisions, the green 106th and the recuperating 28th, were routed. English-speaking Germans in American uniforms caused chaos and panic behind the lines. Bradley rushed two American armoured divisions into the area as reinforcements and Eisenhower sanctioned the release of the 82nd and 101st Airborne Divisions from theatre reserve; the latter, under Brigadier General Anthony McAuliffe, conducted an epic defence of Bastogne that disrupted the Fifth Panzer Army's progress. Likewise, the defence of St Vith by Brigadier General R. W. Hasbrouck's 7th Armored Division cost the Sixth SS Panzer Army priceless time. Montgomery took control of the northern arm of what became known as the Bulge and moved British troops to provide a backstop on the Meuse. Simultaneously, Patton turned his Third Army left through ninety degrees and drove into the left of those besieging Bastogne. On 26 December the skies cleared and the Allied air forces began pounding the German columns. A few of von Manteuffel's tanks almost reached the Meuse but were driven off in an exchange of gunfire. Elsewhere, failure to secure a fuel depot intact indicated that the operation had failed. By 16 January 1945 counter-attacks had eliminated the Bulge altogether. Hitler's gamble had cost Germany 120,000 men killed, wounded or missing, 600 tanks and assault guns, 1,600 aircraft and 6,000 vehicles. Allied losses included 7,000 killed, 33,400 wounded, 21,000 missing and 730 tanks or tank destroyers.

The Allies returned to clearing the left bank of the Rhine, a task that was achieved by degrees in variable weather. On 7 March the US 9th Armored Division unexpectedly found the Ludendorff railway bridge at Remagen intact. It was seized by *coup de main* and troops began crossing at once, securing the high ground on the east bank. Horrified, the Germans tried everything to destroy it, including V-2 rockets fired from Holland. A new bridge was put in alongside the damaged structure so that when it did collapse into the river the flow of men and vehicles continued without interruption.

On 22 March the US 5th Division made a surprise crossing of the river at Oppenheim. Bridges were put in both there and at Boppard, across which Patton's army began streaming into central Germany. On the 23rd the British Second Army crossed on a twenty-mile front supported by the fire of 3,000 guns, followed by the US Ninth Army at Dinslaken. Beyond, resistance was limited to pockets of fanatics, but most Germans seemed happy that the British and Americans had reached them, rather than the Russians.

In the east, all was chaos. Germany's Romanian and Bulgarian allies had turned against her and the return of troops from the Balkans seemed to make little difference. The Red Army, now huge in numbers and adequately equipped, rolled on across middle Europe and Poland into eastern Germany. In the Baltic the German Navy evacuated 1,500,000 fugitives and four army divisions from Kurland, including 157,000 wounded. Further evacuations followed from Danzig, Gdynia, Königsberg, Pillau and Kolberg. On 22 April Berlin was surrounded by Koniev's and Sokolovski's fronts. In recent weeks Hitler's appearances in public had been few. He was now a shambling husk of a man, taking pills to counteract the side effects of other pills, promising that events would finally turn his way, just as they had for Frederick the Great when all seemed lost. He transmitted orders to the commanders of vanished armies and when nothing happened screamed that the German people were unworthy of him. Finally, he retired to his bunker, married his mistress, shot her and then himself amid scenes of burning, collapsing buildings, and incessant explosions as the Russians fought their way towards his Chancellery. This was not the Götterdämmerung, the Twilight of the Gods spoken of in Norse legends, for it marked the squalid end of by far the worst chapter in the entire history of Germany.

# Bibliography

Adair, Paul, *Hitler's Greatest Defeat: The Collapse of Army Group Centre, June 1944* (Arms & Armour, London, 1994)

Belfield, Eversley and Essame, H., *The Battle for Normandy* (B. T. Batsford, London, 1965)

Carver, Michael, *Dilemmas of the Desert War* (B. T. Batsford, London, 1986)

Chandler, David G., *Jena 1806: Napoleon Destroys Prussia* (Osprey, London, 19930

Chandler, David G., *Dictionary of the Napoleonic Wars* (Wordsworth, Ware, 1999)

Cooper, Matthew, *The German Army 1933–1945: Its Political and Military Failure* (Macdonald, London, 1978)

Elliott-Wright, Philipp, *Gravelotte-St Privat: The End of the Second Empire* (Osprey, London, 1993)

Erickson, John, *The Road to Berlin* (Weidenfeld & Nicolson, London, 1983)

Farrar-Hockley, A. H., *Ypres 1914: Death of an Army* (Pan, London, 1970)

Forbes, Archibald et al, *Battles of the Nineteenth Century* (Cassell, London, 1986)

Guderian, General Heinz, *Panzer Leader* (Futura, London, 1974)

Hamilton-Williams, David, *Waterloo: The Great Battle Reappraised* (Arms & Armour, London, 1993)

Howard, Michael, *The Franco-Prussian War* (Routledge, London, 1988)

Kluck, Alexander von, *The March on Paris, 1914* (Frontline, London, 2012)

Kurowski, Franz, *der Kampf um Kreta* (Efstathiadis, Athens, 1977)

Laffin, John, *Jackboot: The Story of the German Soldier* (Cassell, London, 1965)

Larianov, V., et al, *World War II: Decisive Battles of the Soviet Army* (Progress, Moscow, 1984)

MacDonald, Charles B., *The Battle of the Bulge* (Weidenfeld & Nicolson, London, 1984)

McCarthy, Chris, *The Somme: The Day-by-Day Account* (Arms & Armour, London, 1993)

Mellenthin, Major General F. W. von, *Panzer Battles* (Futura, London, 1977)

Mitcham, Samuel, *Hitler's Legions: German Army Order of Battle World War II* (Leo Cooper, London, 1985)

Moltke, Field Marshal Helmuth von, *The Franco–Prussian War 1870–71* (Greenhill, London, 1992)

Perrett, Bryan, *A History of Blitzkrieg* (Robert Hale, London, 1983)

Perrett, Bryan, *Knights of the Black Cross: Hitler's Panzerwaffe and its Leaders* (Robert Hale, London, 1986)

Pitt, Barrie, *1918: The Last Act* (Corgi, London, 1965)

Playfair, I. S. O. and Molony, C. J. G., *History of the Second World War: The Mediterranean and the Middle East, Vol IV* (HMSO, London, 1966)

Richardson, William and Freidlin, Seymour (eds), *The Fatal Decisions: First Hand Accounts by Hitler's Generals* (Pen & Sword, Barnsley, 2012)

Ste Croix, Philip de (ed), *Airborne Operations* (Salamander, London, 1978)

Seaton, Albert, *The German Army 1933–45* (Sphere, London, 1983)

Summerville, Christopher, *Napoleon's Polish Gamble: Eylau and Friedland, 1807* (Pen & Sword, Barnsley, 2005)

Terraine, John, *Mons* (B. T. Batsford, London, 1960)

Whiting, Charles, *Death of a Division* (Arrow, London, 1979)

Whiting, Charles, *Siegfried: The Nazis' Last Stand* (Pan, London, 2003)

Zhukov, Georgi, et al, *Battles Hitler Lost* (Jove, New York, 1988)

# Index